More Advance Praise for Chuck Zito and *Street Justice*

"Chuck is a real bad boy. It takes one minute to live but a second to die."   —Dennis "Bad Boy" Rodman, five-time NBA champion

"Chuck is a great guy and very well respected. He gets the job done wherever he goes."   —Smokin' Joe Frazier, former undisputed heavyweight champion of the world

"I can't think of any man I want to be stuck in a foxhole with except Chuck Zito, who would eat the last bullet."   —Mickey Rourke

"Chuck Zito's story is the quintessential American story—tough, awe-inspiring, and triumphant."   —Tom Fontana, creator of *Oz*

"I have known Chuck Zito for twenty-five years, and we're still friends. You'd be surprised what you could learn about loyalty and integrity from a Hells Angel. Read on."   —Joe Pesci

"Chuck is the coolest guy I know, and he is a very dear and close friend."

—Tony Danza

"I met Chuckie Zito at Café Central about twenty years ago. He was big, tough-looking, and wearing his Hells Angels colors. I must say, I was a tad bit nervous, but then when I got to know him, I realized he was a strange combination of Italian stallion, cuddly bear, and a Renaissance man. Maybe just a tiny bit more cuddly bear."   —Cher

STREET JUSTICE
CHUCK ZITO

WITH JOE LAYDEN

ST. MARTIN'S PRESS ≈ NEW YORK

www.stmartins.com

Book design by Michael Collica

All photos, except where otherwise noted, are courtesy of the author.

Library of Congress Cataloging-in-Publication Data

Zito, Chuck.
    Street justice / Chuck Zito with Joe Layden.—1st ed.
      p. cm.
    ISBN 0-312-30124-3
    1. Zito, Chuck.   2. Actors—United States—Biography.   3.
Hells Angels.   I. Layden, Joseph, 1959–   II. Title.

PN2287.Z58 A3   2002
791.45'028'092—dc21
[B]

                                               2002069830

First Edition: October 2002

10 9 8 7 6 5 4 3 2 1

This book is dedicated to my family.

To my mother: You are the foundation under me. Words cannot express my gratitude and love for you.

To my sisters, Rosanne and Cindy: I love you dearly, and thanks for putting up with me all these years.

To my nephews, Bobby, Anthony, and Dennis, known as the Bad Team: Grow strong.

To my beautiful nieces, Danielle and Candace: You make me proud.

To Kathy and Lisa: Your unconditional love and support has given me the strength and courage to fulfill my dreams and reach my goals. You are the wind beneath my wings.

And to my dad: You gave me your skills, your wisdom, and your attitude. Until we meet again, so I can tell you I love you, rest in peace.

And also, let us never forget all who were lost on 9-11. They took away our towers, but they can't take our freedom, pride, or spirit. God bless America and the families of those lost.

ACKNOWLEDGMENTS

GOD GAVE ME THE STRENGTH TO ACCEPT THE THINGS I CANNOT CHANGE.

For those who have shared my joy when things were good, those who endured my pain when things were bad, and those whom I can call my friend, I thank you all for your support, love, and loyalty.

To those who were in my corner and held me up to fight another day: Danny Aiello, Philip Carlo, Cher, Steven Greenberg, Brian Hamill, Paul Herman, Joan Jett, Joe Kaplan, Kenny Laguna, Terry Magovern, Liza Minnelli, Sean Penn, Chita Rivera, Eric Roberts, Mickey Rourke.

To my friends: Satch Boyd, John Chirachella, John and Debbie DeVito, Frankie and Diane DiBuono, Scotty and Kim Ferrara, Tommy and Janine May, Jimmy and Sally Toglia, John and Janice Tufo, John and Donna Valente.

And to all my relatives: the Bleichs, the Curcios, the Engelmans, the Frangiones, the O'Sheas, the Viscontis, the Zitos.

To the cast and crew of *Oz*: It's a pleasure working with each and every one of you. Without a doubt, you are all consummate professionals, especially Tom Fontana—thank you for believing in me and giving me a chance to work on the best show on HBO.

To the stuntmen I worked under—we gave them the thrills, the excitement, and the danger: George Aguilar, Danny Aiello, III, Peter Antico, Kenny Bates, Peter Bucossi, Eddie Braun, John Cenatiempo, Doug Crosby, Eddie Dono, Frank Ferrara, Jack Gill, Freddie Hice, Buddy Joe Hooker, Joel Kramer, Terry Leonard, Charlie Pircerni, Simon Rhee, Mike Russo, Alex Stevens, and Dick Ziker.

To the martial artists: "I come to you with empty hands . . . I have no weapons . . . if for any reason I have to defend myself, be it right or be it wrong, then here are my weapons—my empty hands." It's been an honor and pleasure to train alongside all of you: Master Butté, Master Chin, Shihan Chris Colombo, Soke Little John Davis, Danny Inosanto, Kyoshi Tommy May, Chuck Norris, Philip Rhee, Professor Florendo M. Visitacion, Bob Wall, Bill "Superfoot" Wallace, Don "The Dragon" Wilson, Benny "The Jet" Urquidez, Chuka Zulu. Thank you for filling my cup with your knowledge. *Ous.*

To the boxers, the warriors of the squared circle—thank you for the excitement you gave me: Muhammad Ali, Iran Barkley, Mark Breland, Hector "Macho" Camacho, Michael Carbajal, Gerry Cooney, Bobby Czyz, Doug DeWitt, Roberto Duran, George Foreman, "Smokin' " Joe Frazier, Arturo Gatti, Rocky Graziano, Larry Holmes, Beau Jack, Jake LaMotta, Zab Judah, Ray "Boom Boom" Mancini, Angel Manfredy, Buddy McGirt, Floyd Patterson, Vinny Pazienza, Freddie Roach, Johnny Tapia, Mike Tyson, Fernando Vargas, Mickey Ward, Chuck Wepner.

To the wrestlers—thank you for inviting me into your world: Bam Bam Bigelow, Big Papa Pump, Buff Bagwell, The Big Show, Eric Bischoff, Booker T, The Disciple, The Dudley Boys, Ric Flair, Mick Foley, Goldberg, Scott Hall, Hulk Hogan, Chris Kanyon, Billy Kidman, Shane McMahon, Vince McMahon, Stephanie McMahon, Kevin Nash, Diamond Dallas Page, Raven, The Rock, Perry Saturn, Macho Man Randy Savage, Triple H, The Undertaker, Rob Van Dam, and X-Pac.

To all the people who made this book possible. My agent, Frank Weimann, who, for the last six years, has been hounding me to write a book. Well, Frank, we finally made it. Thank you for pursuing me. And to my friend, Philip Carlo. Thank you for hounding Frank to hound me. To my editor, Marc Resnick, and the staff at St. Martin's Press. Thank you for believing in me. Book two is on the way. And to my friend and co-author, Joe Layden, it's been a lot of meetings and endless hours of conversation. Thank you for putting my words on these pages.

And a special thanks to my lawyers, Thomas Cascione and Ron Kuby. *What doesn't kill me makes me stronger.*

Finally, to all the Hells Angels in the world:

> *"The world will be on the brink of destruction*
> *And a band of rebels will rise to rule the world.*
> *These rebels will be the angels from Hell.*
> *For the Earth is Hell, and upon it are the . . .*
> *Hells Angels."*

Loyalty, strength, and honor—Charming Chuck.

To anyone I left out, please forgive me, but it's been one hell of a roller-coaster ride.

I don't have to be what anyone else wants me to be. I am free to be
who I want to be.   —*Muhammad Ali*

We'll ride to hell . . . or to glory. . . . Depends on one's point of view.
                                    —*General George Armstrong Custer*

When in doubt . . . knock 'em out!   —*Big Vinny Girolamo*

We'll stand together, or we'll stand alone.   —*Benjamin Franklin*

FOREWORD

WHAT MAKES CHUCK ZITO FUNNY? HE'S AN EX-CON. A HELLS ANGEL. THE thick skin of his fighting hands nearly overlaps the rings on his massive fingers. He's wildly tattooed. Speaks with a deep and imposing voice, and has a long history of physically disassembling those who have crossed or threatened him or his friends (and he'll be the judge of that cross or threat). In short, he's a big, bad American outlaw from New York. So what's so funny about that? What's his contribution? Why should we want to read about him? I'll begin this way: The post–September 11 United States has been one of fear, reflection, loss, bloodlust, pain, and at best, the beginning of a dramatic societal re-evaluation. For many of us, though (and many before us), the questioning of the moral and political status quo began long before September 11, 2001. From the beginning of the atomic age through the emergence of catch phrases like "politically correct" and so on in the 1980s, this country, built on an ideal of individual spirit and freedom, has moved closer and closer to the archaic standards of conformity that the country's forefathers fled in the jolly old English empire, and man, can you track this movement in the fabric when an unprecedented tragedy so swiftly closes the ranks of bipartisan political, religious, corporate, and all other fear-exploiting authorities. So what becomes of those who don't play ball in a culture so homogenized, pasteurized, correct, and careful (so fucking careful)? Those few who still believe that the passionate rap star has the freedom of his speech, that the dissenting opinion is not un-American, that it is the Cheneys, the Enrons, and the Falwells who are obscene. Those who would suggest that the casual cigarette in a restaurant never hurt so many children as the chronic drinking of a parent culture that even occupies offices in our own White House. These people outside the lines of the laws of media, the comfort-addicted masses, or even the land at times. They will be marginalized, censored, discredited, and yes, even imprisoned. So it is now more than ever that we need our original thinkers, our poets, upstarts, and indeed, depending upon your own definition, our outlaws. And it is in that spirit that we should celebrate this very American life that Chuck Zito shares with us on these pages. Chuck is my friend. He has been for nearly twenty years. I've never known him to be anything less than completely honest, direct, and bold. That's more than one can say for the government that took six years of his life in the federal prison system. Don't get me wrong. I am not an apologist for malicious or greedy ways in outlaws, be they on motorcycles or in the Oval Office. I'm just another American who appreciates a little color, and Chuck wears his colors with a rare dignity. So again, what's so funny about that? I guess it's just the unending will to be a round peg in a square hole. An iconoclast and a cowboy. Take a ride in *Street Justice* through Zito's life. It's touching, violent, informative, and yes, sometimes even funny.

—SEAN PENN
California 2002

STREET JUSTICE

PROLOGUE

THIS IS THE WAY IT IS FOR ME. WHEN THE LIGHTS GO OUT AND THE DOORS slam shut and the tier finally falls silent—when grown men take themselves into their sticky palms and become lost in some adolescent fantasy or weep quietly for the lives they've lost and left behind—I drift away, carried to another place by sweet and merciful sleep.

I'm in the driveway of my home in New Rochelle right now, the home I renovated with my own hands and sweat and money. In the garage now I'm flat on my back, tinkering and tuning my Harley-Davidson, chatting and laughing with my beautiful daughter, Lisa, who assists me the way a nurse helps a surgeon, skillfully slapping tools into my hand with a knowing smile and a look of unconditional love.

There is a jump cut, in that odd way of dreams, and suddenly Lisa is gone and I'm on my own again, looking down at someone, a lone figure on a motorcycle, cruising along on a sun-bleached day, Hells Angels jacket flapping in the breeze. The rider unstraps his helmet, one of those flimsy little sheaths we bikers refer to as "brain buckets," and tosses it over his shoulder. It hits the pavement, bounces high into the air, and shatters into a hundred tiny pieces. I can see the rider's face now, and I recognize it as my own. I can feel my hand lean into the throttle as the bike explodes forward, rushing off into the open road, which stretches before me now like a great black carpet—long, empty, forgiving.

"Chuck?"

There is a crackling in my ear as the picture fades and my mind goes dark, like a movie screen when the film breaks.

"Chuck?"

1

I open my eyes and through the haze of sleep see the steel ceiling above me, the bars in front of me, the slow-footed gait of inmates in the hallways, the tentative, wary movement of the corrections officers. I see someone outside my room, looking in through the thick glass door, the one that robs me of any privacy and humanity, the one that never lets me forget that I am a prisoner . . . a convict. That this is a prison and that escape comes only in dreams.

"Hey, Chuck . . . you okay?"

Wait a minute . . . He's in the doorway now, strolling in casually, as if the rules don't apply. He wears jeans and sneakers and carries a clipboard, and I recognize him, by face if not by name. I sit up on my bunk and rub my hands through my hair, try to shake the cobwebs loose.

"Sorry, I must have fallen asleep."

He smiles. "Yeah, well, that's understandable. There's a lot of downtime between scenes. Anyway, you're up in fifteen minutes."

"Thanks."

He walks out, leaving the door open in his wake, and I can see them out there now, the cast and crew of *Oz,* the HBO prison drama in which, starting today, I have a supporting role. I look around my cell, which is startlingly realistic, a fine approximation of the shitholes in which I wasted six years of my life, and I can feel the sweat evaporating on my back. A sense of relief washes over me, and I laugh quietly under my breath.

My name is Chuck Zito, and I am a free man.

1

I KEEP A PICTURE OF MY FATHER OVER THE VISOR OF MY '81 'VETTE, A CRISP black-and-white image of a formidable man in his prime—a boxer, a fighter, a survivor. I take it down sometimes and hold it between my fingers while I'm cruising around New York, through the old neighborhoods: Sheepshead Bay in Brooklyn, and especially the South Bronx, places my dad would barely recognize if he were alive to see them today, to see what they've become, all the old row houses smeared with graffiti, the brownstones with bars on the windows. I know what he'd say if he were beside me in the passenger seat. I know what he'd think. I can almost see him squinting and shaking his head: *How the hell do people live like this? Like fuckin' animals in a cage . . .*

He's maybe twenty-five years old in the photo, thickly muscled, with eight-ounce black gloves on his fists, which are held high, at once protecting and highlighting his Mediterranean features: the thick hair, the heavy-lidded eyes, the splayed nose. You need only a quick glance to understand that this is a man not to be taken lightly, a man who would never run from a confrontation. Although he never lifted weights, he did spend a number of years working as a steamfitter, carrying cast-iron radiators up and down flights of stairs. Consequently, he has the chiseled, tapered look of a bodybuilder: broad shoulders atop a forty-four inch chest, well-defined six-pack, and twenty-eight-inch waist. He's only five feet, eight inches tall and weighs maybe 145 pounds (he's a welterweight), but there is something in his face, something in the way he carries himself, that makes him seem much bigger.

Fighting will do that to you, and Charles Zito was a fighter in the

Al La Barba

truest sense of the word. He became a professional boxer at the age of sixteen, when someone offered him a chance to make a few bucks in his spare time. This was in the 1930s, when work was hard to come by and fighters earned their money in a way that seems almost incomprehensibly harsh today. There were no million-dollar paydays then, no pay-per-view packages that made it possible for a modestly talented fighter to strike it rich and retire with his brain and his looks intact. My father used to sneak out of the house, walk to some dark, smoke-filled club, and mix it up for as little as ten bucks a night. On a good week (depending on how you define the word *good*) he'd do this two or three times.

To hide his new profession from my grandparents, my father fought under the name Al LaBarba. In those days, there was nothing unusual about using a stage name. Rocky Graziano, after all, was really Thomas Rocco Barbella, Rocky Marciano was Rocco Marchegiano, Archie Moore was Archibald Wright, Sugar Ray Robinson was Walker Smith, Jr. and so on. Some fighters wanted to hide their ethnicity; others wanted memorable, poetic names, names that rolled off the tongue or looked good flashing in neon (not that many of them would ever see their names in lights). In my father's case, it was merely a matter of age and opportunity. Legally, he wasn't allowed to fight. So he chose a different name, told promoters he was an adult, and tried to make a living as a boxer. Dad chose Al LaBarba because he liked the sound of it and because it had a successful ring to it (already there had been a featherweight champ named Fidel LaBarba). The scheme worked for a while, until Dad started coming home late at night with his eyes blackened and his cheeks swollen. He'd lie, of course, tell his parents that he'd gotten in a little scuffle on the street or that he'd had some kind of accident at work. My grandparents had no idea he was actually a professional fighter . . . not until the night he staggered home after a particularly brutal bout, his blood-soaked brow held together by twenty-two freshly sewn stitches.

My grandfather, no soft-hearted wimp himself, confronted my father at the door. This time

My mother at Orchard Beach—the day she met my father

Dad didn't even try to lie his way out of it. He was too tired, too sore. So when my grandfather, who was Italian and spoke no English, said, "How did this happen?" Charles Zito just shrugged his shoulders.

"I've been fighting, Pop."

"What do you mean, fighting?"

And then my father went into a stance, held his fists in front of him, and said, through a weary smile, "You know . . . boxing. Professionally."

I don't know exactly what my grandfather said to him then. I've heard the story many times, and the words never seem all that important. What I do know is this: Al LaBarba got the shit beat out of him twice that night. First by some older club fighter in a boxing ring and then at home, at the hands of his own father. And he never denied that he had it coming.

Dad didn't lose many fights, though—not in the ring and certainly not in the street. He boxed professionally for twelve years and compiled a record of 228 wins, 12 losses. Whether fighting as a lightweight or welterweight, he displayed a rare combination of power and speed. My father was a boxer-puncher, which basically meant he could knock out an opponent with either hand. He was a dangerous, intimidating man, both in the ring and out of the ring. Despite his record, he never made it big as a boxer, never had a chance to cash in. Dad trained with the legendary Ray Arcel at Stillman's Gym and was managed by Irving Cohen, who also managed Graziano; Dad was a stablemate of Graziano and in fact used to routinely whip the Rock's ass in sparring sessions . . . until Graziano became champion and suddenly my father was no longer allowed to share the ring with him. Have to protect the merchandise, you know. (By the way, in case you think the source of this information is an old, bitter man bragging to his kid about how he *coulda been*  *a contendah* . . . think again. I have a scrapbook at home stuffed with newspaper and magazine clippings related to my father's boxing career, including several that talk about the unmerciful beatings he used to administer to his training partners, including Graziano.) Had fate not stepped in the way, my father might have become a champion himself. He had the talent, and he certainly had the disposition. But, as it happened, while he was training for the welterweight title held by Marty Servo, he received a call from Uncle Sam. And that was that. Dad went overseas, saw some action near the end of World War II, came home, had a few more fights, and then retired. His one break, his chance for a title fight, dissolved while he was away. Who knows what might have happened if he'd gotten that shot? What if he'd won? His whole life might have changed. There would have been money, prestige, fame.

But that's not the way it worked out. Instead, my father took a string of tough, unglamorous jobs: cabdriver, mechanic, building superintendent. Often he held two or three jobs at once. He did what he could to pay the bills. If my father was pissed about his misfortune, he never let on. I don't mean he was never pissed off—in fact, he was pissed off a lot of the time. He just never revealed the root of

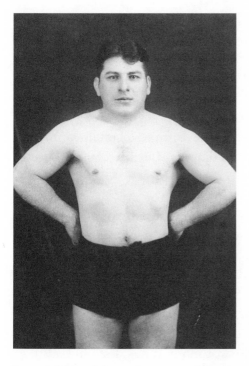

his anger. Maybe he was bitter. If so, well, I suppose he had reason to be.

Dad's retirement came in 1948, shortly after he met Gloria Frangione. She spotted him first, strutting along the sand at Orchard Beach in the Bronx. Charles was twenty-eight, fit, muscular, extremely good-looking in a tough, Italian sort of way (just like the guy in the photo), and well aware of the effect he had on women. Gloria was . . . well, she was sixteen years old, that's what she was. But Charles didn't know that when he saw her, walking with her girlfriend Pat, the two of them staring and giggling like schoolgirls, which, of course, was precisely what they were. Charles and Gloria talked on the beach for a while. He got a name and a phone number, and pretty soon he and Gloria began dating. It's kind of funny when I think about it, my dad, nearly thirty years old, chasing after this teenager . . . a minor, no less! That's dangerous territory. Interestingly enough, years later he would zealously and ferociously try to protect the virtue of his own daughters, but no one ever pointed out to him the obvious double standard. Somehow, I'm pretty sure he wouldn't have seen any humor in it.

Charles was a tough son of a bitch, but he fell hard for Gloria, and no amount of common sense could dissuade him. Nor was he frightened by the prospect of being dismantled by Gloria's father, Leo Frangione, a six-foot-two, 240-pound policeman at the Port Authority who had once made a living as a professional wrestler known as "Young Leo." I would learn over the years that size matters only so much in a fight, that heart and courage and skill are equally important. My father understood that the first time he visited Gloria's house and Leo met him at the door. They were two strong-willed men, each in his own way madly in love with the same woman. Leo understood pretty quickly that Charles would not be easily frightened. More important, he saw that his daughter loved this guy, this boxer from Harlem, and there was no point standing in their way. And so they dated for a couple years, until Gloria turned eighteen, and then they got married. The first baby, Rosanne, was born on January 2, 1952. Charles Zito, Jr.—that would be me—came along fourteen months later, on March 1, 1953, at the Bronx Hospital. Mom was twenty years old with two babies in diapers. Her life changed pretty quickly, I guess.

I have a nasty scar under my left eye, the remnants of an encounter with an unforgiving foe when I was less than two years old. I'd like to say that was my first fight, that I refused to back down from another toddler on the playground. That would make for great copy, huh? Really adds to the legend of a tough guy. Unfortunately, it's not true. The truth is, I fell and whacked my head against a tree branch. Slit my head open and nearly lost an eye . . . practically gave my mother a heart attack, too (the first of many times, I should add).

My sister and I standing in front of 645 Barretto Street

My life has been punctuated by violence and danger. I've been a bouncer, boxer, biker, and bodyguard. In part because of my affiliation with the Hells Angels (I'm a former president of the New York Nomads chapter), I spent nearly six years in jail on a trumped-up conspiracy charge, an experience I wouldn't wish on anyone, even if it has helped inform my work as an actor on *Oz*. I figure there have to be better ways to conduct research. But you live and learn, right? You make the best of life and try to have a little fun along the way. I'm forty-eight years old now, and I still believe what my father taught me: that you stand up for yourself, you do what you think is right, and you take shit from no one. But I've never been a bully. In fact, I like to think that I'm the kind of person who sticks up for those who aren't strong enough to defend themselves. While I've never run away from a fight, I've rarely gone looking for one, either. And when I was a kid, I hoped they wouldn't come looking for me.

They did, of course. I don't know anyone lucky enough to survive childhood without meeting some asshole along the way, someone who wants to steal your lunch money or spit in your face or maybe even beat you up, just for the sheer hell of it. Butch was that kind of kid, and for a while he was my nemesis. Like his namesake, that tough kid from the *Little Rascals,* Butch was always bullying people. He was a little bigger, stockier, than everyone else in the neighborhood, and he liked to throw his weight around. Looking back, I'm amazed that he developed this attitude at such a young age. I mean I'm talking about a kid who was four years old, maybe five, and already he liked to inflict pain and misery on everyone around him. And for some reason I was his favorite target. Maybe it was just a mater of proximity—Butch and I came from the same neighborhood when I lived at 645 Barretto Street in the Bronx. It seemed like every time I saw him, he gave me trouble. He'd call me names, push me around, try to provoke some type of confrontation. I avoided him at all costs, basically because I was a shy kid who was afraid of getting in trouble and winding up across the street, in what is today known as the Bridges Juvenile Home. Back then it was called the Spofford Home (it was located on Spofford Avenue), but the name didn't really matter. This was a detention center, a big, white building with bars on all the windows, encircled by a tall fence topped with razor wire. Whenever I got out of line, my mother would threaten to have me incarcerated: "Wait till your father gets home! We'll send you across the street! *For good!*" As an adult, I ended up in far more brutal cages, but I was never more frightened by the prospect of jail than I was as a child, living next door to the Spofford Home. Sometimes when my friends and I would walk by, we'd see the kids in there, poking their faces through the bars, and we'd hear them yelling, cursing, taunting, promising to tear us apart if we ever came inside. These were mostly

9

Left to right: My sister Rosanne, myself, and my little sister, Cindy, with my Dad's '55 Chevy in the background

kids who'd been caught shoplifting or stealing cars or getting in fights, but to us they seemed as dangerous and deadly as Jack the Ripper or Al Capone. Frankly, the place scared the shit out of me, and I wasn't about to do anything that would give my parents cause to make good on their threat. Getting into a fight with Butch, I was pretty sure, fell into that category.

Butch was a jerk, no question about it, but he taught me a valuable lesson: sometimes, when you turn the other cheek, you get smacked twice. One summer morning before I started kindergarten, I ran into Butch on the front steps of our apartment building. Our family was going out for Sunday brunch at my father's parents' house, at 1032 Wheeler Avenue in the Bronx, as we did every Sunday. (It was a lively place, since Dad's sister, my Aunt Connie, also lived there with her husband, my Uncle Freddie, and their three kids.) So my mom had dressed me like a little gangster, in a suit and tie, with a fedora. She'd also given me strict instructions to stay neat and clean. So, when I saw Butch, I told him straightaway that I couldn't wrestle, argue, fight, or do anything else.

"Why not?" he said.

"Because my mom will kill me if I get dirty."

I can still see Butch sitting there, gnawing at one of those little wax bottles you could buy at any penny candy store, the kind that was filled with a couple ounces of sickly sweet juice. He said nothing, just stood up, broke off the top of the bottle with his teeth, and then squirted the contents all over the front of my nice white shirt. Then he just stood there and laughed.

I remember wanting to hit him but being overcome by fear and embarrassment, and so I turned and ran back into the apartment building. I could still hear Butch cackling as I bounded up the stairs and into our apartment, where my mother greeted me not with sympathy but with a slap to the face and an order to get changed—fast!

Funny thing about Butch, though—he wasn't nearly as tough as he seemed, a fact that was revealed a few months later, on the first day of kindergarten at Public School 48 in the Bronx. It remains to this day one of the more vivid and satisfying images of my life (strange as that may sound), the sight of Butch's mother walking into class, in front of all the kids in the neighborhood, with her son clinging to her leg, the hem of her skirt rising and falling over the brow of his meaty head as he cried and wailed and pleaded for her not to leave him there . . . *"all alone!"* Some of the kids were frightened by his outburst, but most were merely amused by it—the sight of the neighborhood bully whimpering like a baby was comforting, even to a bunch of five-year-olds. Butch's mother eventually dumped him in his seat, gave him a quick kiss on the cheek, and scurried for the door, but he chased her like a lost puppy. The teacher finally stepped in, pried them apart once more, and led Butch back to his chair, still weeping uncontrollably, and I remember thinking, *This is what I've been afraid of?*

I took that image of Butch and put it away for safekeeping, figuring it would come in handy someday. On some level I'd already learned the rudiments of self-defense, for I understood that Butch's public display of cowardice would have repercussions, that it diminished him in the eyes of his classmates and especially in the eyes of those he'd been terrorizing, most notably me. Never again would he seem quite so fearsome, so invincible.

My mother, sister, and I on the front steps of the house where I was born: 1028 Wheeler Avenue

11

My sister and I with my father on Barretto Street

It wasn't long before I had an opportunity to use my new psychological weapon—only a few days, in fact. Butch confronted me outside our apartment building, started teasing me and pushing me around, trying to goad me into a fight. I held my ground, summoned up all the courage I could muster, and said coolly, "I'm not afraid of you, Butch. Everyone knows you're just a big baby, crying in school like that."

Oh, man, it felt great to say that to him, to cut him down to size. And it seemed for an instant to have exactly the desired effect, for Butch froze in his tracks, clearly shocked by what I'd said and the fact that I'd dared to say it at all. I thought it was over at that point. Butch would break into tears again, just like he had on the first day of kindergarten, and run home squealing to his parents. No such luck. After giving the matter some thought, he lunged forward, planted his arms in my chest, and knocked me to the ground. Apparently, my plan had backfired. I'd succeeded only in pissing him off.

It was worth a try, I suppose. But as Butch walked away, giggling like an idiot, it became clear to me that this bully business was more complicated than I'd first thought. So I turned to my father for advice. He'd seen me crying on a few occasions but hadn't ever said much about it, probably because he wanted me to try to work things out on my own. One day, though, after another encounter with Butch, my father finally asked me what was wrong. Through tears I told him all about Butch and his ceaseless bullying. My father hated bullies and in later years would come to my defense (as well as the defense of others in the neighborhood) when he sensed the deck was stacked too heavily in someone else's favor. But this was a couple of five-year-olds; it wasn't appropriate or necessary for him to get personally involved. Instead, he looked me in the eye and said, "Come on . . . I'll show you how to take care of yourself."

Although he'd been retired for nearly a decade, I knew my father had been a boxer. There were pictures on the walls of our apartment, trophies on the mantel, daily reminders of the life he had lived before his family came along. Dad also kept a big steamer trunk in his bedroom closet, and I'd always been told to stay away from it. On this day, though, he pulled out the trunk, popped the lid, and revealed a treasure chest of boxing memorabilia: gloves, shorts, hand wraps, headgear, shoes, robes . . . all kinds of stuff he'd accumulated over the course of a twelve-year career. Staring in wonder and admiration, I ran my hands through his gear. I picked up a glove, held it to my face, and took a deep breath. It smelled musty and vaguely like liniment.

"Go ahead," my father said. "Put it on."

I pulled the glove over my hand, and of course it engulfed most of my arm. My father laughed, picked up a second glove, and covered my other hand. He tied them both loosely and pulled me out into the center of the room. Then he got down on his knees and held his hands in front of his face.

"OK," he said. "Try to hit me."

"No, Daddy, I don't want to."

"Don't worry. You won't hurt me. You might as well learn how to do this right."

I don't know exactly how long that session lasted. I remember only that I flailed away at my father until my arms grew heavy and he started to laugh. Then he removed the gloves, put them back in the trunk, and told me never to use them without his permission. I didn't listen, of course. That trunk became the most important thing in the world to me, the best toy in the whole house. Whenever my father wasn't around, I'd rummage through the contents and pretend to be a boxing champion. I'd put on the gloves and bounce around on our Castro convertible sofa. There was a big mirror on the living room wall, and if I bounced high enough, I could see my reflection in it. So I'd pretend I was boxing, throwing and receiving punches against an imaginary opponent. Sometimes I'd

My dad and Rocky Graziano, thirty years later

smack myself in the face, really hard, until a trickle of blood began to flow from my nostril.

Up and down . . . up and down . . . I could see myself in the mirror, see the welts on my face, and I liked what I saw: My father's nose, my father's face. A boxer's face.

2

ON THE DAY WE MOVED INTO THE HOLLYWOOD, AN APARTMENT BUILDING AT
2750 Homecrest Avenue in Brooklyn, I thought I'd died and gone to
heaven. I was seven years old, and I couldn't believe people actually
lived in such comfort and luxury. In truth, it was really just a nice,
clean building that catered to a middle-class clientele. But compared
to our home in the Bronx . . . well, it might as well have been the
Hamptons.

From a cramped six-story building with no elevators we moved
into a glistening new high-rise with doormen, and porters buffing the
floors, and plenty of elevators, and hallways as long and wide as a
city block.

"I'm gonna need roller skates just to get from one end of the building to the other!" I said. My parents just laughed. They were about
as happy as I'd ever seen them. And why not? They had three kids by
now (my younger sister, Cindy, had joined the family on July 14,
1957), and the Hollywood represented a big step up the food chain.
Not that we'd struck it rich or anything. My father had landed a job
as building superintendent, and with that position came a modest
apartment . . . rent-free. Not long after he accepted the position, he
helped my Uncle Freddie get a job as superintendent of the Belair,
which was owned by the same company and was located right next
door. So it was a great situation: we had family nearby, and we were
living in a much nicer place. In the Bronx, "going swimming" meant
taking a towel, sneaking outside, and cracking open a Johnny pump
on a hot summer day. The Hollywood had a couple in-ground swimming pools—it was almost too easy.

My father wasn't exactly the laid-back type, which is probably why he got the job in the first place. As the conduit between management and tenants, a superintendent has to deal with a lot of shit—complaints come from all directions. My father was responsible for the Hollywood maintaining its pristine appearance, and to that end he ruled the building with an iron fist. If anyone made too much noise late at night, he'd hear from my father. Graffiti or vandalism of any kind was a serious infraction guaranteed to leave the perpetrator with a footprint in his ass. It didn't take long for everyone, kids and adults alike, to develop a healthy respect (maybe *fear* would be a better word) for Charles Zito.

Of course, some people got the message later than others.

I had just come home from school one day when I heard a commotion outside. The Hoch brothers, Bruce and Matthew, were there, as well as Steve Leeds and Bobby Ing. These guys were my best friends. We all lived in the Hollywood or the Belair or one of the nearby buildings, and we hung out together all the time.

"What's up, guys?" I yelled from my window.

"Come on, Chuck!" Bobby said. "There's a fight . . . down the street."

We were boys, so we naturally loved a good street fight. And, this being Brooklyn, we saw our share. In fact, there was nothing all that unusual about it. In the fifties and sixties, people often settled their differences in this manner. Or, at least, in my neighborhood they did. And they did it without guns or knives. They did it without police intervention. They rolled up their sleeves and exercised a little street justice. Everyone accepted the rules.

Anyway, I ran out of the apartment and then sprinted off down the street with my buddies. A couple blocks away I could see a crowd forming, expanding and shifting with each passing moment.

Jeez . . . I hope we haven't missed it!

We pushed our way into the crowd, using our size (or lack thereof) to get a ringside view. We were just sitting down on the curb when I realized I recognized one of the combatants.

"Pretty cool, Chuck," Bobby said. "Your dad's gonna beat someone up." He nudged me in the ribs with an elbow. It was like watching the *Gillette Friday Night Fights*—live and in person.

Only they weren't fighting yet, merely arguing. Later, through conversations with my friends and my father, I found out what had led

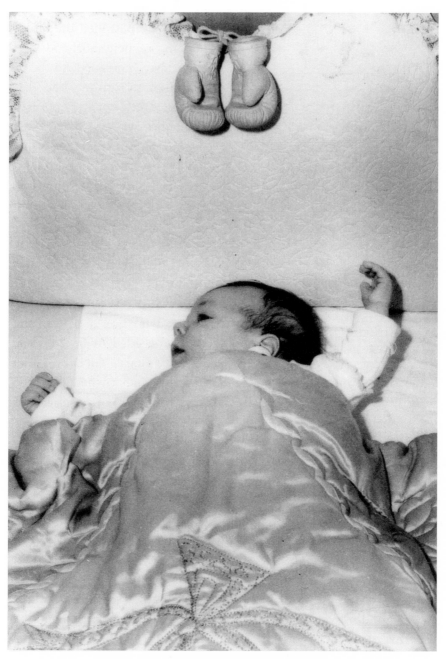

A few weeks old and already I have my gloves.

to this moment. A security guard who patrolled the buildings in our neighborhood, and who also happened to be a friend of my father, had dispensed a little corporal punishment to a wiseass kid. I knew the kid. He was older than me, maybe twelve or thirteen, and he had a big mouth. He was a punk and a troublemaker, and at some point his disrespectful attitude had led to the security guard giving him a good boot in the behind. The kid went home, told his father, and the father, who was a big, strong guy, proceeded to beat up the security guard. Their fight had ended only minutes earlier, when my father had rushed down to break it up. So this is where they all had landed, on a street corner just a few blocks from the Hollywood.

Now, I'm pretty sure the punk's father was new to the area, for he obviously didn't know anything about Charles Zito. Didn't know he was a man with a temper. Didn't know he was a seasoned professional fighter. Didn't know that old adage, you know: *It ain't the size of the dog in the fight; it's the size of the fight in the dog.* If he had known any of this, I'm sure the guy would never have provoked my father. As it happened, though, here they were, nose to nose, shouting at each other, circling each other, preparing for battle.

More words were exchanged, the punk's father saying something about "minding your own business" and my dad saying something like "this is my business." My father let him throw the first punch, a wild roundhouse right hand. He sidestepped it easily, causing the man to lose his balance, and then unleashed a lightning-quick combination—*right to the body, left to the head!* The man slumped to the concrete like so much deadweight, unconscious before he even hit the ground. And that was that. *Show's over!* On the way home, my buddies patted me on the back, told me how lucky I was to have such a tough, crazy father.

I nodded and smiled. "Yeah. That's my dad." Already I could tell that my father's reputation somehow extended to me and that simply by virtue of being his son I was accorded a certain degree of respect. I hadn't earned it, but that almost seemed to be beside the point.

This wasn't the first time my friends had witnessed this kind of behavior from my father. Once, while playing in the street, we saw him jump out our first-floor window, hop over a row of hedges, and corner two kids coming out of the back of the Belair. Dad grabbed them and smacked their heads together, like two melons. They fell to the ground, barely conscious. Later we found out who they were: two kids named Chris and Rocco, from Banner Avenue. They were part of a gang known as the Banner Avenue Boys, and they had shown up with the express purpose of seeing Uncle Freddie's daughter, Rose-linda. My uncle didn't approve, of course, and he chased them away. Unfortunately for Chris and Rocco, my father was waiting for them. Chris was no quitter, though. He wound up marrying Roselinda. They've been together thirty-five years now, and they have three grown children. Funny the way things turn out, huh?

My father's sense of honor . . . his interpretation of right and wrong . . . was untouched by shades of gray. His was a black-and-white world, one in which disrespect was not tolerated and the laws of the street outweighed the laws of the land. I admired him for this, even if I didn't completely understand it. When he believed he had been the target of disrespect, my father's blood would boil. Similarly, if any member of his family had been disrespected (or, worse, hurt), my father was quick to exact revenge on behalf of that person.

We used to hang out at a local luncheonette, me and my buddies. We'd sit at the counter, spin on the stools, drink ice-cream sodas, and generally act like unruly but harmless little boys. Most of the time no one cared; sometimes they did. One day at lunchtime, while we were messing around, pretending to fight, another customer told us to set-tle down. We didn't. So this man got up out of his booth, walked over, and leaned into me.

"I said . . . knock it off! Someone's going to get hurt."

Left to right: My aunt Connie, my father, and my mother

I laughed. "Ahhh . . . we're just fooling around, mister. It's no big—"

Before I could complete the sentence, he smacked me in the face with an open hand . . . knocked me right off the stool and onto the floor. The whole place fell silent—I think everyone was stunned by what he'd done. I mean I was only in second grade and he was a grown man, probably thirty-five years old. What was he thinking?

"I told you someone was going to get hurt!" he yelled. Then, slowly, he backed away, picked up his coat, and walked out the door. Still in shock over having been attacked by a crazy man, I struggled to my feet. Then I went back to school with my friends.

That afternoon, when I got home from school, I told my father what had happened. (I don't recall feeling as though there was anything wrong with telling him; something about the discrepancy in our sizes made it perfectly acceptable, even necessary.)

"Someone hit me today, Dad."

At first he barely looked up from his newspaper. I presume he figured I'd just gotten in an argument with one of my friends.

"Yeah? Who?"

As I revealed the details, the newspaper slid into his lap and his face turned crimson.

"Get in the car," he said. "Now!"

We drove straight to the luncheonette and double-parked in front. My father dragged me out of the car and led me to the front door. We walked in together. My father's jaw was tight, his eyes filled with fury.

"Is he here?"

I looked around. Indeed, the man who had hit me was there. As it turned out, he was good friends with the men who owned the luncheonette, a pair of brothers—big, barrel-chested guys who supposedly wrestled professionally at one time. I don't know if that was true or not, but they sure looked the part.

"Yeah, he's here," I said.

"Show me."

I pointed to the man who had hit me. My father released my hand. "Wait here."

He wasted no time, simply marched up to the man and said, "Did you hit my son?" The two owners quickly intervened, shouting something about how my friends and I had been causing trouble.

"You two," my father said, pointing a finger at the men, "should stay the fuck out of this." It seemed a remarkable sight, my father, only five-eight, 150 pounds, threatening two elephants and apparently getting away with it, for they didn't move on him, didn't order him out of their luncheonette. He turned to face the man who had hurt me.

"Did you hit my son?" he asked again, this time gesturing over his shoulder to where I was standing.

The man stood, hitched up his shorts, and began to speak. "Yeah, but—"

There were no more words. My father straightened the man with a right uppercut, then dropped him with a left hand. As the man lay on the floor, motionless, bleeding from the mouth and nose, my father turned to the owners, his fists still clenched.

"Well?"

Looking on in awe and disbelief, the two men just shook their heads and held up their hands, as if to surrender.

"That's what I thought," my father said. Then he put an arm around my shoulder and pushed me toward the door.

While my father was quick to jump to my defense when I'd been hurt, he was equally quick to punish me when he felt I was wrong. He hit me probably three or four times in my entire life, and each time I had it coming. I remember once, around this same time, when I actually became the bully for a short time. I got involved in a fight with another kid at school, and I wound up giving him a pretty good beating. I don't remember what caused the fight, but I know I was the instigator. I didn't like the kid, and I was looking for some excuse to rough him up a bit. I thought I was being a tough guy, like my father, and that everyone would respect me, the way they respected him. I was far too young to know the difference between "mean" and "tough." But I learned the hard way.

That night, this kid showed up at our apartment with his father. I watched from another room as the three of them talked near the door. My father nodded a lot. After a while, he called my name.

"Did you hit this boy?" he asked.

I cleared my throat, stood as tall as I could make myself, and answered confidently, "I sure did." Honest to God, I thought he'd be proud of me . . . proud that I could handle myself, just like him . . . proud that I wasn't afraid to dish out a little punishment. Instead, he cracked me across the side of the head with the back of his hand, sent me reeling to the floor, right there in front of them.

Despite the ringing in my ears, I could hear him telling the kid's father it would never happen again. And it wouldn't. I had learned another valuable lesson: fighting was acceptable only under certain conditions. If he believed I was defending myself, I'm sure my father would not have objected. But I was picking on the kid, and he didn't approve of that. More important, I think he wanted to demonstrate that the problem was resolved and that he was indisputably, absolutely . . . in charge.

Not that my father was always a hard-ass. He had a tender side—you just had to turn him over a few times to find it. Once, on the way home from school, I got involved in a nasty rock fight. Sounds stupid, I know, but it wasn't uncommon in my neighborhood. Such fights usually began harmlessly enough, one kid chucking a piece of gravel at another, with no more malicious intent than if he were throwing a snowball in the winter. Of course, rocks don't break apart when they hit you, so by definition a rock fight is a more serious and dangerous activity than a snowball fight. But try telling that to a bunch of eight- and nine-year-old boys.

It was in the middle of one of these fights that I took a shot to the head. I saw it coming, too, saw the rock flying straight at me. If I'd stood perfectly still, it would have hit me in the chest and done little or no harm. Oh, it would have hurt, sure—the rock was roughly the size of a golf ball—but it wouldn't have left any scars. Instinct, though, told me to duck, and so I did. The rock struck me in the right side of my head, just above the eye. Within seconds my face was covered with blood and people were screaming, crying, running in all directions. Afraid I might bleed to death, I pressed a hand against my head and staggered home. By the time I arrived a substantial amount of blood had pooled around the site, and when I lifted my hand to reveal the damage to my parents it was as though a dam had broken. *Splat!* A puddle of blood hit the floor, prompting my mother to recoil in horror and scream at the top of her lungs.

"He's dying, Charlie! Do something!"

My father, who could go ballistic over the smallest annoyance, was positively tranquil. It was as if he'd suddenly become this character out of *Father Knows Best* or something. He told my mother to get some washcloths and a first-aid kit. Then he held my hand while she left the room. Before she returned, he whispered, "That's what you get for throwing rocks," but he didn't sound angry, maybe because he sensed how scared I was or maybe because he figured I'd been hurt enough already.

"Hold still," he said.

I clenched my fists as he wiped the wound clean and then shaved a patch of hair from my head.

"This will hurt for a second," he said.

I had an idea of what was coming. We never saw doctors when I was growing up—my father *was* the doctor. He stopped all our bloody noses, patched up all our cuts and scrapes. This was a man who boxed in an era when ringside surgeons were mere fantasy. In Dad's day, when you got cut you wiped off the blood, applied a little grease, and got back in the ring. You stopped only when you lapsed into unconsciousness.

I winced, closed my eyes, and held my breath. There was an instant of deep, searing pain as my father pinched the wound closed and laid a butterfly stitch across the opening. Then he added another . . . and another. Finally, he took my head in his hands, moved it around, as if inspecting a bowling ball, and nodded approvingly.

"Good as new," he said. Then he patted me on the behind and sent me back out to play.

3

Through my bedroom window on the sixth floor of the Shorehaven Apartment Buildings at 8869 Twentieth Avenue in Bensonhurst, I could see them working, building what soon would be known as the Verrazano-Narrows Bridge—men in hard hats climbing and skimming like spiders across webs of scaffolding and ribbons of wire and steel. They were out there even today, on a hot Sunday afternoon in July. It was an amazing, almost incomprehensible thing to see, the way they built a tower at each end and moved steadily toward the middle. These guys had no fear, I thought, working so high above the water, where one slip, one mistake, could cost you your life.

My Uncle Jack (who was the husband of my mom's sister) did work like this at one time, I had been told. He'd even been part of a crew that had painted the tower of the Empire State Building some years earlier. I'd seen pictures of him at work on that project, dangling from the sky, some 110 stories above the street, a smile on his face. He seemed so happy, so full of life. I once asked Uncle Jack how he could do something like that, and he said it wasn't that big a deal. "Just don't look down," he said. "Then it doesn't matter how high you are." There was something to his theory, I guess. Uncle Jack survived the painting of the Empire State Building tower, only to suffer a horrible injury while painting a second-story fire escape in the Bronx. He'd lost his balance and fallen backward, probably no more than fifteen or twenty feet, but his back took the full force of the blow. He broke several vertebrae, spent a year in a body cast, and never did regain the full use of his arms and legs.

As scary as that kind of work seemed, it was nonetheless exciting,

25

My uncle Jack (left) painting the tower of the Empire State Building

and being able to watch the building of the Verrazano-Narrows was one of the best things about living at the Shorehaven, where we moved when I was in sixth grade. Given half a chance, I would have run down there and offered my help.

Instead, I'd have to settle for a game of sandlot baseball. Sundays we always ate at Grandma's house—Mom, Dad, me, and my two sisters. But Mom said we wouldn't be leaving for a couple of hours, so I grabbed my glove and bat and started rounding up some of the guys from the neighborhood. Mom yelled something about not getting dirty as the door slammed behind me, her voice drowned out by the squealing of tires and the screeching of sirens—the summertime music of the street.

I banged on door after door, and pretty soon they were spilling out of apartments and brownstones, one after another, following me across the hot asphalt like I was the Pied Piper or something, all these kids, trailing after little Chuck Zito. We didn't have enough for a real game, but that didn't matter. Five to a side meant more hitting, more scoring, more running, more fun for everyone. Truth is, I didn't even like baseball all that much, didn't even know that much about it. My friends? They collected cards, posters, went to Yankee Stadium whenever possible. They could tell you when and where Mickey Mantle was born, what Roger Maris liked to eat for breakfast, and Yogi Berra's real name. Me? I'd rather have been in the gym, hands taped and gloved, working up a stink, trying to flatten some guy's nose, like my father did all those years. But it was Sunday. It was baseball season. What are you gonna do?

Everything was fine for a little while. We were playing and running, losing track of the score because so many guys were crossing home plate. Then someone hit a line drive up the middle and the ball skipped past the lone outfielder—me—and rolled almost to the edge of the field, where the grass met the street. I ran after it, head down, as the others yelled from behind. But someone beat me to the ball, someone bigger, faster, stronger . . . someone who was not a part of our game. I recognized him from the neighborhood, although I didn't know his name. He was a high school kid, probably seventeen or eighteen years old, and he was leading a bunch of other guys in tank tops and dungarees and greasy black hair.

He put a foot on the ball as I reached down to pick it up, and then shook his head arrogantly, as if I were nothing more than a pest.

"Game's over," he said.

"Huh?" I had no idea what he was talking about.

"What are you—stupid?" he yelled. "Get outta here. We want the field."

I looked past him, noticed that one of the kids was carrying a bat. They were closing in now, laughing, smiling, taking some sort of perverse pleasure in picking on a bunch of kids half their age and size. I could feel the hair on the back of my neck standing on end, taste the cotton in my mouth. With a quick tug, I yanked the ball from beneath his shoe and stood up. He towered over me, but I gave up nothing. My nose was inches from his chest, and the combination of fear and the smell of his shitty aftershave made my stomach rise up into my throat.

He smiled and extended an open hand, palm up. "Give me the ball, and get off the field."

I swallowed hard. His gang was behind him now, half a dozen kids, any one of whom could break me in half. My buddies were huddled around home plate, watching, wondering, but smart enough to stay out of it. I was the one with the mouth, the one with more balls than brains. I was the tough guy.

"No," I said. The word hung in the air for a moment.

He studied me, then laughed out loud. "You're fuckin' crazy, you know that? Go on, before I kick your ass."

I tried to hold my ground. I could feel my legs shaking, and for a moment I thought I might wet myself. But I didn't. I looked up at him, and with as much certainty as I could muster I said, "It's our field. We were here first. We're not going anywhere."

The smile drained from his face. He said nothing, simply balled his hand into a fist and hit me in the stomach, just below my ribs. The air rushed out of me as my knees buckled and I crumpled to the ground. The baseball skipped away. I couldn't breathe, couldn't move.

"Warned you," he said, picking up the ball. As he and his gang walked toward home plate and my friends began to scatter, I rolled over on my side and pulled myself up. There was dirt on my face, tears in my eyes. Doubled over, I could see a fresh hole in my pants, and I thought of what my mother would say when I got home. I hated this kid, hated him for being a bully and for hurting and humiliating me in front of my friends. I tried to speak, tried to call after him, but nothing came out. Then, finally, the air returned to my lungs and the words spilled out, smothered in hiccups, but loud enough to be heard.

"F-f-f-uck you!"

He stopped, turned, and marched back. "What did you say?"

"You heard me."

This time I barely even saw it coming. The blow struck the side of my face, sent me crashing to the ground again. For a moment the lights went out and all I could hear was the muffled sound of laughter. By the time I rolled over, my friends were all gone and the bigger kids were getting ready to play. In the middle of the outfield, an obstacle too small to cause any harm, I lay there, dirty, sweaty, sobbing. Finally, I pulled myself up again and staggered off the field, but before I reached the sidewalk I saw a familiar car approaching, a big 1958 silver Cadillac El Dorado, gleaming in the midday sun. The car stopped at the curb and my father stepped out from behind the wheel. He stood there, waiting for me, staring at me. I wobbled into his arms, wanting nothing so much as a warm embrace, but he stopped me, pushed me back, looked me hard in the face, staring at the mess his son had become.

"Who did this?" he asked coldly.

Unable to speak, I simply pointed toward the bigger kids at the other end of the field.

My father took me by the arm. "Come on."

He pulled me across the field, his pace quickening with each step. I could feel the anger in his touch, the adrenaline flowing from his arm to mine. The bigger kids were playing catch, warming up as we approached. My father took me into the middle of their group and stood there, silently at first, stoically, until he was certain he had their attention.

"Which one of you did this to my son?" he asked.

The biggest kid, the one who hit me, didn't hesitate for a second, just sauntered up to my father and folded his arms across his chest. The kid was several inches taller than my father, and it was obvious he thought he had nothing to fear: *What's this old man going to do me?* But he was wrong.

"I did," the kid said.

29

My father tilted his head a little, as if sizing the kid up. "Why?"

"Because we wanted the field and he wouldn't leave."

My father shook his head in disbelief. "You hit my son just because you wanted this ball field?"

"Uh-huh." The kid turned and looked at his buddies, then faced my father and smiled. It was the smile of a punk, and I knew what was coming next. "What of it?"

There was no warning. My father leaped at the kid with his right arm extended, hit him flush in the nose with the butt of an open hand. There was a crack as the kid's nose shattered and blood began to pour from his face, and then another sound, something like a whimper, as he fell to the ground. By the time he got up, crawling and scrambling and running all at once, his gang was gone and it was just him and my father. The kid put a hand to his face, spit out blood and grass and dirt, and looked at my father, who was just standing there, waiting for the kid to do something stupid. But he didn't. Now just a scared child, he turned and ran.

As the boy disappeared from sight, my father brushed the sleeve of his shirt and walked back to me. He bent down, and for a moment I thought he was going to give me a kiss. Instead, he placed a hand on my shoulder and looked me in the eye.

"Let me tell you something," he began, his tone serious, unsympathetic. "The next time you get hit by someone bigger than you . . . the next time someone tries to hurt you . . . I want you to pick up a baseball bat, a bottle, a brick, whatever. And I want you to crack his skull open." He paused, as if to let the message sink in. "You understand?"

I nodded.

"Don't ever come crying to me again, or I'll really give you something to cry about. You got it?"

"Yes, Daddy."

"Good," he said, wiping the dirt off my back. "Now let's go to Grandma's and eat."

I can honestly say that I never lost another street fight, mainly because—for better or worse—I took my father's words to heart. I learned how to defend myself. And when threatened, I acted quickly. *"The next time someone tries to hurt you . . ."* I've won a lot of fights, quickly, by taking the initiative before that moment occurs, by realizing that confrontation is inevitable and that I might as well throw the first punch. If that sounds less than chivalrous, well, too fucking bad. The Marquis of Queensbury never spent much time on the streets of Brooklyn.

In Bensonhurst, two of my best friends were the Horowitz brothers, Ricky and Lonnie, a couple of tough Jewish kids who shared my budding affinity for fighting. I'd often sneak into my father's room, open the forbidden trunk containing his boxing gear, and borrow his boxing gloves. At first I just wanted to show some of the stuff to Ricky and Lonnie, because I knew they'd appreciate it, but it wasn't long before we began lacing up the gloves. Sometimes we'd spar at their apartment; sometimes we'd go outside. Usually, though, we fought in the basement—it was dark, damp, hot, and smelled like shit. In other words, it felt just like a real gym, which was why we loved it.

We never fought with animosity or anger, although that doesn't mean we didn't try to hurt each other. I'd box with Lonnie while Ricky played the part of referee and timer. Then I'd become the ref while the two brothers whaled on each other. Having received a little instruction from my father, I usually absorbed less punishment than they did, but we all took our lumps (headgear was never part of the uniform). We'd give each other bloody noses, black eyes, and then we'd go down to the store and buy sodas and proudly display our war wounds. We thought we were pretty cool, pretty tough.

I really fell in love with boxing around that time. Other kids dreamed of playing center field for the Yankees; I wanted to be heavyweight champion of the world. When I'd splatter Lonnie's nose, I imagined it was Marciano who'd been vanquished. Some days, when I got home from school, I'd head straight to the closet and begin rummaging through my father's gear. That he'd repeatedly warned me to stay away from the trunk no longer mattered. I was obsessed, and I didn't care about the consequences. Anyway, it wasn't like I was hurting anything. Putting on his headgear, gloves, trunks . . . dancing around in front of the mirror . . . flicking off deadly jabs and unleashing powerful uppercuts—it was all just a harmless fantasy.

Until the day I pulled out my father's robe.

It was at the bottom of the trunk, folded neatly, untouched for years, and when I held it to my face I could almost hear the crowd roaring. The robe was made of satin. It was white with black trim, and across the back, in black letters, was the name AL LABARBA. I put my arms through the sleeves, shuddered at the way the fabric clung to my skin. I stood in front of the mirror, and while I'm sure I looked ridiculous—a four-and-a-half-foot-tall boy in the robe of a grown man—I felt like a titan. I started to bob and weave, the way real fighters do in the anxious moments before the opening bell. But I kept stumbling and falling, tripping on the hem of the robe. Adjustments were necessary.

I walked into the kitchen, where my mother was making dinner. She looked down, shook her head, said nothing, and went about her business.

"Mom?"

"Yeah?"

"Can I have this robe?"

She stopped, turned to face me. "Why?"

"Because if it's mine, then I can do something with it, right?"

"I guess so. What do you have in mind?"

"I want to cut it so it fits right."

This, of course, was a ridiculous suggestion, a request so outrageous that my mother should have knocked me off my feet . . . or passed out laughing. But she did neither of those things. Instead, she merely shrugged her shoulders and went back to preparing dinner.

"Why not?" she said. "Your father never uses it anymore."

In retrospect, her response was a clear signal that something was terribly wrong in our house, that something had happened between my parents. In the past, Mom would have warned me about playing with Dad's stuff and promised there would be hell to pay when he came home. But all she did was open a kitchen drawer and hand me a pair of fabric scissors.

"Just don't cut yourself," she said.

I ran off into the bedroom and prepared the robe for surgery. I laid it out on the floor, tried to flatten it as neatly as possible, and then began cutting the hem. I sliced a few inches, all the way around, and then tried it on.

Still dragging on the floor . . .

I cut again.

Still too long . . .

32

My dad on the right, wearing the robe that I prepared for surgery

And again.

Eventually I got it right—sort of. The robe hung just above my ankles; the hem was frayed and uneven. The sleeves were still too long; the neck billowed like a parachute. I didn't care. I felt like a pro. When my father came home from work, I ran to greet him, somehow laboring under the misguided notion that he'd be proud of what I'd done. As he stood in the doorway, staring in disbelief, I jabbed and punched at the air, held my hands above my head like a champion.

"Look, Dad . . . I'm Al LaBarba!"

His eyes widened in disbelief, then narrowed in anger. He took a big, fast step forward and cracked me on the side of the head with an open hand. I stumbled, caught myself. I didn't fall.

"You stupid kid! What the fuck are you doing?! I told you never to touch my stuff!" He yanked the robe off my back, fingered it for a moment, then threw it on the floor. "It's ruined!"

"Leave him alone," my mother said. "I told him he could do it."

My father seemed shocked. "What? Are you crazy?"

"It's just a robe. What's the big deal?"

They were in each other's faces after that, swearing, screaming,

33

throwing things around the kitchen. I ran out of the apartment, down the stairs, and out the front door, the sound of their fight chasing me every step of the way. My parents had argued before, but never quite like this. Something had happened; something had changed. And it wasn't just my shredding of Al LaBarba's robe that had caused it.

4

WITHIN A YEAR MY PARENTS HAD SEPARATED AND BENSONHURST WAS JUST a memory. My sisters and I moved upstate with my mother (upstate, as any real New Yorker will tell you, being a vaguely defined region that stretches roughly from the northern edge of the Bronx to the Canadian border).

There had been signs that my parents weren't getting along. Not just arguments, but other less obvious indications. My mother's sudden decision to seek real employment (she got a job as a bookkeeper at Fort Hamilton), for instance. And my father's repeated disappearing acts. He seemed to be around the house a lot less than he had been in previous years; sometimes he'd be gone for days at a time. If I asked why, he'd say he had work to do. It never really occurred to me that their marriage was crumbling, not until the day my mother went on a cleaning spree, just started chucking everything that wasn't nailed down, including my father's old boxing gear. When I asked why, she started crying. We were leaving, she explained, and Dad wasn't coming with us.

I was just finishing sixth grade when this happened. That summer we moved in with my mother's parents on Pelham Parkway in the Bronx. Well, not all of us. My grandparents didn't have enough room for three kids, so my older sister was sent to live with my Aunt Connie and Uncle Freddie for a few months. It was hard. Suddenly the family was all busted up, me and Mom and Cindy in one place, Rosanne in another, and my father . . . well, I didn't exactly know where he was. I knew only that he had disappeared from our lives, at least for the time being, and that I was forced to sleep on a Castro convertible with my mother and sister, and that my mother cried a lot and that everyone seemed unhappy most of the time.

Except on weekends, when Mom's friend Pat (the same Pat who was with her when she'd met my father at Orchard Beach) would take us for a ride. Pat had married a man named Eddie Fellini, and although they weren't related to us, they felt like family. In fact, I usually referred to them as my aunt and uncle. Eddie had done pretty well for himself. He owned a construction company and, unlike my father, was never short on cash. He and Pat owned a nice home, nice car, took expensive vacations. They also happened to be members of the Greentree Beach Club in New Rochelle, just north of the Bronx. New Rochelle today is a congested suburb in Westchester County, but thirty-five, forty years ago? Well, it was more like the eastern end of Long Island. At least, it felt that way to me the first time Pat and Eddie invited us to join them at the Greentree. With easy access to Long Island Sound, New Rochelle was home to dozens of swanky beach clubs and yacht clubs. Everywhere you turned, there was money. Not only that, but New Rochelle was so clean. I'd never seen so much green space or breathed air that didn't stink of car exhaust.

Chucky Zito, the alter boy . . . for now

To a kid from Brooklyn, New Rochelle was like paradise, and I looked forward to every trip to the Greentree. Pat and Eddie were great about taking care of us that summer. They came by almost every weekend in Eddie's big red Cadillac and took us out for a day of swimming and sunning and eating. My mother naturally fell in love with the place, too, and after she saved a little money and got back on her feet she decided that she wanted out of the city. Maybe, she figured, if she moved to New Rochelle, she could have a slice of paradise, too.

It wasn't that simple, of course. A single mother couldn't buy a house in New Rochelle, and she sure couldn't afford a membership at the Greentree—or any other beach club, for that matter. Life for my mother was hard. She took a job as a bookkeeper and secretary at a company called Hydroplane and found a modest little apartment at 25 Shady Glen Court. It wasn't exactly a life of leisure. We lived on the first floor, right over the boiler room, and sometimes the smoke would seep through the walls and doors and windows and fill the apartment with a thick, acrid fog. But this apartment was all we could afford. My mother had her hands full. She was trying to raise three kids, ages thirteen, twelve, and eight. We went to school all day, and in the afternoon we were on our own, at least until Mom got home from work. By that time she was exhausted; but she'd always cook dinner for us, help with homework, listen to our problems. And then she'd collapse into bed. My father wasn't helping out too much. He gave Mom a few bucks each week, but it wasn't nearly enough. Sure everything was cheaper back then, but he didn't really help support the family. He just gave whatever the court said he had to give, which was twenty bucks a kid per week.

To help out, I got a paper route when I was twelve years old. My grandpa Leo had an old bicycle in the garage, and he painted it, fixed it up, and gave it to me so that I could use it to deliver papers. I liked the idea that I was earning my own money and that I wouldn't have to ask my

A rare photo of me with my mom and dad years after the divorce

mother if I wanted to buy something. In a way, I felt like I was more of a grown-up than my own father.

Whatever admiration and affection I still had for my father largely dissolved in the coming year, as my parents officially divorced and the truth about their breakup became clear. He was completely absent for a while, as often happens during a divorce, and then suddenly he was back in the picture, at least once in a while, picking us up at Shady Glen Court and taking us out for a day of bonding with Dad. We'd go out for a drive or to a ball game, maybe have dinner. And that was fine. My sisters and I were angry and hurt, but we were happy to at least have some contact with him. After all, he was our father.

One day, though, he picked us up in New Rochelle and we all drove to Bayside, Queens . . . to the apartment of a woman named Shirley Roberts. I recognized her immediately. We'd been neighbors. In fact, she and her husband had been teammates with my parents in a Thursday night bowling league! And now here was my father, holding her hand gently, giving her a little kiss, welcoming us to her apartment.

Are you shittin' me?!

It all came together then. The fights, the sudden and extended absences . . . my mother's reluctance to explain what had happened. My father had been having an affair. And not with just anyone—with a fellow tenant, an acquaintance of the family . . . a bowling partner, for Christ's sake! I wondered how long it had been going on, and I wondered what in the hell my father saw in this woman that he didn't see in my mother. Mom was prettier, smarter, nicer.

Mrs. Roberts reached down to shake my hand. I didn't move, didn't even make eye contact. My father cleared his throat, gave me a harsh look and a nudge in the back.

"Hi," I said.

She smiled and invited us into the apartment. She was now divorced and had two kids of her own, roughly our ages, and they were running all over the place. For the next few hours we hung out there, me and my sisters playing with these other kids, my father and Mrs. Roberts pretty much ignoring us, acting like a couple of lovebirds. It turned my stomach. It was bad enough that my father had been carrying on an affair with this woman—did he have to flaunt it in front of his kids? As I watched them together, I felt an overwhelming urge to hurt him . . . to curse at him . . . maybe even hit him. But I wasn't that brave, that strong. Not by a long shot.

When he dropped us off at Shady Glen Court that evening, my father kissed my sisters and wrapped an arm around my shoulder. He smiled weakly, almost as if he were embarrassed, and said, "Do me a favor . . . don't tell your mother about Shirley. Okay? It'll just hurt her feelings."

He was right. It would have killed my mother to know we had spent the day with the woman responsible for breaking up their marriage. But that wasn't why he didn't want us to tell her. My father also knew that my mother would have been furious and would have forbidden him from taking us there ever again. My father wasn't thinking about his children or his ex-wife; he was thinking about himself, something he did most of the time, as I'd come to realize. But my sisters and I honored his wishes. For months we said nothing to my mother. We endured weekly trips to Bayside, Queens, and dinners with this other family, this other woman. I resented her and I despised her children, not because they were mean or obnoxious but simply because they were who they were: my father's new family. Most of all, though, I resented my father—for breaking up our happy home (in my eyes, anyway), for running out on his responsibilities, for seeing us only on weekends and even then not giving us his full attention. Most of all, I resented him for asking us to lie.

After a while we began to drift apart. One week Rosanne would refuse to leave the house when my father came to pick us up; the next week I'd refuse. My mother rarely asked for much of an explanation, probably because in some weird way it made her happy to see us rejecting him. Or maybe she just figured we'd finally come to our senses and realized our father was a bum. That wasn't the case, and I never really did feel that way about my dad. I loved him and admired him in many ways, but at that time I felt nothing so much as anger toward him. I was twelve years old, which is a confusing enough time for any kid, but to have it compounded by the sudden disappearance of your father . . . well, it fucked me up, no question about it. I'm almost fifty years old now and my father is gone. He was a complicated, intense guy who made a lot of mistakes, most of which I've long since forgiven. But some of the things he did, like breaking up our family and never making enough time for his kids . . . I have difficulty letting him off the hook for that. My dad always said, "Family is the most important thing. Don't ever forget it." But he didn't really mean it. In my father's case (and I supposed this was true of most men), the little head was thinking for the big head most of the time. And the little head didn't give two shits about family.

39

Eventually, after nearly a year of our lying to her, my mother started to wonder what was going on. Weekends with my father became less frequent. Sometimes we'd argue with him, right there in front of my mother, almost like we were challenging him: *"Go ahead, Dad . . . push it. We'll tell you why we don't want to go with you. Because we don't want to spend any time with you and that whore in Queens!"*

It ended when my mother came to me and asked, point-blank, what was going on. I think she suspected something, and I was tired of lying to her; it made me feel dirty, and I knew it was wrong. So I told her the truth: we'd been spending weekends with Dad and Mrs. Roberts and her kids. My mother blew up, of course, and then it was over. We never went to Bayside, Queens, again. And for a while we didn't see too much of my father, either.

I was lucky to make friends pretty quickly after we moved to New Rochelle. The Goodrich family, in particular, accepted me as one of their own, and I spent a lot of time hanging out with two of their boys, Jimmy and Jeff, who were close to my age. Their father was a good, hard working man who later gave me my first real job, and their grandfather was a crusty old guy with a big heart who became a huge part of my life.

Pop, as we all called him, was in his seventies by the time I met him, but he didn't lack energy. He was caretaker of a twenty-acre parcel of land on Davenport Avenue, a big, thickly wooded area that looked and felt like a jungle to us. The "yard," as it was known, sloped down to Long Island Sound. We'd fish for snapper there, hunt for squirrels and chipmunks using homemade bows and arrows. We never caught anything, of course, but we tried. And Pop would sometimes lead the expeditions. He was a big, burly guy who drove a black 1949 pickup truck and was always chomping on a smelly cigar. He tried to act like a tough guy, ruling the yard like he was the warden of a penitentiary or something, but we all knew what a sweet guy he really was. I'll give you a couple examples. There was a dam that separated the sound from the yard, but when it was low tide we could walk right across and go fishing. One day we all went out and, instead of using live bait, we used brand-new lures—we were excited because these were the killer kind, with three hooks dangling from the bottom. We were all standing on top of the dam, casting into the water, tossing our lines out as far as we could, when all of a sudden my line got caught on something. I yanked real hard, and the line snapped.

"God damn it!" I shouted. "I just bought that lure."

At almost the same instant, I heard someone yell, "Shit!" And I turned around to see Jimmy Goodrich dancing around, clawing at himself. *"Yaaaaaahhhh!"* he screamed. "It's in my head!" I realized then what had happened. The lure had snagged on Jimmy while I was trying to cast.

"Jesus, Jimmy . . . I'm sorry," I said.

We gathered around to assess the damage. Two of the three hooks were embedded in his scalp. The third was dangling. Blood was beginning to trickle down through his hair.

So we brought Jimmy back to Pop, who looked Jimmy over, spit out his cigar, and said, "Jesus, Mary, and Joseph! Now I've gotta take him to the hospital."

Jeff and I hopped in the back of the pickup and tagged along. Pop grumbled the whole time as the doctor used wire cutters and a scalpel to detach Jimmy from the lure and then stitched him up. Afterward, Pop chewed us out for not being careful. But he also took us down to Danny's Luncheonette on Pelham Road for hamburgers and ice-cream sodas.

Pop lived on a houseboat, and I'd visit him there often. One day I saw an old, decaying rowboat on shore, near the houseboat, and asked him if I could try to fix it up. Pop said sure. The rowboat apparently had been sitting there for years, rotting away, and no one had ever expressed any interest in rebuilding it. I knew a little something about carpentry from having hung around my father, who was mechanically inclined. I thought I could put this piece of junk back together. And I did—with Pop's help. He taught me how to patch the boat using tongue-and-groove planks; he showed me how to apply waterproof caulking to seal grooves. It took a few months, but eventually we refurbished the boat, painted it, and made it seaworthy . . . or sound-worthy, anyway.

I got my first taste of acting thanks to Pop, too. He was always taking home movies of his grandchildren, and one summer he created a play for all of us. It wasn't much, just a little skit featuring me as Abraham Lincoln, with a big cardboard hat and everything, but I remember thinking it was kind of fun. And looking back on it now, I realize what an extraordinary man Pop was, to have all that energy at his age and to take me under his wing and treat me like one of his own when he already had more than a dozen grandchildren. For a while, Pop was a big part of my life. He filled a gap, made me feel wanted.

I didn't realize just how much that yard meant to Pop until a few years later, when the property was sold and the land cleared to make room for an upscale housing development. He moved into a two-family house less than a mile away, but we didn't see much of him anymore. I remember one day riding my bicycle past the house and seeing Pop sitting by the window, all by himself, staring off into space. Although his wife had long since died, he still had family nearby, but I guess it just wasn't the same. For so many years he'd been busy. He'd had all that property to manage and all those kids to look after . . . and now they were gone. And I remember thinking that Pop looked like the loneliest guy in the world.

IF NOT FOR BOXING AND MY DESIRE TO BE AN ATHLETE, TO FOLLOW IN my father's footsteps, I might well have wound up in the Spofford Home . . . or someplace just like it. Twelve, thirteen, fourteen years old—that's when the hormones start raging and trouble has a way of finding you. Especially when you're the only male in the household, as I was. A boy that age needs a man in his life, someone not only to take him to baseball games and be his buddy but to keep him in line, to give him a good kick in the ass on occasion. I didn't have that, and eventually my mother began losing sleep over what might become of me. Not that I was disrespecting her—I've never done that. And, unlike a lot of my friends, I didn't smoke, drink, or do drugs. (In fact, I never did acquire any of those habits. I tried a sip of beer once and hated it. Tried a drag off a cigarette and almost choked. Drugs? Forget it. Never even smoked a joint.) But I was hanging out a lot at night, cutting classes at Isaac E. Young Junior High School, and generally just looking for anything that would make life a little more exciting.

Boxing served a dual purpose. First, it kept me from getting into too much trouble at too early an age. Second, it *was* exciting. If you're a kid going through puberty and you've got a lot of adrenaline and anger coursing through your veins, the gym isn't a bad place to be.

My career was born at a gym in New Rochelle run by Scoop Gallello, a former boxer who now owned a bar called Ring 30 on Drake Avenue and who liked to work with kids in his spare time. I was twelve years old the first time I wandered into Scoop's gym, more out of curiosity than anything else. I'd learned the basics of boxing from my father and done a little sparring with my friends, as I mentioned, but I'd never received any formal instruction. My father had never really wanted me to become a boxer, had never pushed me in that direction at all. He'd done all right as a fighter, but he hadn't made any money and he'd suffered a fair amount of pain. I don't think he wanted that life for me. Learning the art of self-defense, knowing how to protect yourself . . . that was all well and good. But fighting professionally? Trying to earn a living by beating people up? It was savage, unforgiving work, and my father never once suggested otherwise.

I went to Scoop's on my own, and almost from the moment I walked through the door I was enthralled by the place: the smell, the heat, the sound of leather on leather. It didn't hurt that while I wasn't a loud or cocky kid (not yet), I didn't lack self-confidence. I was pretty sure that I already knew more about boxing than most of the kids who were working with Scoop. I'd picked up a lot just talking with my father, working out on my own. But I was far from a polished fighter. I was strong for my age and size (125 pounds) and I moved pretty well, but I wasn't in very good shape and I lacked discipline. Under Scoop, I came to understand the importance of training and I learned to think of boxing as a science, a craft, as opposed to merely an explosion of violence.

My first official amateur boxing match was at the Southside Boys Club in New Rochelle—I still have a poster advertising the show. My father, who remained a flittering, inconsistent presence in our lives, found out about the show and demanded that he be allowed to work my corner. I didn't mind. In fact, I was happy to have him there, in part because I wanted to show him how far I'd come but also because I knew he'd be an asset. Whatever his faults, my dad was a hell of a boxer. He knew the sport.

To this day, I don't know if I've ever been more nervous about anything than I was in the moments before the opening bell of that fight. The Boys Club was packed with about three hundred people, including most of my buddies from school and several of my relatives. In the locker room, before the fight, my stomach rolled as I thought about the possibility of getting embarrassed in front of all these people. It didn't help matters any that my opponent was a sixteen-year-old kid from Pelham named Charlie Izizzion. A few years later Charlie joined the armed services and was killed while training during a military exercise. He was a small, tough, wiry kid, and I really had no business being in the ring with him. We were the same size, but he

That's me on the right about to get hit with a left hook by Charlie Izizzion.
Credit: Scoop Gallello

was four years older, stronger, and a more seasoned fighter. I knew he had the potential to hurt me, and the fear made my knees weak as I walked from the dressing room to the ring. I understood instinctively the need to control my emotions, my fear, since fighting—whether in the ring or in the street—is about the harnessing and fueling of emotion, but I hadn't yet learned how to do that.

"Hands up," my father said. "Move and stick. You'll be fine."

The fight was supposed to be short: three rounds, each two minutes in duration. It didn't last nearly that long. The bell rang and we met in the middle of the ring. I tried to take my time, get my breathing under control, and get a feel for Charlie's strengths and weaknesses. He wanted none of that. He was the stronger, older, more experienced fighter, and he knew it. Less than a minute into the round he caught me flush on the nose with a right hand. My head snapped back and my eyes fluttered from the sting, but I thought I was all right . . . until the blood began flowing from my nose into my mouth. I'd never been popped like that before, never had any reason to believe that I'd bleed so easily. But that's what happened. Like a shark, Charlie saw the blood, smelled victory, and charged right in.

Pop! Pop! Pop!

Three consecutive shots to the nose. The bleeding became more profuse. I tried to bob and weave; occasionally I got off a feeble punch that caught nothing but air. The first round wasn't even over yet and already I was thinking, *Why am I doing this?* Boxing, which I'd always loved, now seemed like the most ridiculous sport in the world.

Pop! Pop! Pop!

My trunks were now splattered with blood. I hoped only that the bell would ring before Charlie knocked me out and humiliated me in front of my friends. But the bell never did ring. Instead, the referee stepped in and stopped the fight, putting an end to the carnage. The next thing I knew we were in the middle of the ring together and the referee was lifting Charlie's arm, declaring him the winner by technical knockout. I went back to the locker room, beaten and bloody, and aware, for the very first time, of what it really meant to be a fighter.

I have only two major regrets in my life. One . . . well, I'll tell you about that later. The other is this: that I didn't take boxing more seriously. It is, without question, the most challenging and brutal of all sports, but I truly believe that if I had applied myself, if I had been committed to becoming the best boxer I could be (as opposed to the best "fighter"), I would have become a champion. I had the talent and the ability to withstand pain. Even as a kid, I had a technical understanding of the sport that eludes most adults. What I lacked was the desire . . . the focus.

Boxing remains my favorite sport, and it's a big part of my life even today; however, throughout my adolescence and early adulthood I never gave it the time and respect it deserved. I continued to train at Scoop's gym, but only sporadically. There were more shows, more fights, and fewer bloody noses. I won more often than I lost. I got bigger and better. I had promise, Scoop said, and I knew he was right. But there were too many distractions, too many diversions.

Like . . . well . . . girls.

Although I felt like I lagged behind some of my friends in this regard, in retrospect I realize I was actually an early bloomer. In Bensonhurst there had been a ten-year-old girl named Claudia who had begged me to "take her out." I wasn't sure what she meant, wasn't interested in girls in the least at that time. When she cornered me one day on the way home from school, pressed herself up against me, and promised to "show me a good time," I felt nothing so much as embarrassment. I wanted to get as far away from her as I could.

Middle school brought changes (as it inevitably does). Changes in the way I looked and felt, changes in the way I viewed girls, who suddenly began to sprout curves and bumps in all kinds of interesting places. On some level I began to understand how my father had been guided by the little head instead of the big head, although I didn't consider my casual lust to be the equivalent of his flagrant cheating. I was a kid going through puberty. He was a grown man trying to get some tits and ass outside his marriage. Big difference.

I didn't ask girls out—I was still too shy for that—but things began to happen anyway. There was a cute girl named Mary who invited me over to a house where she was baby-sitting. I was so scared of what might happen that I took two of my friends, Billy Reily and Jimmy Goodrich, with me; just so I wouldn't be alone with her. When we got to the house, Billy and Jimmy both went in and I stayed outside, shuffling and pacing nervously. They came out about a half hour later,

Billy pumping his fist, shouting, "I got her, man! I got her!" and Jimmy asking me if I wanted to smell his finger.

"Bullshit," I said. "You guys didn't do nothing." I believed that, too. No one got laid at twelve. Except in the movies.

"Go on in," Billy said. "She'll take care of you."

"Yeah," said Jimmy. "Don't be a chicken."

Suddenly Mary was at the door, smiling at Jimmy and Billy, saying good-bye to them, and asking me if I'd like to come in. Jimmy nudged Billy in the side with an elbow, laughed, and the two of them bounced down the front steps and sprinted up the sidewalk.

Mary and I talked for a while on the front porch and then went inside and watched television. Nothing else happened. I didn't even consider making a move, and Mary didn't exactly throw herself at me. Later I walked her home, and just as we said good-bye I decided to give her a kiss. I don't even know where I got the nerve. Regardless, as soon as our lips touched, Mary took control. She jammed her tongue into me, pulled me close, and we began making out right there on the street, kissing and caressing like crazy for the better part of ten minutes. She finally said good-bye and walked away smiling and giggling, leaving me there standing alone, flushed with excitement and wonder, thinking maybe Billy and Jimmy weren't lying after all.

I happily surrendered my virginity the next year, when I was in eighth grade, although it was not Mary who took it. (Sadly, she moved away and I never had another opportunity to walk down that path.) The girl with whom I first shared the joy of carnality was in fact the younger sister of one my friends (and that's why she'll remain nameless here, in these pages). She was twelve; I was thirteen. We'd known each other ever since I'd moved to New Rochelle and had merely been friends, but one day we wound up at her house, just the two of us, sitting together on the couch, hanging out, listening to music, watching television . . . and our hands began to wander. It was completely spontaneous, at least on my part. I remember thinking for a few moments that there was something very wrong about what I was doing. Not because of our ages or anything I'd been taught in school or church—frankly, I didn't give a shit about any of that—but simply because of my friendship with her brother. You weren't supposed to mess around with your buddy's sister—that much I knew.

But . . . sometimes the brain shuts down, doesn't it? There's no reasoning with most men when the blood rushes south . . . and a thirteen-year-old? Fughetaboutit!

Our first time was clumsy and fast and messy, which is to say . . . it was great. I mean let's be serious . . . is any sex bad sex when you're thirteen? And it pretty quickly became a regular occurrence. We'd meet at her house, my house . . . anywhere . . . anytime . . .

I used her and she used me and neither one cared . . . we were getting our share.

Night Moves indeed. Working . . . practicing . . . On some level I guess I felt bad about what we were doing, but I enjoyed it too much to stop. Funny thing, though. It wasn't like we were in love. We were just hooked on each other's bodies and on sex. This went on for several years, and although I'm sure our friends suspected something, there were never any accusations. In public we were never boyfriend and girlfriend, never held hands or passed notes or exchanged friendship rings or any of that gooey, romantic high school nonsense. But alone, at night, we were lovers. It was a strange relationship, one that finally ran its course when I was sixteen and she was fifteen and we both found other people. There was no big fight, no angry breakup. We just stopped, as if the lesson was over.

There were other distractions. I was really into music for a while. In Bensonhurst I had learned how to play the drums and actually joined a drum and bugle corps. Wore a uniform, marched in parades . . . the whole thing. I thought it was kind of cool, too. When we moved to New Rochelle I continued to play the drums, although my taste in music naturally shifted to rock 'n' roll. In the basement of our apartment building at Shady Glen Court I found a pearl white Ludwig drum set. It once was owned by the son of one of our neighbors, but he had long since grown up and moved away, so they were happy to part with it. For a price, of course. They wanted a hundred dollars for the complete set, which was a ton of money to me and my family but still far less than it was worth. Hell, the chrome snare drum alone was worth that much. I used the money from my paper route to pay for part of it; the rest I borrowed from my mother.

I set up the whole kit in our apartment and practiced all the time, drove everyone in the building crazy. My friend Mike Sabella already knew how to play the drums, so he helped teach me. He'd play the floor drum, and I'd play the bass and the snare. Billy and Jimmy later joined us and we formed a band. We'd play for hours (usually covering the Young Rascals) and create an unbelievable racket. The cops used to stop by all the time because of complaints from the neighbors. They were cool about it, though. I think they knew we were just having fun and that there were far more dangerous and annoying things for a bunch of teenage boys to be doing: like running with gangs and getting in fights. Real fights.

By eighth grade I was hanging out with some hard-nosed kids. We weren't bad kids, but we were tough, or at least we wanted to think so. We used to dress neat, too. All the tough kids, even kids in gangs, bought their clothes at a place called Frombury's on Hugenot Street in New Rochelle. It was almost like a contest, a source of pride to see which group could look the sharpest. Not like today. Kids dress like slobs, even in school: jeans hanging off the ass, guinea T-shirts . . . anything goes. We would have gotten smacked for dressing like that, but I guess today teachers have more important things to worry about—like not getting shot in the classroom.

Anyway, we used to go to these dances at the Blessed Sacrament Church on Maple Avenue—BS dances, we'd call them. We'd hang out, act tough, maybe even dance a little. Groups of kids represented various neighborhoods, and there was always a lot of talking and chest thumping and strutting around. To us, it was all pretty dramatic, like the Jets and the Sharks, you know? It all seemed fairly innocent until one night a friend of ours, a kid named Joey Fortuna, got jumped by a bunch of guys from Mount Vernon and tossed through the side window of Karl Ehmer's meat store (located directly across the street from Mayflower Doughnut Shop on Leroy Place and Center Avenue, where we used to hang out with other tough guys from the neighborhood, like Frankie DiBuono, Johnny Tufo, Bobby Brower, Gary LaPore, and Anthony Raffa, and listen to rock 'n' roll blaring out of one of the many hot rods parked in front). We were still at the dance when we heard about it, when someone came running in and started screaming about Joey getting beat up. By the time we got to the Mayflower, Joey had been taken to the hospital and there was glass and blood everywhere.

Even though I wasn't that close to Joey, I was enraged by what had happened to him. He was one of us, a New Rochelle kid, and nobody had any business hurting him like that. We decided there would be payback . . . and soon. I was pissed off and scared by the prospect of a gang fight; I was also excited as hell.

The confrontation came a few weeks later, after several attempts were aborted by the cops, who seemed always to be one step ahead of us. We met in New Rochelle, a dozen guys on each side, armed with sticks and rocks. We all wore Garrison belts, too, the kind you'd buy at an Army-Navy store, with a big, heavy brass buckle that could be filed down and sharpened at the edges. In battle you could remove the belt, wrap one end around your fist, and use the other as a whip-like razor. It was rare to see anyone use the Garrison belt, though, because it was capable of serious mayhem. We were thirteen, fourteen years old—we wanted to fight; we didn't want to kill anyone. The Garrison belt was more for effect than anything else.

We fought at an abandoned house near the Blessed Sacrament Church, known as the White House. We stood in two rows, a few feet apart, and traded insults until Billy Reily decided he'd heard enough. Billy was a tough Irish kid with a reputation for knowing how to use his hands, and he proved worthy of that reputation on this night. He leaped at one of the Mount Vernon kids, threw a big, wild right hand, and dropped the kid to his knees. At that point we all jumped in and the battle was on, a flurry of wild punches and kicks, and pretty soon we were all on the ground, wrestling and squirming and trying to catch our breath. It was over almost as soon as it began, thanks to a neighbor who had called the cops. As the sirens screamed in the distance, we struggled to our feet, cursed and spit at one another some more, and took off in opposite directions. Billy patted me on the back as we ran, told me I did a good job. My first gang rumble was history, and I'd survived. More than that, actually. I'd found it exhilarating!

There was something about being part of a group—*a gang*—that was alluring. Of course, we weren't really a gang, just a bunch of guys from the same neighborhood who liked to hang out together. But we knew what we wanted to be. We wanted to be like the gangs depicted in movies—tough sons of bitches who didn't like authority and weren't afraid of anyone, guys who looked out for one another and fought for one another . . . who knew what friendship really meant.

For me, though, that was only part of it. For me . . . it was also about bikes.

The same year I had my first real boxing match, I also went to see the movie *Hells Angels on Wheels,* starring Jack Nicholson and Sonny Barger, the founder of the legendary Oakland chapter of the Hells Angels and a man widely considered to be the most influential personality in the history of the club. I was mesmerized. I remember coming home from the theater that day and turning my bicycle into a mini bike. I used a lawn mower for the engine and some chrome vacuum cleaner pipes for the exhaust. I bought a dungaree jacket at Jack's Army-Navy store for six bucks, cut off the sleeves and collar, and wrote something I thought was pretty cool on the back of the jacket: HEAVEN'S DEVILS. Get it? The opposite of "Hells Angels."

OK, what do you want from a thirteen-year-old? The point is, I was hooked on bikes in general and the Hells Angels in particular. Then, one day while I was riding around on my minibike, I happened to see this big chopper parked in front of a house not far from where Jimmy Goodrich lived. It was an amazing bike, a big-ass Harley-Davidson with the high-rise handlebars. I'd never seen anything like it—not up close—so I pulled in with my minibike and started doing little circles around it, staring, memorizing every line and curve. I got off my bike to get a closer look. I put my face right down near the engine, so close that I could see my reflection in the chrome.

"Hey! What do you think you're doing?"

Startled, I straightened up and jumped back. There, walking toward me from the house, was a monster of a man, at least six feet, four inches tall, with long hair, a beard, and wearing a dungaree jacket covered with patches and medals.

Oh, man! There's a Hells Angel in my neighborhood. How cool!

"You like the bike?" he asked.

"Yes, sir."

He looked at my minibike. "Yeah, well, maybe someday you'll have one just like it."

I smiled and nodded. We talked for a while more, and he turned out to be a real nice guy. His name was Paul Westermeyer—everyone called him Tall Paul—and he wasn't a member of the Hells Angels. He belonged to another club called the Bronx Aliens. Still, he was a real biker from a real club, and I couldn't have been more impressed. Paul was about eighteen years old at the time, but he didn't treat me like an annoying little kid. He was friendly, polite, and seemed to appreciate my interest in him and his bike. So I asked him if it would be okay if I stopped by sometime to watch him work on the bike. I promised not to get in the way.

"Sure," he said. "Why not?"

The very next day, first thing in the morning, I came out and started waxing his bike. When Paul walked out the door of his house, he was shocked but not angry.

"What are you doing?" he said incredulously.

"Putting a new coat of wax on it."

He smiled and shook his head, obviously amused. "Come on. Hop on the back. Let's go for a ride."

"You mean it?"

"Sure."

I jumped on and Paul hit the throttle. The engine let out a roar, that distinctive guttural sound that is the Harley trademark, and we took off down the street. Scared shitless, I wrapped my arms around Paul and held on for dear life. But after a few minutes the fear subsided and the feeling of freedom set in. It was like we were flying. I'd never experienced anything like it.

My mom wasn't happy about any of this. She saw the jacket, went nuts, and took it away from me. She forbade me to ride with Paul. Then, inevitably, a cop pulled me over while I was riding my minibike and just yanked it out from under me and threw it in his trunk. "Tell your father to come to the police station and get it," he said. My parents had split, of course, and like most divorced couples they didn't agree on much, but I was pretty sure they would have been united in their response to my having been inspired by the Hells Angels. So, needless to say, I never saw my minibike again. Didn't matter, though; the seed had been sown.

6

INTERESTING THING ABOUT THAT FIRST RUMBLE WITH THE GANG FROM Mount Vernon: We were all white guys. Every one of us. Race has never been much of an issue with me. If you're a stand-up guy and you treat people with respect, you're okay in my book. Doesn't matter whether you're black, white, Hispanic, Asian, Middle Eastern. The same holds true if you're an asshole. I don't know of any ethnic or religious group that owns the franchise on bad behavior. Personally, I believe in judging a person by the way he acts, not by the color of his skin.

That said, I can't deny that there are times when race is a great divider, as well as a spark for confrontation. This is especially true when you put a large group of people in a confined space for an extended period of time—say, in prison.

Or junior high school.

I was in eighth grade the first time I was exposed to this phenomenon. There were two kids at Isaac E. Young Junior High School, cousins, who walked around as if they owned the place. Their names were Rob and Tony Richards. They were tall, muscular, mean, and black. And they scared the living shit out of a lot of kids in school (a lot of teachers, too, for that matter). Rob was the more sadistic of the two—he liked to play practical jokes on people, jokes that were sometimes funny but often involved physical pain. One day in the school cafeteria, for example, he spent the entire lunch period torturing people with thumbtacks. Whenever someone walked by Rob's seat, he would reach out and jab the person with a tack. That person would naturally scream or curse, turn to face his tormentor, see that it was big, bad Rob Richards, and keep right on going.

A glaring exception was my buddy John O'Mara, another feisty Irish kid, like Billy Reily, who took no shit and was willing to fight with little provocation. John saw what was happening and decided to deliberately cross Rob Richards's radar screen on the way out of the cafeteria. We watched with bated breath as John sauntered down the aisle and Rob started to lean back. Suddenly John stopped, a step in front of where Rob was sitting.

"You stick me with that thing, you black motherfucker, I'll beat your ass."

And there it was, a race riot waiting to happen. I don't think it mattered to John in the least that Rob Richards was black, but the fact that he *was* black became fuel for the fire, a way for John to get his point across. Within seconds the cafeteria had turned into an arena, with these two teenage warriors circling each other and a few hundred bloodthirsty spectators screaming their lungs out. Black kids cheering for Rob, white kids cheering for John.

Unfortunately, our bloodlust went unsatisfied, as half a dozen teachers and aides rushed in to break up the fight before it even began. But that wasn't the end of things—not by a long shot.

That afternoon, while I was walking from one class to another with John and Billy Reily, we passed a group of black students. At the center of the group were the Richards cousins. Clearly they'd been waiting for us. Rob jumped out in front of John, blocking his path, and put his nose right in John's face (he was a good four inches taller than John, so he had to bend over to do this; it was an intimidating sight).

"Who the hell do you think you are?" Rob said. "I'll fuck you up!"

John wasn't much of a diplomat. The words had barely escaped Rob's mouth when John blasted him. He threw two punches with everything he had, knocking Rob off balance, and then jumped on top of him. The two of them crashed to the floor and wrestled for a while as the rest of us looked on. Remarkably, no one jumped in and no other fights broke out. When they were pulled apart by a handful of teachers, it was obvious who had won. Rob was bruised and bleeding; John was unmarked.

But this wasn't just a battle; it was a war. I'm not exactly sure why—maybe he was provoked by his friends or maybe he was embarrassed or maybe he just enjoyed fighting—but Rob Richards came back for more the next day. And the day after that. And the day after that. For at least a month, he and John went at it. Sometimes they fought in school, and sometimes (after they'd been suspended) they fought on the street. It didn't matter. Rob instigated virtually all of these encounters, and he lost almost all of them. John O'Mara was smaller, but he was a better fighter, a more skilled boxer. I won't say he had a bigger heart, because obviously something compelled Rob to keep coming back for more, despite getting his ass kicked on a regular basis. I guess you could say he was brave . . . or maybe just stupid.

I wasn't a serious troublemaker in junior high school. Like I said, I didn't drink or do drugs, and I wasn't into theft or vandalism. I wasn't even the kind of kid who took pleasure in making life miserable for his teachers. I was just a fuckup. Aside from the fact that I got to hang out with my buddies while I was there, nothing about school held any appeal for me. So I started cutting classes. I stayed out late at night, which caused my poor mother undue stress. I got a couple of different jobs on the weekends. One was at a hamburger joint called Mr. Topps on Boston Post Road in New Rochelle. When they asked to see my working papers, I lied and said I was sixteen years old. I stalled as much as I could, but after a while they discovered I was only fourteen, and the owner let me go. The other job was with Carroll Brothers Roofing, which was owned by Jimmy Goodrich's stepfather, Bob. The work was much harder, but the pay was better, so I didn't mind. I realized right away that I liked having some real money in my pocket. It never occurred to me that by studying hard, staying in school, and getting good grades I might someday have a chance to earn a far better living. I just didn't think that way. I was too unfocused, too hyperactive, too concerned with immediate gratification. And while my mother tried to keep me in line, she just didn't have the time or energy. I needed a good whack on the side of the head, and there was no one around to deliver it.

Tenth grade was a waste of time for me and for most of my friends. I was into cars, hanging out, having a good time. My buddy Fred Martinez was the oldest in our group—he'd been left back a couple times—and so the first one to get a set of wheels, a gorgeous '57 Chevy that he reconditioned. He also helped me build my first car, a '63

Chevy. I got my license at sixteen, in the spring of that year, and borrowed Fred's car whenever I could. We'd cut class and drive around all day, sometimes stopping for a burger and a soda at Leo's Delicatessen on North Avenue. To say I lacked purpose would be a big understatement. Aside from my friends, who had become like a surrogate family, I didn't care about much of anything. I wouldn't even go to gym class—that's how bad it got. Here I was supposed to be this big physical fitness nut, a kid who wouldn't touch a cigarette because he had dreams of being a professional boxer, and I didn't even have the energy or ambition for gym!

Truth is, I wasn't even training very much then, either. I'd go to Scoop's gym once in a while and I lifted weights in my basement, but that was really just a way to get a little definition in my biceps so I'd look better for the girls. There was no discipline, no plan, no order. Most of my friends were the same way. We liked fighting, acting like a street gang, trying to be tough guys, but we were all looking for something more.

In Fred's case, responsibility was heaped upon him without request. His girlfriend, Kathy, whom I'd known since seventh grade, when I first moved to New Rochelle, became pregnant at the age of fifteen. She and Fred got married a few months later, and by sixteen Kathy was a mom. I was best man at their wedding, and as much as I liked both Kathy and Fred, I knew there was no way their marriage would last. Fred wasn't ready for a wife and family. They had problems from the start and wound up getting a divorce less than a year after they walked down the aisle.

Billy Reily and Jimmy Goodrich were the next to go. I was sitting in social studies class one afternoon in the spring of my sophomore year, and I saw Billy and Jimmy in the hallway. They were jumping up and down, waving to me, acting all excited about something. When the bell rang I met them in the hallway.

"What's going on?" I asked.

"Come on," Jimmy said. "We're going down to enlist."

I was shocked. This was 1969, the height of the Vietnam War, and nobody in his right mind wanted to be over there.

"Are you nuts?"

Billy shook his head. "Nah, man. We're gonna join the marines. It'll be cool."

Whether I wanted to enlist was beside the point; I wasn't old enough. Billy and Jimmy, however, were seventeen, fed up with school, and looking for adventure. They enlisted that very day. My circle of friends was shrinking, my attitude growing worse. By June I had pretty much stopped going to school at all, and the inevitable happened: I flunked tenth grade. My mother was furious and frustrated. On the day she was informed by the school that I'd have to repeat tenth grade, Mom called me into the living room and sat me down. She looked sad and tired.

"I can't control you," she said. "I don't know what to do anymore."

Unfazed, unrepentant, I just shrugged my shoulders. I wasn't worried about being punished or held accountable for my actions. What could my mother do—send me to the Spofford Home? Not likely.

But Mom surprised me. She had something else in mind.

"You're going to live with your father for a while," she said. "Maybe he can straighten you out."

This was bad news, and not simply because I was still angry with my father and thoroughly uninterested in sharing an apartment with him. You see, Dad no longer lived in Brooklyn. He'd taken a new job managing a different apartment complex . . . in Rochester, New York! Sending me there was like sending me to the moon. Who the hell wanted to live in Rochester?

"I won't go," I said.

Mom looked me in the eye and nodded. "Oh, yes, you will."

I was wrong about Rochester. It wasn't like being sent to the moon; to me, a kid from New York, it was closer to Mars. Wearing jeans and a silk shirt, with my hair swept up in an Elvis pompadour, I'd never felt like more of an outcast than I did the first time I walked into Henrietta High School. I was a cocky Italian kid from the city, and now I was stuck in farm country. If this was supposed to improve my attitude, well, it didn't work. I was pissed about moving, pissed about living with my father, pissed about being the oldest kid in tenth grade . . . I was pissed about a lot of things. And I didn't mind letting other people know it. That whole year I walked around school with a big chip on my shoulder. If I didn't exactly go looking for fights, neither did I pass up any opportunity to flex my muscles, to let everyone know I was the real deal: a guy who had grown up in Brooklyn and the Bronx and who could easily beat the fuck out of anyone who disrespected me. A shitty attitude? You bet, but I felt like I'd earned the right to be angry. By confronting anyone who so much as looked cross-eyed at me . . . by cutting no one any slack at all I'm sure I gave the impression of being a bully. But I didn't care. I took no shit from anyone. If I heard that another student had said something behind my back, I challenged him immediately.

"Repeat it to my face," I'd say. And they rarely did. Compared to where I'd come from, Rochester seemed a weak and flacid place, which only made me despise it more.

I sensed most of the teachers were afraid of me, too . . . with one notable exception. One of the shop teachers was a big, muscular man who had no trouble keeping his students in line. He wasn't exactly a fan of mine, and after a while he grew tired of my tough-guy routine. So, in the springtime, he devised a clever way of dealing with it. Our masonry class had been involved in erecting a flagpole in front of the school, and this teacher decided, after watching me argue with another kid, that my talents would be of more use outside the classroom.

"Zito," he said. "You're such a tough guy . . . why don't you go outside and guard the flagpole."

"Guard it how?"

"You know . . . make sure no one puts their hands in the wet cement."

I straightened up, believing for a moment that this was some kind of honor. "And if they do?"

The teacher smacked his right fist into the palm of his left hand. "Let 'em have it."

"Really?"

He nodded. "Absolutely. Anyone touches the cement, tries to draw their names in it or mess around with it in any way, you have my permission to beat them up. Just stand guard until I call you back in." Other kids in the class were starting to snicker, though I wasn't sure why. "Can you handle that?"

"Yes, sir."

After about three hours of guarding the flagpole as a butt-chilling wind whipped off Lake Ontario, I finally got the message: this was a punishment, not an honor. But I can't say the experience taught me a lesson. It just made me harder, angrier.

At least I got to reconnect with my father while I was in Rochester. He managed a place called the Fairways, a typical suburban apartment complex with swimming pools, tennis courts, and a gym. It was clean and comfortable. I'd taken a lifesaving course at the YMCA back in New Rochelle, so I was able to get a job as a lifeguard at the Fairways. The money wasn't bad and the work was easy. There was tension between me and my father, but he didn't give me a hard time, didn't ride me too badly, maybe because he knew he'd screwed up himself. By sticking his dick where it didn't belong and by ripping apart our family my father had forfeited at least a portion of his parental power.

Nevertheless, we grew close again. My father decided to teach a boxing class at the complex, and to do that he had to get in shape. So he started training again, at almost fifty years of age. I trained right along with him. It was kind of cool—he'd teach the residents how to box; I'd teach them how to swim.

It was perhaps inevitable that my father and I would end up in the ring together, and that's precisely what happened one evening after class. The suggestion came from me, of course, and when he declined the offer I pushed the issue.

"Why not?" I taunted. "Afraid you can't keep up?"

I've analyzed my motive for this a few times over the years. On one level, I just wanted to see how much I knew, how much I had learned. My father had been a great fighter, and now he was back in shape. What better way to test myself? On a far more emotional level, I wanted a chance to hit him, to hurt him . . . to pay him back for what he'd done.

"Okay," he said—you could only push my father so far. "Let's see what you've got."

I weigh about 195 pounds today, but back then I was a wiry kid, maybe 155 pounds, roughly the same size as my father, although a couple inches taller. It figured to be a good match. And it was. But it quickly became much more than a technical exercise. With a few dozen people watching, we touched gloves and began boxing. We circled, bobbed, threw a few halfhearted jabs. Dad was in control—

emotionally and physically. He moved me around the ring, trying his best to maintain a clinical air in the proceedings. There was no fire in his punches, no seriousness.

My attitude was significantly different. I danced, moved, waited. When an opening came, after I slipped one of his jabs, I dug in and hit him with a hard uppercut to the solar plexus. There was a distinct cracking, and then the air rushed out of his lungs with a *whoosh!*

Oh, shit!

My father was in severe pain, but he didn't stop, didn't say a word. Not yet. Instead, he collected himself and hit me with a combination—a straight right followed by a left hook that hit me flush on the jaw and lifted me right off my feet. I never saw it coming. The next thing I knew I was on my back, looking up at my father. He spit out his mouthpiece and started yelling at me.

"You stupid son of a bitch! What are you doing? This isn't supposed to be for real." He pawed at his ribs with his glove. "Christ, you broke my ribs."

My head was spinning. I'd almost lost consciousness. My father finally reached down and offered a hand. The sparring session was over. Dad walked around holding his side for a week or so, grunting every time he laughed or coughed. I don't know what made me prouder, the fact that I'd hurt him or the fact that he had nearly knocked me out. We had a strange relationship, me and Dad. But at least we had come to some sort of an understanding. I never asked him for an explanation, never asked him why he had messed up our family. And we never sparred again. There was no need.

7

THAT SUMMER, AFTER I'D COMPLETED TENTH GRADE FOR THE SECOND TIME,
I flew back to New York to spend some time with my old friends.
Rather than imposing on my mom, I stayed with the Goodriches, who
were like my second family anyway. After a few days I got a call from
my father in Rochester. I could tell the moment I picked up the phone
that something was wrong.

"How's the trip going?" he asked, though it didn't sound like he
really cared.

"Okay . . . why?"

"Because you're going to be there for a while. I just got fired."

The apartment complex had just been sold, and the new owners
were going to be working with a different management company. My
father was given only a few days' notice to pack his bags and clear
out of the apartment. He told me not to worry—he'd already lined
up a new job managing a building at 1000 Park Avenue in Manhattan.

I wasn't worried. Although I felt bad that he'd lost his job, I couldn't
have been happier about getting the hell out of Rochester. One year
was more than enough. I was a New Yorker, and I belonged in New
York. Or at least in New Rochelle.

I moved back into my mother's Shady Glen apartment and tried to
resume my old life, but a lot of things had changed. For one thing,
most of my old buddies had put New Rochelle High School in the
rearview mirror. Billy Reily and Jimmy Goodrich were still in the
service; others had either graduated or dropped out. I was seventeen
years old and still several dozen credits short of a degree. At this rate,
I'd still be in high school at age twenty. No thanks. I'd had enough.

The plan, such as it was, went something like this: I'd work during the day, put away some money, and take courses at night. Before long I'd have my GED and I wouldn't have to worry about the stigma of being a high school dropout. It seemed like an easy shortcut, one that would allow me to help my mom out with the rent at the same time.

And then Kathy came along.

Not for the first time, of course. As I said, Kathy and I had been friends since junior high. She and Fred had even visited me in Rochester, along with their baby daughter, Lisa (who was also my goddaughter). By the time I got back to New Rochelle, however, Fred and Kathy were history. Their marriage had ended the way most shotgun marriages end (especially those involving teenagers): in divorce. Kathy was now living with her mother (who helped take care of Lisa) and trying to hold down a job while raising a child. She was only seventeen. Most kids in that situation fall apart, but Kathy was tough and tireless; she wasn't much for self-pity. Under her picture in her high school yearbook, it read, "Only the strong survive." I loved that about her.

Fred and I were still the best of buddies, but that all changed one

Kathy's high school picture

night at John Magotta's birthday party in the West End. Kathy and I talked for a while, the way we often did, and when the party came to an end, I asked if she needed a ride home. It couldn't have been more innocent (although I don't deny that I was attracted to her, and I think she was attracted to me). I drove Kathy to her mother's house, dropped her off, said good-bye, and went home. That was it.

The next day I got a call from Fred. "I'll be there in five minutes," he said. I could tell by the tone of his voice that he was pissed about something, but I couldn't imagine what it was. I was waiting outside when Fred pulled up, got out of his car, and said, "You give Kathy a ride home last night?"

"Yeah. What of it?"

Fred stared at the ground, shook his head. "That's wrong, man, and you know it."

First of all, I didn't think it was wrong. Kathy needed a ride home, and I gave it to her. Second . . . nothing happened. Fred was my friend, though, so I tried to be considerate of his feelings.

"What's the big deal, Fred? It was just a ride home, that's all. Who cares?" I paused, gave him a little tap on the shoulder. "Come on, man . . . I've known Kathy as long as you have. What's the problem?"

He stiffened. "The problem is, you shouldn't be taking her anywhere. Don't let it happen again."

Now he was starting to piss me off. Fred was my friend, but he was out of line, implicitly accusing me of something I hadn't done and, worse, telling me what I could or could not do in the future. No one did that—not even one of my best friends.

"Freddy," I began, knowing that what I was about to say was going to cut him to the bone, "you guys are divorced. You can't tell her what to do anymore." I paused. "And you sure as hell aren't going to tell me what to do."

Well, that was all Fred needed to hear. He went fucking wild, started threatening me, challenging me, demanding that I stay away from Kathy. I took it pretty well, I thought. Usually, when anyone talked to me like that, I gave him one chance to apologize before responding with a slap to the face. But Freddy and I were friends, and I figured he had a right to blow off some steam at my expense. That's not to say that I backed down. Far from it. After Fred had vented for a minute or so, I held up a finger and said, clearly and forcefully, so as to make sure he got the point, "You know what, Fred? Nothing happened last night. But because you're acting like such an asshole, I'm going to take Kathy out on a date. What do you think of that?"

Fred shook with rage, but he didn't make a move on me. For one thing, he was smaller than me and not nearly as good a fighter. If things got physical between us (which was not my intention), Fred was going to get the worst of it. And he knew it. Second, I'm sure he also knew that he was making no sense at all. Logically speaking, Fred's argument had no weight. He and Kathy were divorced; he'd wanted out of the marriage.

Now, I suppose you could argue that honor among friends would dictate that I not have anything to do with Kathy, at least romantically. And, to tell you the truth, I never intended to fall in love with her. I just wanted to teach Fred a lesson.

"Don't do it, Chuck," he said. "You'll regret it."

I laughed at him. "Fred, you and I are friends . . . but don't you ever tell me what do."

He stormed away and I went back in the house. I walked right into the kitchen, took the phone off the hook, and dialed Kathy's number.

"Hey, it's Chuck. You free tomorrow?"

Funny how something you do basically out of spite can evolve into something so profound. I picked up Kathy and Lisa the next morning, and the three of us had a great little day, the kind of day you never forget. We drove around for a while, and then we went to the Bronx Zoo. Kathy and I talked and laughed and quickly came to the realization that we liked each other—a lot. It's hard for me to describe the way I felt, walking with Kathy by my side and Lisa in a stroller between us. I wanted to protect them, to shield them from whatever pain the world might have in store for them. I don't know that I was really equipped for the job—shit, what seventeen-year-old is?—but I wanted to do it anyway. It was like I'd been searching for some sort of purpose in my life, something to give my days meaning, and here it was: an instant family.

Within a few weeks I knew this was a serious relationship,

My daughter, Lisa

unlike anything I'd ever experienced before. In the past, my interest in girls had been almost exclusively sexual. What I felt toward Kathy was much more complex, much more intense. I loved her, and her daughter, in ways I'd never imagined possible.

I grew up fast that year. I moved in with Kathy, who already had an attic apartment in her mother's house at 153 Franklin Avenue, and we became a family. I wanted to work hard for Kathy and Lisa, to take care of them and make their lives better. I don't ever remember feeling like Lisa was anything other than my own child. She called me Daddy, and I loved her as my own daughter, raised her as my own; like any good parent, I would have walked in front of a bus for her.

We were pretty happy, although the cloud of nostalgia tends to obscure the difficult times. Kathy and I both worked very hard. She was a telephone operator, a dental hygienist; I held down a variety of jobs, all involving manual labor. I went back to working for Carroll Brothers Roofing; I painted and sanded boats at the Castaways Yacht Club. Later, when my mother started seeing a man named John Felice, whose brother Frank was supervisor of the refrigeration department at Finast Supermarkets, I became a refrigeration apprentice. Then I got my own truck to drive, my own route, a degree of autonomy. I liked that. And the money wasn't bad.

There was, predictably, fallout from my relationship with Kathy. For one thing, my friendship with Fred dissolved. He maintained contact with Lisa for a while—he'd pick her up on weekends, take her out—but that ended years later. My being there might have had something to do with his dwindling interest—it was awkward for all of us. But I didn't really care. I didn't think of Fred as Lisa's father anyway, and when he moved out of state and disappeared from her life completely I was actually kind of relieved.

School wasn't high on my list of priorities, either. I had intended to pick up my high school equivalency degree by taking courses at night. But when I came home from a long day of work, the last thing I wanted to do was open a book and study. So I dropped out again.

I clung to boxing a bit longer, for I still had dreams of being a champion. I had become a good street fighter. I was tougher than most people and I knew how to use my hands. I figured with my background in boxing and my desire to make something of myself

I'd take one more shot at cracking the big time. But that meant serious training, hours and hours of sparring, skipping rope, and running. Hundreds of sit-ups and push-ups each day. It meant making a commitment that a young working father couldn't realistically make. Nonetheless, I tried. I'd get up at five in the morning to run. Then I'd leave for work at six. In the afternoon and on weekends I'd hit the gym to train. At first I went back to Scoop's place, but he was working primarily with younger kids, so I switched to Cage Recreation in White Plains, where I trained under a guy named Charlie Caserta.

Once again, I have to admit that I'm using the word *trained* loosely. It was never a twenty-four/seven kind of thing. Some days I was just too tired to work out. Other days I had family or work responsibilities that kept me from going to the gym. My father eventually found out that I was boxing again and urged me to work with him. The truth was, he didn't want me to be a boxer, didn't think it was worth my time and energy.

"But if you're going to do it," he said, "let's do it right."

By the time I was nineteen years old, Dad had moved to an apartment at Seven West 14th Street, which wasn't far from the Gramercy Gym. So I started training there, with my father guiding my workouts. I fought my first match in the Golden Gloves, the king of all amateur boxing tournaments, on January 30, 1973, my father's birthday. I was nineteen years old . . . almost twenty. I'd fought before, of course, so I knew what to expect. I knew what it felt like to get hit in the face and to have my nose splattered. Still, that first night, sitting in the dressing room at Madison Square Garden's Felt Forum, I was so nervous that my stomach was doing somersaults.

It was an interesting scene. There were several fighters in the room. Like gladiators preparing for battle, we shared the same space, which meant we all tried to hide our fear and anxiety, for we didn't want any potential opponent to sense our weakness. As my father taped my hands and slid my gloves over my fists, I looked around the room. Everyone seemed to be lost in their own world, and, quite frankly, no one looked all that intimidating.

With one notable exception.

In a far corner of the room, sitting on a milk crate, rubbing his gloves together, staring off into space, was a thickly muscled black man with a receding hairline and a nose that appeared to have been broken about fifty times. He looked like he couldn't wait to get into the ring and do some damage.

"Jesus Christ," I said to my father. "I'd hate to be the poor sap who's fighting that guy."

My father looked up briefly, grunted, and went back to working on my hands. I laughed a little at my own joke, mainly because I knew I wouldn't be facing the killer in the corner. This guy had to be a middleweight—he looked like he weighed at least 160 pounds. I was 147, a welterweight. My opponent was some guy named Joe Pratt. I looked around the room.

Pratt . . .

An ordinary name. Could have been just about anybody.

Mine was the very first fight on the card (in fact, since this was opening night, it was the first fight of the entire tournament), so it wasn't long before an official came into the dressing room and summoned me to the ring.

"Okay, gentlemen," he said, looking at a clipboard. "First up—Zito and Pratt. Let's go!"

I stood up. Out of the corner of my eye I saw movement in the distance, someone rising from a milk crate.

Oh, no. . . .

Yup. The big guy in the corner, the one with muscles on top of muscles . . . that was Joe Pratt.

Holy fucking shit! He's gonna kill me.

My father gave me a little shove, and the next thing I knew we were both in the ring, me and Joe Pratt, the welterweight who looked like a middleweight, bouncing around, throwing jabs at the air. I wore my father's old shoes that night, as well as his old trunks. I even wore a robe bearing his name (I'd given it to him as a present a few years earlier, to replace the one I'd destroyed when I was a little kid). Well, actually, not his name, but the name of the fighter he'd once been.

"Al LaBarba?" the ring announcer said to me. "Who the hell is Al LaBarba? I thought this was Zito and Pratt."

"Yeah, it is. I'm wearing my father's robe."

He nodded, shrugged his shoulders, and introduced us to the audience, which, by the way, included all of my friends, my family, and even my boss. As my name echoed throughout the arena, I sensed a completely different atmosphere from anything I'd experienced in

This is where I saw stars from Pratt's overhand right—and they weren't movie stars either.

boxing. I'd had plenty of amateur bouts, but this felt so much bigger, so much more important. Not just because it was the Golden Gloves, but because I was standing in the same ring where so many great boxers had fought in the past, including Joe Louis, Rocky Marciano, Muhammad Ali . . . and my dad, Al LaBarba. To me, it was like being in the Olympics.

My father didn't provide much in the way of instruction. He just put in my mouthpiece, smacked me on the back of the head, and said, "Move and stick."

The bell rang and Joe Pratt seemed to leap off his chair and into the middle of the ring in a single motion, like a tiger pouncing on its prey. I'd barely taken a step when I felt a stinging sensation in my left temple—he'd hit me solidly with an overhand right, so hard that I saw stars and for a moment I thought I might go down right there, ending my Golden Gloves dream in approximately fifteen seconds. I took a drunken step backward to give my head a chance to clear, and as the fog lifted I thought, *What the fuck am I doing here anyway?*

Instinct took over soon enough, though, and I began moving and punching, moving and punching. He was bigger and stronger than I was—older and more experienced, too—so I couldn't afford to get into a brawl with him. I had to box. I landed a few right hands, which gave me confidence and seemed to frustrate him. Then I threw a jab, and he came down underneath it. For an instant, his head was wide open, and I knew I had him. He was strong, all right. But he was reckless. Eventually, there would be another mistake, another opportunity, and I'd be ready. The nervousness drained from my body. Now I was confident, excited.

It was the second round before the window opened again. Joe Pratt, tired and irritated that he hadn't been able to put away this smaller Italian kid, came down underneath another right jab. And this time I hit him as hard as I could with an uppercut. His legs buckled and he crumpled to the floor. Out cold.

As my friends screamed their lungs out, my father jumped into the ring and wrapped his arms around me. After all we'd been through, I have to admit that it felt great to win his approval and to make him proud. It turned out that we had more in common than I'd been willing to accept or believe. Like Al LaBarba, I was a boxer with a

71

Nailing Pratt with a right uppercut in the second round

heavy punch. And like Charles Zito . . . I had a taste for blood. The next day, a story on the Golden Gloves tournament appeared in the centerfold section of the *Daily News,* which was sold at virtually every supermarket on my route. Everyone seemed to know that I had won, and they were quick to offer their congratulations. I felt like a champion of the world.

Boxing brought me closer to my father, helped heal some of the wounds that had opened and festered over the years. We spent a fair amount of time together while I was training. We even joined a bowling league together; we competed at the rec bowling alley above the Lowe's movie theater on Main Street in New Rochelle, on a team sponsored by Carroll Brothers Roofing. In fact, we were supposed to bowl on the night of the second round of the Golden Gloves. It was a single-elimination tournament, which meant you fought until you lost, and thanks to my knockout of Joe Pratt, I was still alive. So we urged our bowling teammates to try to find a couple replacements for us.

"We're going to be busy," I proudly explained.

The fight was held at the Audubon Ballroom, most famous for being the site of the assassination of Malcolm X. The Audubon is located in a predominantly black and Hispanic neighborhood. And, by this time, I was one of the few remaining white guys in the tournament. My opponent was a tall, lean Puerto Rican kid, and not surprisingly, the crowd was heavily in his favor. The bell hadn't even rung when the taunting began:

"Whip that honky's ass!"

"Kill that white motherfucker!"

I figured the best way to shut them up was to end the fight quickly, so that's what I did. Even though this was a second-round match and presumably the quality of competition was better, this kid wasn't nearly as good a fighter as Pratt had been. I knocked him out in the first round, and afterward, as the official raised my hand and the ring announcer declared me the winner, more insults rained down upon me.

"You're lucky, white boy!"

"Better watch your ass when you leave tonight, punk!"

As I laughed at them, my father wrapped my robe around me and pulled me close. "Keep your mouth shut," he said. "Let's get to the dressing room and get out of here."

We hustled not only because we wanted to avoid getting jumped by the crowd but also because we hoped to get back to New Rochelle in time to make our bowling match. We walked in just as our league was getting started, prompting everyone to ask what had happened.

"Didn't you have a fight tonight, Chuck?"

My father smiled. "Yeah," he said, throwing a little jab. "First-round knockout."

Then everyone surrounded me, patted me on the back, treated me like a hero. And I thought to myself, *I could get used to this.*

Unfortunately, and predictably, the sporadic nature of my training caught up with me in the next round, and I was eliminated from the tournament. Without a tangible goal in sight, I trained even less over the next few months. That was pretty much the story of my boxing career: long periods of inactivity interrupted by bursts of intense training and occasional competition. I fought in the Golden Gloves four times, even made it to the semifinals of the New York competition one year. After that, I stopped boxing seriously. There just wasn't time. It still bothers me to this day that I never reached my potential as a boxer. I don't know for sure whether I would have won a professional championship, but I know that I had talent, and I know that I would have been a formidable presence in the ring.

Even though I stopped boxing competitively, I never stopped training completely. I continued to work out at the Gramercy Gym (which was owned by Al Gavin and a corrections officer from Sing Sing Prison named Bob Jackson). I also began to study the martial arts. Hand-to-hand-combat, in all its forms, fascinated me. As much as I admired my father and countless other great boxers, a man I held in even higher regard was Bruce Lee. Like many people, I'd been introduced to Bruce through his role in the *Green Hornet* television series and then through his starring roles in martial arts films. In the way he combined style and power Bruce was light-years ahead of his time. He was so fluid and strong and capable of such quiet destruction. He was amazing, especially when you consider his size. Not many people realize what a little guy Bruce Lee was: about five-foot-five, 130 pounds. Think about that. He was roughly the size of a thirteen-year-old. And yet, despite his stature, he was capable of absolute mayhem. Bruce could destroy people . . . three, four, five of them at a time. I wanted to be like Bruce, to move like him, to have his confidence and grace. And, let's be honest, I wanted to command the type of respect that Bruce commanded.

Myself with Chris Colombo at the Great Gorge Playboy Club in New Jersey

One night, while driving home from work, I stopped at the Aaron Banks Karate Academy on 47th Street. I went in and looked around and immediately liked what I saw. The room was divided into two groups. On one side, Aaron was teaching a karate class; on the other, an instructor named

Master Chin was teaching a class in kung fu. Well, this was the early 1970s, when millions of Americans tuned in each week to watch David Carradine kick some Western ass in the television show *Kung Fu,* so it wasn't surprising that Master Chin's class was filled almost to capacity. Everyone wanted the combination of tranquillity and self-confidence displayed by Carradine's character. So they said, anyway. In reality, what attracted most people to kung fu—the television show and the martial art—was the violence. That's part of the appeal of the martial arts: the fact that anyone, even someone lacking size, can learn how to defend himself.

I studied two forms of kung fu, White Crane and Tiger Claw, and became proficient in both. Later, I joined Tommy May's Westchester Academy of Self-Defense, where I studied jujitsu and karate. I trained alongside some impressive guys, including Chris Colombo, who went on to become a world martial arts champion in kata and weapons. I'd been at Tommy's place only a few weeks, studying jujitsu under Master Butté, when we were informed that a tournament was coming up. Master Butté asked for volunteers, and I immediately raised my hand.

Master Butté cocked his head. "You're new to this," he said. "Are you sure you're ready?"

My jump split kick while holding my kamas (a Japanese weapon)
Credit: Big Joe Kaplan

"I've got some boxing experience," I explained. "I'll be okay."

The tournament was held at the Great Gorge Playboy Club in New Jersey, and I wound up beating every white belt and yellow belt there (I was a white belt), primarily because I used the skills I had learned as a boxer. I beat people with my hands. I confused them. So, naturally, when I returned to class the next week and the other students saw my trophy, they all wanted me to teach them how to box. But that wasn't my job. I was there to learn, just like them. And I did. I progressed to black belt in jujitsu and karate.

As with boxing, I lacked the time to become a top-notch competitor in martial arts, but what I learned would come in handy down the road. You see, even though my career was over, my fighting days had just begun.

THERE'S AN OLD SAYING AMONG MOTORCYCLISTS: *"YOU HAVEN'T REALLY* ridden until you've had your first accident." I don't know if that's quite true, but I appreciate the sentiment. There's something about being thrown from your seat and scraping the highway that makes you understand what it means to be a biker. It isn't just the freedom, the speed, the wind in your face, and the power at your fingertips. It's about the danger, too. If you're a reasonably cautious and defensive driver, I suppose riding a motorcycle is a fairly safe activity. But most people who ride motorcycles are not prudent, conservative people; it's not their nature. The truth is, I don't know anyone who has ridden for twenty, twenty-five years who doesn't have a few battle scars. It's part of the game.

Mandatory helmet laws are intended to minimize the risk of riding a motorcycle, but the risk is undeniably part of the appeal. When I was younger, if I was visiting someplace where they didn't have a helmet law I'd ride around without a helmet. Sometimes I still do. And I have to tell you, it's a hell of a rush, knowing that if you lose control there's nothing between your brain and the asphalt except a thin layer of bone and skin.

But I'm not completely crazy. I've had three accidents in close to thirty years of riding motorcycles, and each time, thank God, I was wearing a helmet. I was christened in 1974, less than a year after I started riding. Tall Paul Westermeyer helped me build my first bike, a '69 Sportster. I traded that for a '74 Panhead, which I then rebuilt into a big, customized chopper with a rigid frame. A real biker's bike, although I wasn't involved with any club at the time and had no idea just how much of a part of my life motorcycles were about to become.

One day I was riding my Panhead up North Avenue in New Rochelle, not far from where Kathy and I lived, when I hit the gas. I just started cranking, probably going thirty-five, maybe forty miles an hour in a thirty-mile zone. Too fast, yes, but not so fast that I couldn't control the bike and avoid any potential trouble. Or so I thought. All of a sudden I saw a car coming in the opposite direction, with his turn signal on. It never occurred to me that the driver wouldn't stop and wait. I mean he was trying to make a left turn across traffic and into a shopping center. So I didn't even slow down.

Oh, shit!

The car, a big dark sedan, lumbered into the intersection. It's funny how time really does seem to slow down when something terrible is about to happen, how you see and process three or four things at once, right before the world collapses. I glanced quickly into the rearview mirror and saw a line of traffic behind me. I looked across the road: more traffic. I looked at the sidewalk: pedestrians.

Fuck!

There was only one place to go: down. I hit the brakes and leaned to the side, trying to take the bike down as smoothly and painlessly as possible. At forty miles an hour there's bound to be some damage, to both the rider and the bike—I was just hoping to avoid a head-on collision. I held on to the handlebars and slid along the road for at least thirty feet. The driver must have finally realized what was about to happen, because he hit the brakes. Too late, of course. If he'd kept going, he might have made it through the intersection without hitting me. Instead, he gave me a big target, and I hit it squarely. Well, actually, I slid right under it, me and the bike.

The next thing I knew, a huge crowd had gathered around us and people were yelling, screaming, trying to hold my hand and comfort me.

"Lay still," someone said. "There's an ambulance on the way."

At first I couldn't move at all. The impact of hitting the ground had knocked the wind out of me, and my arms and legs were raw from skidding along the ground. I think I was in shock, too. But after a minute or so, my head began to clear and the feeling returned to my extremities. I wiggled my fingers and toes—*good, I'm not paralyzed.* Then the pain set in. And then the anger.

I pushed away from the bike and crawled out from beneath the car, much to the shock of the crowd of onlookers, most of whom tried to convince me to get back on the ground. I think they expected me to collapse in a heap, but I was reasonably sure that I hadn't even broken any bones. I had a good dose of road rash and I'd be sore for weeks, but I had avoided serious injury. Maybe I should have been grateful, but I wasn't. I was pissed. I yanked off my helmet, which was cracked and ruined, and threw it to the ground.

"Who the fuck was driving that car?" I shouted.

Into the crowd stepped a large black man. I don't know whether he was contrite or self-righteous or what. And I didn't care. I knew only that someone had cut me off and destroyed my bike and very nearly gotten me killed So, when the words, "I was," escaped his lips, I lit into him. Didn't even give him a chance to explain.

"You stupid motherfucker!" I shouted, and then I dropped him with a single punch.

The poor guy struggled to his feet and I hit him again. I hadn't just lost my temper—I'd gone crazy. But I felt my actions were reasonable under the circumstances. This guy's recklessness had nearly cost me my life, and I was going to let him know about it. Was I right? Depends on how you look at things, I guess. In the world in which I was raised, you didn't get away with shit like that.

I'd beaten him bloody and unconscious before I realized that I was at the corner of Lincoln and North, a predominantly black section of New Rochelle. Pretty soon the crowd pressed in again, started yelling at me, shouting, "Grab that crazy son of a bitch!" Before a full-scale riot erupted, however, the cops showed up and got everything under control. They issued a ticket for crossing a double yellow line to the driver of the car, which made me feel vindicated; however, they also charged me with assault. I was handcuffed and taken into custody. A few hours later I paid a $100 fine and was released. I suppose the judge cut me some slack because . . . well, because I'd nearly been killed and was therefore justified in losing my temper (if not in actually trying to kill the driver of the other vehicle). Nevertheless, I now had a record.

*   *   *

Did I learn anything from that incident? Yeah, I learned that once you get the itch to ride motorcycles, you can't help but scratch it. The accident, the arrest—they did nothing to dissuade me from getting right back on my bike (after I'd rebuilt it, of course). I wasn't alone, either. Several of my old buddies had also gotten into bikes, including Billy Reily (who had returned from the service unharmed), John Magotta, and Pat Catulo. I loved the freedom and excitement of riding a motorcycle, but I also enjoyed the camaraderie of hanging out with other bikers. It was more than just friendship—it was a brotherhood, the hallmarks of which were a passion for riding motorcycles and an attitude and outlook on life that's hard to describe. Bikers have their own rules, their own code of ethics, their own definition of right and wrong.

I sensed all of this from the very beginning, even before I'd become part of a club. The motorcycle serves as a bond between like-minded friends. A club merely formalizes that bond. We spent a lot of time on our bikes. We'd go for long rides late at night, after work. Sometimes we'd just cruise around the boroughs; other times we'd ride all the way out to the Hamptons or to Bear Mountain in the Catskills. As often as not, our wives and girlfriends would join us. We were like a big extended family. It was only natural that after a while we wanted a place to hang out, to gather on a regular basis, and that's how the New Rochelle Motorcycle Club was born. There were three of us who served as a driving force: me, Tall Paul, and Tony Lamboy. Together we found an empty storefront on Westchester Place and transformed it into a clubhouse. It was nothing more than a place to call our own, a place where we could gather at night before heading out on a run, where we could have parties or just watch TV.

At first, Kathy didn't mind my growing obsession with motorcycles. She liked riding with me, spending time with Paul's girlfriend, Paula, and Tony's girlfriend, Laura. As my commitment to the club intensified, however, Kathy became less tolerant. I began spending more time away from home, more time at the club, and that put a strain on our relationship. Kathy didn't mind going for a long ride once in a while, but she had no desire to make motorcycles the center of her life. She had a job and a daughter and she was serious about both. Meanwhile, I was losing interest in just about anything unrelated to motorcycles. My job, boxing, my family—everything took a backseat to the club and my passion for riding. I don't say that with pride. I'm just stating it as a fact.

One night Kathy's resentment boiled over and we had a huge fight, complete with thrown plates, broken glass, and nasty comments that would be hard to take back. It started with a meeting at the club-house, during which Tony, Paul, and I decided that we wanted to go on a long solo ride. No wives, no girlfriends. Just the boys. Now, Kathy and I were husband and wife by this time (after six years of living together, we'd gotten married on January 30, 1977—my father's birthday—at the Marina Del Ray Club in the Bronx), and we'd moved into our own place at 463 Pelham Road. So we didn't have to be quite so careful about restricting the noise level when we fought. And, boy, did we cut loose that night.

It started when I was getting ready to go out and I saw Kathy looking for her jacket.

"What are you doing?" I asked.

"Going with you. My mother will watch the baby."

I waved a hand. "No, you're not. The guys aren't taking their girl-friends tonight."

"I'm not your girlfriend. I'm your wife." She paused, gave me a hard look. "And I'm coming."

Well, things spiraled down from there. I remember Kathy opening the refrigerator and heaving a carton of grapefruit juice at me. I ducked just in time, and the carton exploded against a wall. When I left, Kathy was on her knees, crying and cursing at me while cleaning up the mess. I felt bad about it at the time, but not bad enough to stay and help her, not bad enough to invite her to come with me. Hell, I was a man, and there was no way I was going to let my old lady tell me what I could or could not do. What would the other guys say? I could just imagine arriving at the club, with Kathy in tow, and getting abused by Paul and Tony for not having the guts to stand up to my own wife.

So I started my bike, hit the gas, and roared off in anger. Two minutes later I was on Westchester Place, in front of the club. Stand-ing outside, next to their bikes, were Tony and Paul . . . along with Laura and Paula.

I jumped off my bike, pulled Tony and Paul into the club, and jumped all over them.

"What the hell is going on?" I shouted. "I thought we had a deal: no old ladies."

At first they said nothing. Tall Paul looked at Tony, and Tony looked at Paul. They scuffed the ground with their feet, stuffed their hands in their pockets. What a sight, these two big, bad bikers, humbled by their women.

"They wouldn't take no for an answer," Tony finally said. "What were we supposed to do?"

"That's just great," I said. "Kathy didn't want to take no for an answer, either. And now my wife is up there in the house, cleaning up a big mess, crying her eyes out, and you guys got your old ladies here."

They shrugged, said they were sorry, but they weren't about to lay down the law now. A part of me wanted to go back to the house and apologize to Kathy, help her clean up, and take her for a ride. Or, maybe, just stay home. But my pride wouldn't allow it. And, to be honest, I think it might have only made things worse if I'd gone back at that moment and told Kathy, "Uh . . . Paul and Tony wimped out and invited their girlfriends, so you might as well come, too."

Nope. I was on my own. So we took off, Paul and Paula, Tony and Laura . . . and me. We rode out to Sheepshead Bay in Brooklyn, and I fumed the entire way. I was pissed at my friends, and I felt stupid for having fought with my wife. We wound up at a bar, and since I don't smoke or drink, I did what I often do in those situations: I hung around outside. I was about to leave on my own when I was approached by a girl.

"Nice bike," she said with a smile.

Next thing you know, I'd become an even bigger heel. I borrowed a helmet from Paul, gave it to this chick, and took her for a ride down to my old neighborhood in Bensonhurst. Nothing else happened—it was just a ride—but it felt like a betrayal nonetheless. I hadn't allowed Kathy, my own wife, whom I adored, to ride on the back of my bike that night, but I'd welcomed a complete stranger. By the time I returned, after maybe forty-five minutes, Tony and Paul were standing outside with their girlfriends, just waiting on the sidewalk for me to get back so they could retrieve their helmet and leave. I could tell by the way Paula and Laura were looking at me, shooting daggers with their eyes, that Kathy would soon hear about this little escapade, and in the retelling it surely would become more than it really was.

I wanted to talk to Kathy when I got home, but she was already sleeping and there really wasn't much to say. I slid under the covers, turned my back to her, and stared at the wall until the sun came up.

9

REMEMBER WHEN I SAID I HAD ONLY TWO GREAT REGRETS IN MY LIFE? NOT reaching my potential as a boxer and . . . something else? Well, here's the something else: I could have been a better father and a better husband. It's interesting . . . sometimes you look back on your life, and you wonder about the decisions you've made. Motorcycle clubs, riding—they've given me a lot in life, and I'm thankful for it. But they've cost me some things, too.

I grew up believing that when you commit to a certain lifestyle, like being a husband and father and raising a family, you stick with it. You follow through, regardless of how long it takes and the sacrifices you have to make. I was angry with my own father for years because of his failure in this regard, and I was determined not to make the same mistakes. That's one of the reasons I was so eager to move in with Kathy. I would prove that even at seventeen I was already more of a man than my father had been. I would protect both Kathy and Lisa, provide for them, and never let them down.

But what do you know when you're seventeen? I thought I was all grown up, that I didn't need or want anything else. By twenty-two everything had changed. Well, not everything. I still loved Kathy and Lisa, but I also felt trapped. I'd missed a good chunk of my young adult years, the period during which most guys are out living it up, raising hell, chasing tail, and generally acting like red-blooded American males. A part of me felt as though I had earned the right to demand a taste of freedom. It wasn't so much that I was interested in other women, but I did want some time to myself. Check that—I wanted time to ride my motorcycle and hang out with my buddies in the club. It didn't seem like such a terrible thing to me.

But, of course, I was just being selfish. I used to stop at the club-house almost every night on my way home from work, just to unwind a little. One evening Kathy came bursting through the doors, a wild look in her eyes, and at first I thought we were going to have a big fight because I was late for dinner again or something like that. Instead, she just started crying uncontrollably.

"What's wrong,?" I asked.

She held me close and explained that my grandfather, Leo, had died of a heart attack. He was a big, strong guy and had never been sick a day in his life, but he'd just fallen over on a New York City street. I couldn't believe it.

"Where's Mom?"

"She's home," Kathy said. "She's pretty shook up."

The worst part of that day, to me, was not so much hearing the news that my grandfather had died, but the way in which I had heard it. My mother had called for me, and I wasn't home. I wasn't there to help her, as she had been so many times for me. No, I was down at the club, and my wife had to get her mother to baby-sit so she could go out into the night to find me. That's not the kind of thing a responsible father would do. And I knew it. But I was torn: old family on one hand, new family on the other.

There's a fair amount of weirdness surrounding the insular world of motorcycle clubs. A small, relatively disorganized group of guys who like to hang out, ride bikes, and drink beer (or whatever) . . . they pretty much go unnoticed. But the moment that group becomes a "club," it begins to attract attention. Sometimes it's good attention; sometimes it's bad attention. A new club with strong leadership and significant numbers in its membership can be seen as either a threat or an opportunity. Within a year the New Rochelle Motorcycle Club was being recruited by several older, more established cubs, including the Tribe, from nearby Port Chester, New York, the Bronx MC, and the Ching-a-Ling Nomads (*nomads*, as you might expect, is a term adopted by clubs, or chapters of a club, that are not restricted by geographic boundaries). One night we had a party at our club in New Rochelle and we invited all of these other clubs. That's kind of the way it works: when a club hosts a party, members of other clubs are usually welcome, provided there's no existing animosity between the groups and provided the guests exhibit the proper amount of respect while visiting another club's turf. Of course, when there's alcohol involved and the hour gets late, things don't always work out as planned. Respect is an important thing among bikers, and transgressions are not tolerated.

We in the New Rochelle MC understood the rules. We knew our place in the pecking order (at the bottom) and acted accordingly. At the same time, we had a nice clubhouse and several people who had the potential to make any club more formidable (in terms of muscle and commitment). As a result, a lot of clubs were considering offering us a patch (a patch is a vest or jacket bearing a club's name and logo; when one club is absorbed by another, its members remove the patch representing the old club and replace it with one signifying membership in the new club). The interest was nice; we were flattered. And we viewed this party as a way to assess the other clubs, to determine which one we wanted to join . . . or even *if* we wanted to join another club. Maybe we'd just remain independent.

Events made the choice an easy one. It began when one of the guys from the Tribe got a flat tire on his car and dispatched some of his club's prospects to find a replacement tire. They found a tire, all right—what they didn't realize, however, was that it came from a car belonging to a member of the Bronx MC. That naturally ignited a battle. Pretty soon they were all in one another's faces, shouting accusations; predictably, a fistfight broke out. And then, even more predictably, knives were unsheathed. Before someone was killed—and, more importantly, before our clubhouse was destroyed—we broke up the fight. Tony and I jumped in right away . . . followed by the rest of our brothers.

As the fight ended, without any bloodshed, I noticed several members of the Ching-a-Ling Nomads hanging out in a corner, laughing. Not one of them got involved. When I asked them why, they said, simply, "It's your clubhouse, man. We're not gonna bust it up. That shit's wrong."

By morning the Bronx MC had offered us a patch and we'd turned it down. Instead, we joined the Ching-a-Ling Nomads, mainly because they'd been so cool in the way they had handled the fight. Also . . . *Ching-a-Ling* is slang for "Fuck everybody!" and we liked the sound of that. We also liked the history of the Ching-a-Lings, a legitimately ferocious band of bikers with impeccable credentials in the outlaw world. See, before the Ching-a-Lings became a motorcycle club, they were a street gang on the Lower East Side of Manhattan. On December 5, 1969, when the Alien Nomads, a motorcycle club from New York, were absorbed by the Hells Angels, the Ching-a-Lings were granted the right to call themselves Nomads and wear patches emblematic of this status. Had the Alien Nomads not given up their patches, of course, the Ching-a-Lings could not have adopted the Nomads moniker without provoking a turf war. Simple as that. You see . . . it's about respect. The Ching-a-Lings' attitude may have been "Fuck everybody," but they weren't stupid. They knew how to choose their battles, and they understood the rules of the street. That we were a bunch of Irish and Italian guys from New Rochelle and the Nomads were Puerto Rican and black guys from the Bronx didn't matter. We liked their reputation and thought it seemed like a good fit. So it was good-bye to the New Rochelle MC and hello to the Ching-a-Ling Nomads. No longer were we just a bunch of ordinary guys banding together to ride motorcycles and shoot pool. We were part of a legitimate, even notorious club. In the eyes of law enforcement—hell, in the eyes of just about everyone—we were a motorcycle *gang!*

In fact, one of the first things I noticed about being a member of the Ching-a-Lings was how much more likely I was to get pulled over and hassled by the police. Now, let me make one thing clear: I am not a copbasher. Far from it. I have a lot of friends who are cops, and I have nothing against those whose job it is to enforce the law (even if their interpretation of right and wrong doesn't always correspond with mine). Believe it or not, I even took the police test myself when I was younger. And, as I said, my grandfather was a Port Authority cop, so you might say there was blue blood in my family. Over the years my relationship with the cops has quieted down and evolved into one of mutual respect. It used to be common for cops to stop me and demand my signature on a traffic ticket. Now they ask for my autograph. It's kind of amusing.

But there are certain cops who are crooked—always have been, always will be. And there are cops who are just looking for an excuse to exercise their power. Wearing the patch of the Ching-a-Ling Nomads, I discovered, provided a convenient excuse. Kathy disliked my involvement with the Ching-a-Lings and basically stopped riding with me altogether after I joined the club. She saw potential problems far before I did. A few years earlier, when I'd first gotten involved with motorcycles, she thought it was just a phase, and a cute one at that. But she thought I'd grow out of it. My involvement with the Ching-a-Lings changed her opinion. This wasn't just a bunch of guys messing around with bikes. This was a legitimate, hard-core motorcycle club, and there was nothing cute about it. Membership in the Ching-a-Lings involved commitment, and my time at home began to shrink even further. We'd go on long rides—sometimes we'd be away for the entire weekend. I had an obligation to take part in these events, and while I might have felt some guilt about it, I can't say I didn't have fun. The camaraderie was even more intense and spirited than it had been in the New Rochelle MC. If there was danger involved, well, that only made it more exciting. But it wasn't until several months into my membership with the Ching-a-Lings that I fully understood the risks and consequences of being part of an outlaw motorcycle club.

A little background, first. There is a club on Tremont Avenue in the Bronx called the Black Falcons, comprised entirely of African-Americans, as you might have guessed. Well, one night while the Black Falcons were having a big party, one of the Ching-a-Lings, a guy named Chester, made the mistake of picking up a girl and taking her for a ride past the Black Falcons' party. When he stopped at a red light near their clubhouse, he quickly found himself surrounded by dozens of bikers, guys from the Black Falcons and another black motorcycle club, the Wheels of Soul. They circled Chester, taunted him, tried to intimidate him. Chester tried to play it cool—he was outnumbered and he had a guest on the back of his motorcycle—but when one of the Wheels of Soul reached across Chester's bike and turned off the ignition, Chester got pissed.

"You guys want to fuck with me?" he asked. "Let me drop this lady off and I'll be right back." (This is Chester's version anyway, and I don't doubt it for a second.)

They all laughed, but in reality the Black Falcons were neither happy nor confident about the situation. They knew that the Ching-a-Lings were not to be taken lightly. And, like most clubs, the Falcons weren't into rumbling with women. So they gave Chester some room, shouted, "Get the fuck out of here!" as he drove off, and went back to their party. I'm sure they did not expect to see Chester again that night.

Boy, were they wrong. Chester did exactly what he said he would. He brought the girl home and then drove straight to the Ching-a-Lings' clubhouse on 187th Street. There were perhaps a half-dozen of us there when Chester walked in, red-faced and eager for action. He related the story and then asked if any of us wanted to join him, although he said he really didn't care, because he was going back either way, even if it meant taking on the Black Falcons and Wheels of Soul all by himself.

"I'm with you," I said. The others nodded, too. Within minutes we were on our way downtown, armed with knives, guns, brass knuckles. This was serious shit. Between the Black Falcons, the Wheels of Soul, and whatever friends and guests they'd invited, there were probably more than 200 people at this party.

There were six of us.

This wasn't going to be just a fistfight, that's for sure. When outlaw motorcycle clubs meet to settle a grievance and they're armed with guns, people can and do get killed. It's part of the culture, part of the risk. It's also part of the appeal.

A strange thing happened, though. Both clubs turned out to be far cooler than we'd expected. We met a large group of them near their club and immediately engaged in the sort of banter that leads to gunfire.

"Go ahead," Chester said. "Fuck with me now."

I was sweating, anxious, just like in the nervous moments before a boxing match. Except something far more important than mere victory was at stake. I waited for someone to move, to do anything that would give us an excuse to engage in battle. To my amazement, one of their biggest guys, clearly a leader, started laughing. And then they all started laughing. "The Falcons said you guys are crazy," the big guy said.

I didn't say a word, didn't move.

"Come on, take it easy. My name's Cliff." He pointed to the guy next to him. "This is Wino. No disrespect intended."

I looked at my brothers, made eye contact with Chester. In a way, this was his decision, since he'd been the target of their abuse . . . their joke . . . whatever you want to call it.

"Cool with you, Chester?"

Chester nodded. "Yeah, it's cool."

And that was it. The entire situation was defused. We shook hands, talked a little, and, believe it or not, became friends. That's the way it is with motorcycle clubs: one minute you're ready to kill each other; the next minute you're swapping war stories over a beer. Hard to believe? Well, consider this: A couple weeks later the Wheels of Soul invited us to their clubhouse in Philadelphia, where they were hosting a big party. About twenty-five of the Ching-a-Lings went on a weekend-long run, including me, which didn't exactly sit well with my wife. Adding to her disapproval was my insistence on volunteering the use of my truck from work (it's common when clubs go on long runs for someone to drive a van or truck, in which supplies and equipment are stored, both for partying and to help with repairs in the event that a bike breaks down; sometimes you just have to throw the bike in the back of the truck and keep going). My employers would not have approved of my using the van for this purpose, obviously, so I placed masking tape over the word FINAST. And off we went.

The trip down was uneventful, and the party was all right. But all hell broke loose on the way back. You have to picture twenty-five Ching-a-Lings (and a handful of guys from the Wheels of Soul, who had joined us for the return trip), accompanied by a big van, cruising along the interstate on a Sunday afternoon. Whether we were doing anything illegal (we weren't) was beside the point. When that many representatives of an outlaw club are together in one place, it's bound to attract attention. When we stopped to gas up, we quickly found ourselves confronted by a handful of New Jersey state troopers. They walked around us, asked a lot of questions—*"Where are you going?" "Where have you been?" "What's in the van?"*—and generally treated us like criminals. They didn't detain us, though. They had no right to do that. They just wanted to harass us, bust our balls a little.

Eventually we began to pull out of the rest area, a few at a time, and return to the highway. The first to leave were David Sansoni, a Ching-a-Ling, and a guy named Rick, one of the Wheels of Soul. Big, strong, with long red hair, David was basically a fun-loving kid, although he did have a temper, which got him in trouble from time to time. His nickname, not surprisingly, was Big Red.

A couple miles beyond the rest stop we came upon what at first appeared to be an accident. I was at the front of the pack, so I approached slowly, at first, with the rest of the group behind me. There were lights flashing, and I could see a Harley partially hidden by one of the trooper cars.

Shit . . . it's Red. He's hurt!

I cut the engine, jumped off my bike, and started running. Along the way I noticed a few things, like the absence of an ambulance or any other cars. Then I saw Red's bike . . . and Rick's bike, both up on kickstands, in perfectly good shape. But I couldn't see either Rick or Red. Something was very wrong here. As I reached the police car, one of the cops turned quickly and put a gun in my face.

"Get the fuck out of here!" he shouted.

I stopped in my tracks, put my hands in the air. The cop looked scared. When I glanced over, I understood why. Rick was on the ground, handcuffed, and Red was facedown on the pavement, blood pooling around his head.

"Jesus Christ!" I said. "What's going on?"

The cop pushed the gun against my temple. There was a wild look in his eye. I tried to stand perfectly still.

"Okay," I said. "Take it easy."

Within minutes the scene was flooded with cops, six cars, more than a dozen troopers. They put us all in a group and instructed us to ride, slowly, carefully, to the nearest state police barracks. To prevent anyone from riding off on his own, they surrounded us with their cars—one in the front, two on each side, one in the back. And that's the way we traveled, some thirty motorcycles surrounded by flashing lights. When we arrived, they separated us and brought us into an interrogation room one at a time. In addition to the usual background shit, they wanted to know what we saw on the highway. The truth is, we hadn't seen anything. As the first to arrive, I had the best view, and all I saw was a dead Ching-a-Ling. How he got that way I didn't know, although I had a pretty good idea.

Here's Rick's account of that incident. Whether it's completely accurate or not I can't say for sure. But I'm inclined to believe it, es-

Red's funeral procession. That's me on the left and Giuseppe on the right.

pecially given the way the cops acted that day and in the weeks and months that followed, when they seemed to be in heavy-duty cover-their-ass mode. According to Rick, he and Red had been pulled over shortly after leaving the interstate rest area. At first, they didn't know why they had been stopped, especially since they'd just been hassled minutes earlier, or what the cop wanted. Soon, though, they realized what was happening. Red recognized the cop—he'd stopped him on the same highway a week earlier and had warned him never to ride on his turnpike again. Red hadn't listened, and now the cop was throwing his weight around. He ordered Rick and Red to get off their bikes and move away from the shoulder of the highway, which they did. The cop put them up against a fence and was in the process of putting them in handcuffs when Red asked what the problem was.

"Shut up and turn around or I'll blow your fucking head off!" the cop said (again, according to Rick).

Red, who didn't like being told what to do, wasn't easily intimidated. According to Rick, the cop raised his gun and fired a single shot into Red's head. He died instantly. I don't call that justifiable homicide. I call it an assassination. Unfortunately, a jury disagreed. The cop was indicted, and after many months a trial was held, at the end of which the officer was found not guilty of all charges. He went

Red's funeral

back to work; meanwhile, Red Sansoni was dead and buried at the age of seventeen.

That incident opened my eyes about precisely what it meant to be part of an outlaw motorcycle club. Running with the big boys was a whole different game from anything I'd experienced with the New Rochelle MC. If there was more prestige attached to being a Ching-a-Ling, there was more danger, too. And I wasn't the only one affected. Kathy had heard about the shooting on the news. The early reports even identified the victim as a member of the Ching-a-Ling Nomads. Not revealed, however, was the victim's name, so, for a few hours Kathy had no idea whether I was alive or dead. She knew I had been part of the Pennsylvania run, and she knew I was likely part of the group that had been involved in this incident. But since we all were detained for several hours and not allowed to make phone calls, I had no way of letting her know that I was all right.

When I finally got in touch with Kathy, she was both relieved and furious, which was understandable. I spent a lot of time over the next few days thinking about what happened. What if I'd been the one who got stopped first? That could have been me lying facedown on the pavement. I had a wife and kid at home. They needed me, depended on me. What was I thinking?

Kathy was asking most of those same questions, although she didn't really expect any answers. "I love you," she said. "But you have to stop this."

I couldn't reasonably argue with her, so I didn't. I just kept doing what I'd been doing. I loved Kathy and Lisa, but I loved riding, too. The freedom, the brotherhood, the thrill of the open road (a cliché, I know, but absolutely true nonetheless)—it had sucked me in and held me tight, and I felt warm in its embrace.

When my supervisors at Finast discovered that not only had I been involved in the incident that led to Red's shooting, but I'd also used one of the company vans in the process, they responded about as you might expect they would: they fired me. So, now I was on unemployment, which made things even harder at home. On the plus side (if you can call it that, which I did), it left me with more time for boxing and hanging out with the Ching-a-Lings. This was around the same time that I took my last shot at the Golden Gloves, when I was training with at least some degree of seriousness, if only for a short while. It was through boxing that I found my way to the granddaddy of all motorcycle clubs: the Hells Angels.

It happened one day while I was shooting some pool at the Ching-a-Lings' clubhouse in the Bronx. One of our guys walked in and said, "Hey, somebody from the Hells Angels just pulled up outside!" Now, this was a very big deal, because the Hells Angels, as everyone knew, were the ultimate motorcycle club, membership in which was coveted by many, obtained by few. *Oh, really? Well, let's go see what this guy looks like.* I walked out, half-expecting to be disappointed, and all of a sudden I saw this guy coming around a corner, and he was without question the biggest, scariest guy I'd seen in my entire life—about six-two, 350 pounds, with tattoos all over his body and nothing but a leather vest covering his torso. I took one look at him and thought, *Holy shit! Is this what every Hells Angel looks like?*

His name was Vinnie Girolamo, and while he was a frightening and legitimately tough son of a bitch (whose well-deserved nickname was the Beast from the East), he was also a good guy. We started talking, and after a while we went inside and shot some pool. When Vinnie saw the Golden Gloves insignia on my jacket, his interest was piqued.

"You a fighter?" he asked, his voice as rough as sandpaper.

Big Vinnie Girolamo with his dog, Satan

"Sometimes."

"No shit! You should meet my club president. He's a boxer, too."

"Yeah? Where's he train?"

"Gramercy Gym."

So, you see, my switch to Gramercy Gym was due only in part to its proximity to where my father lived. The truth was, I wanted to meet Sandy Alexander, the president of the New York City chapter of the Hells Angels Motorcycle Club. I did a little homework first, and I was shocked to discover that not only was Sandy a fighter, but he'd also actually fought in the last Golden Gloves tournament on the same night that I'd fought. We'd been in the same arena, on the same night. Our lockers might have been right next to each other, for all I knew, although I couldn't say for sure because, quite frankly, I had no recollection of ever having met Sandy.

When we finally did meet, at Gramercy Gym, Sandy and I hit it off right away, literally and figuratively. We sparred together in the gym several times, and even though Sandy was a good ten years older than I was, he had the strength and spirit of a young man. We trained hard together under Al Gavin and soon became good friends.

(Al, by the way, also trained another New York City Hells Angel by the name of John "The Baptist" LoFranco. John had spent countless long nights in bars and many hours in hospitals getting stitched up after battling with anyone and everyone who crossed him. One night in March of 1980, I asked John to come with me to the Golden Gloves finals at Madison Square Garden. Well, actually, I had to beg him to

go. Like I said, John did his fighting in the street and could have cared less about the rules in the squared circle. While watching the finals, John turned to me and said, "I could beat these guys." I looked at him and said, "Oh, yeah? Well why don't you come to the gym with me tomorrow and prove it?" So we went to the gym together the next day and worked out for a while. Same thing the next day and the day after that. John became a regular, and our gym workouts became battles, just like those between Al LaBarba and Rocky Graziano. After a few rounds of sparring,

John "The Baptist" LoFranco

blood would be pouring from our noses, and Al Gavin would jump in the ring and say, "Hey, you guys are brothers! Stop trying to make it a war." It was only a matter of time before John fell in love with boxing. In fact, the prediction he'd made that first night at the Garden came true the following year, when John became a silver medalist in the 1981 *New York Daily News* Golden Gloves tournament. He liked the sport so much he turned professional and became a serious threat in the heavyweight division, compiling a record of 14–2 before his career was cut short in 1985, when Uncle Sam tapped a bunch of us on the shoulders and invited us to take a vacation at Club Fed. But we'll get to that later. The point is, John became a hell of a fighter. And it's interesting to note that on the undercard of one of John's fights in Albany, New York, making his professional debut, was a kid by the name of Mike Tyson.)

Before too long, Sandy invited me to become a "hang-around," which is the first step on the road to becoming a full-fledged member of the Hells Angels. This presented something of a quandary for me— I liked the Ching-a-Lings, some of whom had been my friends for years. I didn't want to leave that club if it meant leaving those guys behind. At the same time, I was thrilled with the idea of becoming a member of the most feared, famous, and respected motorcycle club in the world. I'd been fantasizing about what it would be like to be a part of the Hells Angels since I was a kid, from the moment I sat in that darkened movie theater and watched Sonny Barger team up with Jack Nicholson. Now my dream was about to become reality. How could I turn it down?

There was one other possibility: convince all of the Ching-a-Lings to give up their patches, disband, and join the Hells Angels. No small task, since not all of the Ching-a-Lings wanted to be Hells Angels; similarly, I knew the Hells Angels might not want everyone in our club. But with a little time and effort I was able to convince the entire membership of the Ching-a-Ling nomads—close to thirty people—to become prospects for the New York City chapter of the Hells Angels.

"We consider ourselves to be the best club in New York," I said by way of explanation. "But let's be honest—the Hells Angels are the most well known motorcycle club in the world. Let's join them. It'll be good for both clubs."

And it would have been . . . if it had worked out right.

As it was, the proposed merger (actually, it was more like an absorption, but I didn't want to put it that way, since it would have been something of an insult to the guys in our club) never really got off the ground. It died one night in Bridgeport, Connecticut, site of a party to celebrate the second anniversary of the Bridgeport chapter of the Hells Angels. Sandy Alexander invited us to the party, so we thought everything would be cool. Not quite true. We showed up around midnight, thirty of us wearing our Ching-a-Ling patches, and it was fairly obvious from the moment we walked into the clubhouse that we weren't going to be welcomed with open arms. It was a typically wild party, with dozens of drunken Hells Angels, and when they saw us moving through the door their reaction was like something out of a movie. The music abruptly stopped and all conversation ceased. Everyone stared at us.

Looking back on it, I can't help but laugh at my own hubris and ignorance. Walking into a Hells Angels party at midnight, wearing the colors of another club . . . well, it's just not the smartest thing in the world to do. And, of course, it had been my idea. "Sandy said it's no problem," I had told my brothers. "Don't sweat it—we're hang-arounds now."

Unfortunately, most of the people in that clubhouse didn't know me from Adam, and they were understandably suspicious. More than that, really. They were hostile. After all, we were in their territory. I can only imagine what they must have thought: *Either these guys have some kind of death wish, or they're just plain stupid.*

Several of them were ready to confront us right away, and I thought for a moment that not only were our days as Ching-a-Lings numbered but our days on this planet as well. Before any blood was spilled, however, Sandy Alexander appeared out of nowhere, stepped in front of us, and gave us a hearty welcome.

"It's cool," he said, loudly enough for everyone to hear. "They're hang-arounds for our chapter."

And just like that the tension melted away. The music returned and the party went back into high gear. The worst, I thought, was over. I took a seat near the pool table between Paul Casey and a guy named Mike the Bike, two Hells Angels from New York City. I grabbed a Coke and tried to relax. Not fifteen minutes later I saw one of the Ching-a-Lings, a guy named Roy, lurch past me on his way to the bathroom. His head was tilted back, his hand pressed against his nose. Blood streamed down his face.

"Jesus . . ." I said, starting to get up.

Mike put a hand gently on my shoulder. "Relax. He probably had an argument with one of our guys. Stay out of it."

My first instinct was to help my brother, and I was surprised to see these guys responding so calmly, reasonably. *"Just an argument,"* they said . . . like it happened every day. Maybe the rules here were different.

I leaned back and tried to forget about Roy. But ten minutes later I heard shouting and cursing, and across the room I could see another Ching-a-Ling, a guy named Chopper, going at it with another Hells Angel. All of a sudden the music stopped again and someone yelled, "Get the old ladies out of here and lock the fucking door!" I looked around the room. There were at least 200 Hells Angels there . . . 200 of the biggest, baddest motherfuckers on the planet, and thirty Ching-a-Lings. And I thought, *Oh, shit . . . we're all going to the hospital tonight.*

But an amazing thing happened: no one jumped in. Without any assistance from his brothers, this Hells Angel beat the dog shit out of Chopper. A big circle was formed and they were allowed to settle whatever differences they had the old-fashioned way. No knives, no guns, no outside help of any kind. It became clear to me that this wasn't some kind of test or even an attempt to intimidate another club. It was just business as usual at a Hells Angels party. People got drunk, said stupid things, got into fights. No big deal. My Ching-a-Ling brothers didn't see it that way, though. When the fighting stopped and Chopper was scooped off the floor, our club president, whose name was George, said, "That's enough; we're leaving." Virtually all of the Ching-a-Lings nodded in agreement and began filing out the door. I didn't move.

"Come on, Chuck," George said. "Let's go."

I shook my head. "You go. I'm staying."

George shrugged. "Big mistake, brother."

The only other Ching-a-Ling to hesitate was Giuseppe, another headstrong Italian. He looked at the door—most of our brothers had disappeared. "You sure about this, Chuck?"

I leaned into his ear. "We walk out of here now, we look like a bunch of scared jerk-offs. That what you want?"

"No way, brother," Giuseppe said. "I'm with you."

When the last of the Ching-a-Lings was gone and the door closed, Giuseppe and I became the center of attention. Several of the Hells Angels, people I did not know or recognize, formed a tight circle around us. I was prepared for the worst.

"Why don't you go with your punk-ass friends?" one of them said.

"Yeah, get the fuck out of here," added another.

Giuseppe and I stood shoulder to shoulder. This was pucker time, as they say in the military (a reference to the way a man's sphincter reflexively closes when danger is imminent).

"You know what?" I began. "I was invited to a party. When that party is over, I'll leave. And I don't care if that doesn't happen until the sun comes up."

For a few moments, no one moved. I looked across the room, saw Sandy sitting on a chair. He wasn't about to ride to the rescue now, and frankly I didn't expect him to. When you disrespect a Hells Angel, you face the consequences. Simple as that. But I meant no disrespect to anyone. I was merely standing up for what I felt was right. I know a lot of bikers who would not have demonstrated the restraint I had witnessed that night, who would have jumped right in and turned a one-on-one altercation into a riot. In fact, with a lot of clubs, that's standard behavior. I was impressed that the Hells Angels had shown more class than that. They were the number-one club in the world, and they had the confidence and self-respect to stay out of whatever it was that had led Chopper and Roy to get their butts kicked. The Hells Angels understood the difference between a simple, meaning-less barroom brawl and a turf war. Despite the fact that two of my Ching-a-Ling brothers had been beaten and humiliated, I felt a strong and sudden kinship with the Hells Angels. They were the best, and they knew it. Their attitude reflected what I wanted to be. If I had to stand up to 200 of them to earn their respect, then so be it.

One of their biggest guys was standing in front of me now, inches away from my face. Dozens of his brothers, all equally menacing, were right behind him. Then, to my surprise and relief, he let out a little laugh.

"You guys are cool motherfuckers," he said. "Come by anytime you want."

Over the next few hours Giuseppe and I were introduced to almost everyone at the party. We had a good time, and when the sun came up we said good-bye, drove straight to the Ching-a-Lings' clubhouse in the Bronx, ripped off our patches, threw them on the floor, and said, "Adios." No one said a word to us, because there was nothing to be said. They had left with their tails between their legs, and we no longer had any respect for them. From that point on, Giuseppe and I were no longer Ching-a-Ling Nomads. We were Hells Angels–in–waiting.

10

OK, HOW ABOUT A LITTLE HISTORY LESSON?

Let's go back in time, to July 4, 1947, to Hollister, California, and the Gypsy Tour Run, a national off-road motorcycle championship event sanctioned by the American Motorcycle Association. Local police and town officials anticipated a crowd of maybe a few hundred people. What they got was something else entirely. More than 3,000 bikers came to Hollister on that holiday weekend and held a party that gave the town a hangover that would last for years. Lost in the retelling of this story is the fact that the bikers weren't the only ones causing trouble, that they were joined in their debauchery by several hundred "regular citizens."

Doesn't matter, though. Legends have a way of taking on a life of their own, and certainly there's no denying that these bikers did indeed take over the town of Hollister for the better part of three days. They partied and brawled and rode their bikes into places where they weren't invited and where bikes typically aren't allowed. The town's law enforcement agency was thoroughly unprepared to handle this onslaught. Half a dozen police officers, after all, are no match for a few thousand bikers. When the panic-stricken cops began arresting some of the revelers, the bikers threatened to storm the jail. Cops soon descended on Hollister from all over the region, and the riot, such as it was, came to an end. (This incident would later serve as the inspiration for the Marlon Brando film *The Wild One*.)

Two months later, when many of the same motorcycle clubs gathered in Riverside, California, for another AMA-sanctioned event, there was a repeat performance. Bikers roaring up and down city streets and into public buildings; guys pissing in public and beating the crap out of each other with little provocation, just for fun, really. Once again the cops were outnumbered, reserves were called in, and bikers were thrown in jail.

Well, after that, there was a predictable amount of criticism heaped upon anyone who owned a motorcycle. Carl Rayburn, a Riverside sheriff, put the blame on "a bunch of punk kids" who disrupted his peaceful town. "They're rebels," the sheriff said. "They're outlaws." And so, from an angry lawman's mouth, the term *outlaw motorcyclists* was born.

The AMA gets credit with coining the infamous "one-percenter" designation so often applied to the Hells Angels. It was the AMA, desperately trying to do a little spin doctoring after Riverside and Hollister, that issued a statement denouncing the behavior of the California troublemakers. Ninety-nine percent of motorcycle owners are good people enjoying a clean sport, the AMA asserted. It's the 1 percent that are antisocial barbarians.

What the AMA hadn't considered was that some bikers might actually consider that tag to be a compliment . . . a badge of honor.

Who were these proud and defiant outlaws? The "one-percenters"? A lot of them were social misfits, including a number of World War II veterans who, for one reason or another, just couldn't cope with the idea of returning to society and living a "normal" life. Maybe they were scarred by battle. Maybe they'd become addicted to speed and danger and anger. Maybe they just couldn't find meaningful employment. Whatever the reason, when they got back to the United States they formed motorcycle clubs and spent most of their time cruising around, fighting, drinking, and living outside the law. There were many clubs, and they all had angry, irreverent names, such as the Pissed Off Bastards of Bloomington (POBOB), the Market Street Commandos, the Gypsy Jokers, Satan's Slaves, and the Booze Fighters.

On March 17, 1948, in San Bernadino, California, the POBOB became the Hells Angels. Most people have no idea where this name originated. They figure it's just the product of some crazy biker's imagination. Wrong! The name is derived from a 1930 movie starring Ben Lyon and Jean Harlow. Directed and produced by Howard Hughes, *Hell's Angels* tells the story of a group of World War I aviators. In World War II, when it became common practice for bomber

Picture taken of the camera crew for Howard Hugh's epic film *Hell's Angels* at Oakland Airport, circa 1927

squadrons to name their planes (*Memphis Belle*) and their outfits (Panda Bears, Flying Tigers), "Hell's Angels" was adopted by a crew headed by Capt. Ira Baldwin. As the story goes, Baldwin was hanging out with his men, trying to think of a clever name. Finally he came up with a suggestion everyone liked.

"How about the name from that Howard Hughes movie, *Hell's Angels*?"

One member of the crew said it sounded good to him, since "this is the closest to hell we'll ever get," and the others all agreed.

Like the bomber squadron after which it was named, the Hells Angels Motorcycle Club lived on the edge and seemed to fear almost nothing. Its ranks swelled over the next decade, with chapters forming in San Francisco in 1954 and Oakland in 1957. The Oakland founder and president was Ralph "Sonny" Barger; it was his ambition and vision that helped transform the Hells Angels into the most powerful and well known motorcycle club in the world. Sonny arranged a meeting with representatives of all the major motorcycle clubs in 1959 and suggested an alliance that would benefit everyone. With an eye toward the future, Sonny said, in effect *"Why settle for this? Why be just a bunch of loose, disconnected guys riding motorcycles around*

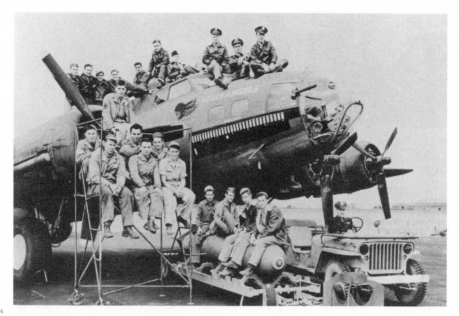

One of the original bomber squadrons from World War II whose name was inspired by Howard Hugh's epic film *Hell's Angels*

California? Why not work together? Why not have some type of national organization?"

Within a year Sonny was not only the president of the world's biggest motorcycle club but also a man smart enough and tough enough to understand the appeal of the outlaw image. It was Sonny's idea to ally the various clubs under a diamond-shaped "one-percenter" patch. He took it a step further by becoming the first Hells Angel to have the famous "one-percenter" tattoo drawn on his arm.

It wasn't an act with Sonny, either. Although he wasn't a big guy, Sonny was strong and charismatic. When you met him, as I did in 1979, shortly after he'd finished serving a few years in prison, you knew right away you were in the presence of someone special, someone who walked the walk. Meeting him was a thrill for me—it was like shaking hands with a living legend. Sonny had been chiefly responsible for my becoming a Hells Angel. I'd admired him ever since I was a kid, sitting in that darkened theater, watching *Hell's Angels on Wheels.* If, as law enforcement would have you believe, the Hells Angels are like the Mafia on wheels, then I guess Sonny Barger is the Godfather. Guys like Sonny and some of his contemporaries from Oakland, hard-core bikers like Johnny Angel, Cisco, Moldy Marvin and Terry the Tramp, Big Albert Boomer and Denkon . . . those guys shaped the Hells Angels. They made their own rules, lived the way they wanted to live. They're heroes, as far as I'm concerned.

Let's talk a little bit about myths and misconceptions. Understand, of course, that I can only speak about the things I've seen and encountered, but there have been so many stories over the years, so many lies and half-truths and comical characterizations, that I feel compelled to address some of the nonsense.

First of all, nothing makes me madder than when I hear someone talking about how all Hells Angels are into drugs, how we're the biggest methamphetamine dealers in the world. Me? I don't smoke, I don't drink, and I've never taken any drugs. I can tell you right now that I've never inhaled and it's the God's honest truth. So I like to think that I'm walking, talking proof we're not everything people say we are. And yet because I wear a Hells Angels patch some people automatically assume I'm a drug user and a drug dealer, which is complete and utter bullshit. Think about it? I don't drink, smoke, or take drugs, and yet I'm supposed to be this crazy, drug-taking, drug-dealing Hells Angel who willingly supports and feeds a criminal organization whose primary source of income is derived from the sale of methamphetamine? Give me a break! It's funny how every time I read a newspaper article or magazine story or even a book about the Hells Angels, it's always loaded with information provided by the government or some law enforcement agency and written by some asshole trying to cash in on our name and reputation. But they're ignorant. They don't know jack shit about what really happens inside the Hells Angels. As a result, the average person has this warped image of the club and its members. Sometimes a story is published and it's so bad, so inaccurate, that we'll raise a stink or file a lawsuit, and maybe, if we're lucky, that eventually leads to some sort of retraction. But it really doesn't matter, because the damage has already been done. People want to believe the worst, and so when they hear it, it stays with them. Whether it's fact or fiction is almost irrelevant.

Don't misunderstand me. I'm not naive, and I don't expect you to be, either. A lot of the members have a problem with authority. In that sense, I was no different. Like my father and a lot of the people I saw when I was growing up in Brooklyn and the Bronx, I tried to

Photo taken in front of the Hells Angels clubhouse in Manhattan's Lower East Side. Left to right: Charming Chuck, Terrible Ted, Pinball, John the Baptist, and Lightfoot. Credit: Hells Angels Club

adhere to my own personal code of conduct. Admittedly, the rules governing that code did not always mesh with the laws of the land. I never thought of myself as a criminal in the everyday, garden-variety sense of the word. I considered a true criminal to be someone who robbed liquor stores and pistol-whipped clerks or molested children or beat up people who couldn't defend themselves. You know . . . a scumbag. I've always loathed people like that. They're filth, and given half a chance, I'd kick the shit out of any of them.

If you want to know whether I've broken any laws, well, that's a different question altogether. I've been arrested on several occasions. Sometimes I've been guilty of the infractions; sometimes I have not. Let me put it this way: when it comes to the issue of respect, I am utterly without flexibility. I've always had a taste for fighting, and my willingness to stick up for my brothers and to wreak havoc in a street brawl did wonders for my career with the Hells Angels. You see, while I don't go looking for battles (most of the time, anyway), I've never shied away from one. I'll defend myself and those I love (and sometimes those who just happen to be in the proximity when an asshole is at work) with every tool at my disposal, regardless of whether the law says I have this right. When I use the word *defend* I am not talking exclusively about protection from physical harm. I'm talking about a personal set of beliefs that compels me to take matters into my own hands when confronted with a situation that is potentially harmful to my health or reputation. You want to pick a fight with me? Fine. But understand what you're getting into. You want to spread rumors and gossip about me? You want to question my honor and integrity? You want to insult me to my face? Okay . . . go right ahead. But don't expect me to walk away. Don't expect me to take it. Hell, don't expect me to hire a lawyer to do my fighting for me. Some people are inherently peaceful. They're capable of swallowing their anger or letting the legal system take its course. Maybe they believe in some sort of Judgment Day, when we all have to account for our transgressions.

Me? I'm not that patient.

I've been criticized for this attitude, but I've also been rewarded for it—and not merely by the Hells Angels. I built a successful career as a bodyguard, and I'm in the process of building a successful career as an actor; neither of those things would have been possible if not for my affiliation with the Hells Angels, which reinforced my reputation as a man with little or no tolerance for insulting, disrespectful behavior. The way I live my life . . . the fact that I am willing to not only stand up for myself but also accept the consequences of my actions . . . I think a lot of people admire that, even if they don't want to admit it publicly. Society in general and law enforcement in particular hammer into our heads the idea that justice is a slow, deliberate process, one requiring thoughtful, professional oversight. Justice is rarely to be meted out passionately, quickly, and never by the hand of the person who has been wronged. In my not-so-humble opinion, that's a load of crap.

Here's a hypothetical situation, one you may have encountered at some point in your life (or something like it, anyway). Let's say you're driving home one night, both hands on the steering wheel of your nice, clean Ford Taurus, adhering to the speed limit posted in your neatly manicured suburban neighborhood. Suddenly, out of nowhere, two dark figures appear in the middle of the street. They look like older kids, sixteen, seventeen years old, and they're stepping right out into traffic. You can't believe your eyes, at first—this isn't an intersection; there's no traffic light, no crosswalk. The kids know exactly what they're doing. Acting as if the world is their own private play-ground, they saunter across the street, causing you to slam on your brakes and veer off to the side of the road. Another car coming in the opposite direction does precisely the same thing. As you lean on the horn, the kids both give you a dismissive look, flip the bird, and con-tinue strutting on their merry way.

What do you do? In all likelihood, you shake your head, curse under your breath, maybe pound the dashboard in frustration. Then you go home, crack open a beer or mix a martini, and complain to your wife about the two punks who nearly got you killed.

Here's what I'd do. I'd stop the car, get out, and confront them both. They're kids, so I'd give them one chance to apologize. And one chance only. If they copped an attitude, I'd smack them both in the face. I don't care if they're minors, and I don't care if the law says I'm not allowed to touch them. Their behavior was reckless, selfish, and deserving of immediate response. I'd give it to them. Maybe part of you finds that repugnant, but let's be honest: you'd like to do the same thing . . . wouldn't you?

Let me give you another example, this one not so hypothetical. One Sunday afternoon in the early 1970s, Kathy and I went for a ride on my motorcycle; Tony and his girlfriend joined us. We were just mind-ing our own business, cruising up Pelham Road in the Bronx on our way back to New Rochelle, when another car passed us and cut us off, coming so close to Tony's bike that he nearly lost control and flipped. Tony stopped momentarily, but I kept right on going, leaning into the throttle in an attempt to catch and confront the driver. I was absolutely enraged, so I pulled alongside the car and signaled for the driver to roll down his window, which he did.

Before I could say a word, the driver brandished a knife and yelled, "What's your problem, buddy?" There were three other men in the car, all of them laughing.

I'm not the one with the problem, asshole. You are.

Back then, I used to keep a set of nunchakus in a pouch on the left side of my bike. Nunchakus, in case you don't know, are standard weapons in the martial arts arsenal—essentially, they're two short rods (made of wood or steel or heavy rubber) connected by a chain. In the right hands, they're lethal, which is why they were eventually outlawed. Anyway, when this guy pulled a knife, I reached into the pouch and withdrew my nunchakus. In a single motion, I flipped them from my left hand to my right and then I snapped them against the guy's windshield. As Kathy screamed in horror, the windshield shattered and the driver lost control of the car. His passengers howled in fear as the car jumped up onto the sidewalk and careened into a nearby park. The driver eventually righted the vehicle and took off down a side road. Figuring he'd learned his lesson and not wanting to frighten Kathy any more than I had, I let him go.

Admittedly, sometimes my temper clouded my judgment, as in the time when Kathy and I were driving through White Plains in our '71 Supersport Chevelle, a gorgeous car, blue with black stripes, that I'd customized with a 454 engine and big Mickey Thompson tires. This was also in the early seventies, when I was at times wild and reckless and, undeniably, madly in love with my wife. We were just driving along, listening to the radio, enjoying our bad-ass car, when suddenly another car pulled up next to us, on the passenger side, and I noticed the two guys in the front seat staring, pointing, smiling.

"What the fuck are those bozos doing?" I said.

Kathy rolled her eyes. She'd been through this before. "Relax, Chuck," she said.

Relax, shit. They're looking at Kathy. They're disrespecting me!

So I rolled down the window. They did the same.

"Pull over, man."

"What for?"

"Pull over!"

I cut him off and yanked the car over onto the shoulder. Then I jumped out and waited for the other car to follow, which it did. With Kathy yelling, banging on the horn, doing anything to stop me from getting in another fight, I marched up to the driver's window, figuring I'd hit him first, and then the passenger.

As I approached, however, I could see that the driver was confused, frightened. "What's wrong?" he shouted.

"What's wrong? What's wrong is the way you're looking at my girl, asshole."

He held up his hands submissively. "Whoa, pal. We were just admiring your car, that's all."

I stopped in my tracks. I could feel the blood draining from my face.

Oh, shit!

"My car?"

The guy in the passenger seat leaned over. "Yeah, man. It's awesome."

I hung my head. Rarely had I felt like such a dummy, such a complete jerk. I'd come within a breath of kicking the shit out of these two guys simply because they liked my car, which was precisely the reaction I'd hoped to provoke by putting so much work into it. So I did something I'd done only a handful of times in my entire life.

I apologized.

Then I went back to my car, feeling two inches tall, and took a tongue-lashing from Kathy.

"You see," she said. "Your temper is going to get you in big trouble someday."

She got no argument from me.

The Hells Angels were a good fit for me. I loved the camaraderie, and, yes, I liked the notion that my affiliation with the club gave me instant credibility and respect on the street. I was a tough guy, and I wanted to be part of the toughest motorcycle club around. But I wasn't willing to compromise my own beliefs to make it happen, that's for damn sure.

The fact that I did not smoke or drink or use drugs could have presented a serious obstacle to my membership in the Hells Angels. Not everyone in the club uses drugs or alcohol, of course, but some do, just as in any walk of life. I know lawyers who do drugs; I know cops who do drugs. And I know Hells Angels who do drugs. But I don't and never have. In fact, in the New York Nomads chapter, of which I was a member—I now belong to the Hells Angels New Roc City chapter—we took one hell of a strong stance against drugs. If any club member was caught selling drugs, he was immediately thrown out. And with dismissal comes the mandatory removal of all Hells Angels tattoos; you don't leave the club with the tattoo. Sometimes the tattoos can be obliterated with black ink, and other times more invasive procedures are necessary, such as a body grinder. It's not pleasant, but that tattoo belongs to us, and we're taking it—one way or another.) Some of the guys were a little surprised that I was so squeaky clean, and a few of them were even suspicious.

"What are you, a fucking cop?" they'd say.

"I ain't no cop. I just don't do drugs. And I'm not gonna start just because you're doing it."

Along those same lines, I'm not going to sit here and pretend that there aren't some individuals in the Hells Angels who sell drugs. Shit, individuals do a lot of things in a lot of different organizations. I can remember when more than a dozen cops from a single New York precinct were indicted for all kinds of nasty, illicit behavior: extortion, shakedowns, illegal search and seizure . . . basically acting like the scum they were supposed to be hunting. But I'm not going to go around condemning the entire police force just because of the behavior of a select few. There are rotten apples in every barrel, right? All I'm asking is that we get the same consideration. If one or two guys get caught selling drugs and they happen to be Hells Angels, that's their business, their problem. It's not representative of the entire membership, and it sure as hell ain't representative of me and the way I live my life.

One other note on this same subject. Think about it logically. If the trafficking of methamphetamine and other narcotics is such a spectacularly efficient and profitable business endeavor for the Hells Angels . . . if we're moving hundreds of millions of dollars of this shit all over the world . . . then why are so many of our members dead fucking broke? How come it seemed like half the guys I met when I was prospecting for the New York chapter had to sleep at the clubhouse because they couldn't afford to make their rent payments? How often do you see big-time drug dealers working long hours at back breaking blue-collar jobs, the way so many Hells Angels do? You know what drug dealers do? They sell drugs. That's it. Or they oversee others who sell drugs for them. And they do it primarily to make easy money while avoiding the kind of hard labor I've done most of my life.

There have always been some individuals in the Hells Angels who have taken drugs and sold drugs (for their own personal gain and profit), and there always will be. But as for that type of activity being the hallmark of the club and the primary source of income . . . well, that's just a bunch of bullshit. The club doesn't support its members, and the members don't support the club (not financially, anyway; emotional support is another matter). Each member attends a weekly meeting and pays dues of approximately fifteen to twenty dollars per week, which is used primarily for parties and supplies when we go on a long run. Think about that: fifteen bucks a week. It ain't much, is it? Hardly enough to drive the machinery of a major criminal organization.

I do think the perception has changed some in recent years, and not just for me (because I've been able to sustain a career in the public eye) but for everyone associated with the club. Thirty, forty years ago, the Hells Angels were the outcasts of society, rough and tough bikers riding around, taking over towns, and scaring the crap out of anyone who got in their way. In those days only the Hells Angels and other outlaw motorcycle clubs were riding Harley-Davidsons. Today, Jesus . . . you have everybody and their mother riding Harleys. The culture of motorcycles has changed, and Harley-Davidson is at the forefront of that change. You see these romantic, dreamy Harley advertisements in magazines, on televison. You see yuppies sipping Pinot Grigio at the Harley-Davidson Café in Midtown Manhattan. Back in the day, we were the only ones supporting Harley-Davidson—the outlaw bikers. Funny thing was, Harley pretended not to like the connection between its product and the outlaw motorcycle clubs. But it was good for business, and Harley-Davidson knew it.

Nowadays, of course, everyone likes to ride Harleys. That's fine with me. Harley-Davidson makes a great bike and this is a free country. There will always be weekend warriors, guys who run out of the office on Friday night, strip off the coat and tie, and strap on the biker regalia: leather jacket, brain bucket, boots . . . whatever completes the fantasy. Good for them. I don't care in the least, just as long as they don't wear anything related to the Hells Angels. That is simply not allowed. We don't let anyone else wear red and white or the skull and wings—the "death head." That's our trademark. It's copyrighted, it's patented, and we—the Hells Angels—are the only ones who wear it. Everyone seems to understand that, especially the weekend warriors. Many of them, I think, have a deep, dark secret desire to be a Hells Angel, if only for a little while. But they aren't stupid enough to impersonate the real deal.

That's one thing that hasn't changed. In the early days the Hells Angels represented a society within a society that lived by its own rules, its own bylaws. We just wanted to be left alone, to ride as a brotherhood . . . and for the most part, whether out of fear or intimidation or genuine admiration, people did give us that respect. And they still do to this day. Average citizens, including the average motorcycle rider, want no part of a confrontation with anyone wearing the mark of the Hells Angels. Even if the image has been softened just a bit, the message remains the same: *Do not fuck with me.*

Part of this image stems from the commonly held belief that anyone who is welcomed into the ranks of the Hells Angels has either done something horrible (like committed an act of murder) or survived something horrible (inhuman hazing rituals, for example). That brings us to one of the great myths about the club, that there is some sort of gruesome secret initiation rite involving pain, degradation, and crime or some combination of the three. I don't mean to spoil the myth, but that's just bullshit. People always ask me, "What do you have to do to become a member of the Hells Angels?" Well, you don't have to *do* anything. First of all—and this is the most important thing—you've got to be a man . . . a man who is at least twenty-one years old, owns a Harley-Davidson motorcycle, and is willing to stand up for what he believes in. That's really about it.

Oh, and one other thing: you have to win the approval of everyone else in the club. It takes only one "no" vote to deny a prospect membership. That's why the hang-around process is so important, so you get to know them and they get to know you. I used to paint cars on the side and I was pretty good at it, so I ended up painting motorcycles for some of the guys in the New York chapter, including Sandy Alexander. I didn't consider that to be a humiliating experience. In fact, I was happy to do it. The guys in the club saw that I did a good job and they asked me to paint their bikes. They respected my ability, and they respected me. You have to understand—a prospect is the same thing as a Hells Angel. He's just not wearing a patch yet. We don't treat prospects like dirt; we give them the same respect we do a member of the club. We don't make them wash motorcycles or run to the store to pick up beer at all hours of the night. We don't demean them or embarrass them. Think about it: We want them to be like us; we want them to be proud of being members of the Hells Angels. So why would we disrespect them?

This isn't *Animal House*. This is the greatest motorcycle club in the world. We don't need stupid, juvenile initiation rites. And we neither need nor want the publicity that would come with compelling each prospect to prove his mettle by breaking the law. It makes for good copy, I know; it adds to the legend of the Hells Angels as reckless, sociopathic warriors. But it's just not true. One of the greatest myths about the Angels surrounds the significance of the "Filthy Few" patch. As the legend goes, only those who have taken the life of another human being are allowed to wear the Filthy Few patch. Well, if that's so, then there must be roughly ten thousand bodies unaccounted for. It's laughable, really. You want to know what the patch means? You want to know who the Filthy Few are? They're the ones who have a reputation for being the first to show up at a party and the last to leave. They're big-time, hard-core drinkers. Not murderers.

And then there are the stories about wild, scatological stuff. Prospects getting pissed on, shit on, and generally abused in the most repugnant manner imaginable. All I can tell you is this: No one has ever done anything like that to me, including the Hells Angels. And I would do serious damage to anyone who tried.

The sexual stuff you might have heard is equally ridiculous. Are there biker groupies? Sure. There are women who, for whatever reason, like getting fucked by tough guys. And the Hells Angels are the toughest of the tough. I'm not going to tell you I've never seen a gang bang, but it's always been consensual. And it has nothing to do with the hang-around process. Peter Weller, the actor who starred in *RoboCop*, among other films, once approached me at a nightclub, when I was wearing my Hells Angels jacket, and asked, in all seriousness, "Is it true you have to share your wife with the other club members before you can get in?" I liked Peter and I understood the fascination some people (most people) have with the darker aspects of biker lore, so I didn't smack him. But I did set him straight.

"Hey, if a guy so much as looks at my wife," I said, "I'm gonna knock him out. No hesitation."

The idea that we'd share our women with other club members . . . it's just ludicrous. The Hells Angels have more respect for one another, and for one another's wives and girlfriends, than any other group in society. I really believe that. I don't care if you're talking about wise guys, strict religious sects . . . whatever. We have a rule in the club: If you fuck around with somebody's wife, you get thrown out. And you get a serious beating on top of it.

To understand just how ridiculous some of these myths are, you have to understand what it means to be a part of the Hells Angels. It's more than just a motorcycle club; it's an international brotherhood . . . the world's largest extended family. Support and friendship among members is unconditional, transcending all geographic and socioeconomic boundaries. When a club member needs help, he has it . . . no questions asked.

Let me give you an example that illustrates what I'm trying to say. I have a close friend named Philip Carlo, a writer who has done a lot of good work involving missing and abused children. In the early 1980s Phil got a lead on a New York City boy who had disappeared a year or two earlier, at the age of eight, while walking to school in SoHo. Phil had reason to believe the boy had been abducted and taken to Amsterdam by members of the infamous North American Man-Boy Love Association, a bunch of twisted fucks who advocate legalized sexual activity between adults and children. NAMBLA's motto is: Sex after eight is too late. That's all you need to know.

Anyway, Phil traveled to Amsterdam on behalf of the boy's family and began rooting around in the city's notoriously kinky red-light district. To say Phil met resistance would be an understatement. No one wanted to talk to Phil, and those who did were interested primarily in threatening him with serious bodily harm. So Phil called me at my home in New Rochelle, explained the situation, and asked if there was anything I could do.

"Wait right there," I said. "I'll make a few calls."

Within half an hour, there was a knock at Phil's hotel room door. In the hallway were four of the biggest, scariest bikers you'd ever want to meet. Or not meet, depending on your point of view. Hells Angels in that part of the world tend to look like Vikings: about six and a half feet tall, thick chests, long hair, beards. Absolutely terrifying. But Phil had no reason to be concerned.

"We're on your side," they told him. "Whatever you need, we're with you. If this kid is here, we'll bring him home."

That night Phil returned to the red-light district, four bodyguards in tow. He knocked on doors, asked a lot of questions. No one laid a hand on him. No one threatened him. No one hassled him in the least.

I'd like to be able tell you the story has a happy ending, that together they found the boy and returned him to his parents. But it didn't work out that way. After exhausting all leads, Phil returned to the United States. The child was never found. Life is tragic that way sometimes. But I think it's worth noting that without the assistance of the Hells Angels, Phil might have become a casualty as well. His work was important; I wanted to help in any way I could. And I knew my brothers in Amsterdam would feel the same way.

It's difficult for anyone who isn't part of the Hells Angels to understand the emotional and psychological pull of the club. I loved being part of it, so much that I was willing to risk losing my family. Early in our relationship Kathy had found my fascination with motorcycles to be an exciting, harmless diversion. She liked riding with me, hanging out with my buddies and their girlfriends. But she also figured it was just a fad and that eventually I'd grow out of it. Kathy was a good, hardworking mother—when she came home after a day at the office, she wanted nothing more than to spend some quality time with Lisa. Naturally, Kathy wanted me to be part of that time. I had a different notion of what it meant to be a husband and father. Convinced I'd somehow been cheated out of all the good times my friends had experienced, I began trying to play catch-up. I stayed out often and late. I took out my own frustrations on my wife, which put a serious strain on my marriage.

Adding to the stress in our lives—especially Kathy's—was my investment in the Hells Angels. As a prospect, I was expected to make the club a priority in my life. And I did. Meetings, runs, hanging out at the clubhouse—I did everything that was required to assure membership. Not that I considered any of these obligations to be a burden; far from it. I wanted in the worst way to be accepted, to be part of the Hells Angels. It became the focus of my life.

Kathy and I fought all the time while I was prospecting. She worried about the club's outlaw reputation and what my membership might mean for her and Lisa. "The club will never hurt you," I said. But she wasn't so sure. She envisioned a husband in prison, an absentee father . . . or worse, a father who had been killed in some sort of gang conflict. I told her she was being melodramatic, that I would always be there for her and Lisa.

None of my protestations swayed Kathy in the least. In the seven years since we'd begun dating, she had evolved into a responsible, mature woman who saw no reason to share her husband with a motorcycle club, especially the most notorious club in the world. It was obvious to her that motorcycles were not just a fad to me; they represented a way of life.

"You're never going to grow out of this, are you?" she asked me.

"No, I'm not."

And with that Kathy gave me an ultimatum: *"It's me or them."*

I never really made a choice, never responded to her demand. I simply continued to live the way I'd been living. One night I came home to find the apartment on Pelham Road cleared out. Within days Kathy started divorce proceedings.

Until then I hadn't understood the depth of Kathy's resentment, or I simply didn't care. Even when faced with the reality of the situation—that I was about to lose my wife and daughter—I continued to prospect with all the energy and enthusiasm I could summon. If anything, Kathy's actions only made me crave acceptance in the club even more, in part because I wanted to prove to her that she couldn't dictate my behavior or actions but also because I now considered the Hells Angels to be my only family. I needed them more than ever.

Here's the way it works. After you spend a year hanging around, earning trust and acceptance, while the Angels try to determine whether you're a good fit for the club, a decision is made. You go to a meeting, your name is brought up, and the entire membership votes on you. You're outside the room while all this is happening, pacing back and forth, wondering whether you've made it. Prospects, you see, aren't allowed to attend meetings.

On the night of May 10, 1979, two prospects were proposed as full members of the New York City chapter of the Hells Angels. Phil Kramer, also known as Lightfoot, was one of the prospects. I was the other. They brought us in together after the vote had been taken, and Sandy Alexander introduced us with the following words: "Welcome. You are now members of the Hells Angels, New York City chapter.

Phil "Lightfoot" Kramer and I
Credit: Ken Nahoum

Congratulations!" The official ceremony was followed by a lot of bear hugs, handshakes, and a long night of partying.

The next day I got my patch, as well as a brand-new tattoo, right over my heart (some chapters today do not require that new members get an Angels tattoo; when I joined, it was mandatory, although I would have gotten one anyway). I got on my bike and rode all over metropolitan New York and lower Westchester County . . . just cruised around for hours on end. I remember the way people stared, the way they averted their eyes when I stared back. And I remember every time I stopped at a traffic light, I couldn't help but turn my head and try to catch my reflection in a store window. I'd see myself astride my Harley, see the skull and the wings stretched across my back, the logo of the biggest and baddest motorcycle club on the planet, and a feeling of pride and exhilaration would sweep over me. In one day, it seemed, the world had changed.

I was now, and would forever be, a part of the Hells Angels.

11

THE BIGGEST PROBLEM WITH LIVING LIFE BY YOUR OWN SET OF RULES, YOUR
own personal code of conduct, is that occasionally you're going to
encounter resistance, if not outright resentment. It's always easier to
march lockstep with the masses, to be a good boy and behave the
way society expects you to behave. I long ago came to the realization
that I couldn't live that way, and I've come to terms with the fact that
my pride and stubbornness are going to get me into hot water once
in a while.

Like the time I lost my job with Five Towns Refrigeration, which
serviced most of the bigger supermarkets in the tristate area. I hooked
up with Five Towns approximately six months after I was fired by
Finast and stayed with them through my early days with the Hells
Angels. It was the same kind of work—installing, repairing, and
maintaining commercial cooling and refrigeration systems—and I
was pretty good at it. It was hard work, but the pay was decent and
the customers usually appreciated our efforts.

Most of them, anyway.

I was on my way home one evening when I got an emergency call.
The dispatcher said the air-conditioning unit at a grocery store in
Manhattan had shut down, and the place was quickly becoming a
sauna. I arrived as I always did, carrying only a screwdriver and a
flashlight (since that was usually all that was required to diagnose,
and even fix, most cooling problems; tool belts were strictly for show).
I was met at the door by a big, fat sweaty guy with greasy hair and
a patchy beard.

"You're from Five Towns?" he asked.

"That's right."

"About fuckin' time . . . follow me."

It had been a long day and I was in no mood to take any shit from anyone, but I understood his frustration. The store was cooking—it was probably eighty degrees in the store, and rising fast. Customers were melting in line, and the half-dozen checkout girls working the cash registers looked like they were going to pass out. If it had been my store, I'd have been pissed, too. (Of course, if it had been my store, I'd have known how to fix the problem, but that's another story.)

We walked to the rear of the market, passed through a set of doors and into a back room, where the air-conditioning unit sat quietly, almost lifelessly, on the floor. I got down on my knees, flipped on the flashlight, and went to work. It took me all of about thirty seconds to fix the problem. I just hit the reset button and the whole system belched and spit and then roared back to life. Behind me, I could hear the fat guy laughing in disbelief.

"Well, how about that?" he said. "What the hell did you do?"

"No big deal," I answered. "These things are like car radiators. When they overheat, they just shut right down. If it happens again, let it rest for a few minutes, and then push the reset button. It's right here."

I motioned for him to come closer, so I could point it out and save him the cost of another service call down the road. Grunting and groaning, he crouched as low as he could, which wasn't nearly low enough to see where I'd aimed the flashlight.

"Ah, fuck these things," the man said, wiping a hand across his forehead, and as he did so one of the checkout girls stepped through the door, a cute girl in her early twenties.

"We're dying out there," she said. "And the customers are complaining like crazy."

"Don't worry," I told her, gesturing toward the air-conditioning unit, which was now humming nicely. "You're back in business."

She smiled. "Oh, that's fantastic! Thanks so much."

After she walked away, the big man inched closer to me. He smiled, gave me a poke in the ribs with his elbow, and said, "Puts you in the mood for a blow job, don't it?"

Figuring he was probably just a typical fat middle-aged lech who wasn't getting enough at home (given his appearance, it would have been a shock if he was getting *any* at home), I smiled. *This poor bastard probably goes home every night and yanks the goalie while fantasizing about all these hot young chicks he'll never touch.*

"Uh-huh," I said without really thinking.

The guy chuckled. "Yeah, I could really use one right about now."

Just to sort of play along with his fantasy, I backhanded him lightly in the chest and said, "Me and you both, pal."

With that, the guy lunged at me clumsily and began pawing at my crotch. Stunned, I didn't move at first, until he managed to get a handful of my package in his grip.

"Well then," he said, grinning like a crazy man. "How about I give you one right now?"

Holy Christ!

I tend to walk around with my antennae up, always ready for trouble or confrontation, but this guy had caught me completely off guard. I was just trying to do my work, get paid, and go home, and now here I was, getting molested by some stupid, greasy slob in the back room of a Manhattan supermarket. This was not part of the job description, and I was not about take it . . . lying down, standing up, or any other way. That he was about six-foot-four, 250 pounds, didn't bother me in the least. In one motion I switched my flashlight and screwdriver to my left hand, balled my right hand into a fist, and swung as hard I could. I hit him just under the chin, right on the button. He sailed backward, leaving one of his loafers on the floor where he had stood, and crashed into a stack of canned goods. Then he slumped to the floor.

I didn't check him for a pulse, didn't bother to see if he was alive or breathing or anything else. I simply marched to my truck, withdrew a clipboard and sign-out sheet, and then went back to get a signature from the store manager verifying that I'd completed the work. A well-dressed young man near the door seemed to fit the bill, so I thrust the clipboard in his face.

"You'll have to give that to the manager," he said.

"I thought you were the manager."

He chuckled, as if he was embarrassed. "Nah, I'm just the assistant. The manager is a big guy."

"Fat guy? All sweaty?"

"Yeah, that's him."

Jesus!

123

I grabbed the clipboard. "Never mind. He ain't signing nothing."

"Why not?"

"Because I just knocked him out, that's why."

Aghast, the assistant manager ran toward the back of the store. I followed, though I'm not sure why. The manager was struggling to his feet when we arrived, his face split from his lip to his cheekbone; blood soaked his shirt and trousers.

"Oh, shit!" the assistant manager said, holding a hand over his mouth, like he was going to puke or something.

The manager took a step, mumbled something, and then fell to the floor again. It must have made quite a noise, because now the butcher was standing in the doorway, a meat cleaver in one hand, a whole chicken in the other.

Okay . . . this is about to get ugly.

The butcher nodded toward the manager. "Who the fuck did that?"

"I did," I said. There was no point in lying about it. If the butcher wanted a piece of me, I'd give it to him. I only hoped he had so much gore on his hands that he wouldn't be able to hold on to the cleaver.

"Oh . . ." the butcher said, and a smile slowly crossed his face. "What did he do . . . grab you?"

"Uh . . . yeah, as a matter of fact. How did you know?"

The butcher wiped the cleaver on his robe, waved it at the manager, as if he'd thought once or twice in the past about using it on the fat piece of shit. "He does that to everyone."

"Yeah?" I said. "Well, he doesn't do it to me."

And with that I walked out, started up the truck, and headed for home.

By the time I arrived I'd received a call from the dispatcher. The boss wanted me in the office by eight o'clock the next morning. It was important, he said, that I be there on time. I didn't have to guess what it was that we'd be discussing.

I arrived at Five Towns headquarters promptly at eight and was summoned immediately to the administrative offices. There were four people in the room: the manager, two supervisors, and me. I can only speculate, of course, but I presume they anticipated a spirited meeting and that's why I was so heavily outnumbered. As expected, they voiced their displeasure with my behavior the previous night.

"Chuck, you can't just go around beating up anyone you don't like,"

"Who said I didn't like him? I don't even the know the guy. I just didn't like what he *did*."

Exasperated, the manager rubbed his forehead. "They could sue us, you know? They could put us right out of business, all because you couldn't control your temper."

I had expected the meeting would go this way, and for that reason I had thought about not even bothering to show up. But I needed the job and thought there was a chance, if I explained my side of the story, that they'd be reasonable. I could see now, however, that they were only concerned with protecting their own bank accounts.

"Look," I said. "Anybody puts their hands on me, I'm knocking them out. That's all there is to it."

They exchanged serious glances and then focused their attention on me. I felt like I was back in high school again.

"I'm sorry you feel that way," the manager said. "Because we have no room in this organization for anyone with that kind of attitude."

At this point it was obvious that the game was over, that there would be no more discussion. I wanted no part of any company that expected me to laugh it off when a client grabbed my balls. So I stood up and reached into my pocket, prompting all three men to recoil in surprise and fear, as if they figured I was going to pull out a gun and bust the place up or something.

"Here's your fucking keys," I said, tossing them on the desk. "I quit."

The manager scooped them up and said, nervously, "Too late . . . you've already been fired."

I shrugged. "Whatever."

Then I turned and walked out, my career in refrigeration now in serious jeopardy after two consecutive dismissals. Not that I really gave a flying fuck. I was tired of the job anyway.

For a while it seemed as though all I had going for me in my life was my affiliation with the Hells Angels. I'd lost my job; I'd lost my wife and daughter. As it often does in these situations, though, the club offered support and encouragement. I started hanging out at Big Joe's Tattoo Shop on First Avenue in Mount Vernon, where Vinnie Girolamo was already employed as a floor manager. Vinnie invited me to help out, and pretty soon we were splitting days. It was easy, enjoyable work in an atmosphere I liked—tattoo shops, after all, attract a lot of bikers. My job was to roam the floor and offer assistance to customers. I'd help them look through catalogs and choose a tattoo. Then I'd get the stencil, give it to one of our artists, Big Joe himself, Louie Lombi, or Carl "Shorty" Haloi, and he would create the tattoo. I got a commission for working the floor, usually about ten bucks per tattoo. I could get as many hours as I wanted, mainly because Vinnie, while nice enough, wasn't the most ambitious man in the world. He often asked me to fill in for him when he needed some extra sleep or simply didn't feel like working. I needed the cash, so I almost always said yes.

I moved into a small apartment above Big Joe's because the rent was reasonable and the commute to my job was ideal: downstairs and through a back door. I could hang out with some of my friends and do work that didn't really feel like work. At the same time, I began studying the craft of tattooing. I'd watch closely as Big Joe, Shorty, and Louie created art on the bodies of their customers—beautiful, precise lines and bold, vivid colors. One day while I was closing up the shop, Big Joe offered me an opportunity to become an apprentice: "You're here all the time, anyway, Chuck. You might as well learn how to draw."

So, thanks to Big Joe, Shorty, and Louie, I became a tattoo artist. I started out as all artists do: by giving my work away. I'd recruit guys on the street, other bikers, mostly, to come in after the shop was closed, and I'd make a deal with them: *Be my guinea pig, and I'll give you a free tattoo.* Amazingly enough, it wasn't hard to find people willing to accept this arrangement. Tattoos can be expensive, and the offer of a freebie—even a freebie that might be a little off balance or otherwise imperfect—is hard to resist.

It didn't take long for me to realize a couple things: First, sketching a tattoo is more difficult than it looks. Even if you know how to draw . . . if you're a legitimate illustrator or painter . . . that's no guarantee you'll make a good tattoo artist. It's all about having a steady, strong hand, following the stencil, and manipulating the skin—stretching, pulling, and twisting. Like any craft, its mastery requires discipline and practice, as well as talent. And that brings us to the second thing I discovered: I had some talent. Before too long I had more guinea pigs than I needed, so I started charging a small fee. While it might cost a customer fifty bucks to get a small tattoo from Big Joe, I'd do it for twenty-five bucks. Within a year or so I was working right alongside Big Joe and Louie, charging full price for tattoos.

In addition to working at Big Joe's, I also went back to the refrigeration business, this time with a company called Comfort Cooling. You see, there aren't many tattoo artists who can support themselves—let alone their families—exclusively through their craft. That, I discovered, was the bad news. The good news was I had a family to support, or at least help support. Kathy and I were completely separated for only a few months. She had divorced me primarily out of anger and spite, because I had refused to divest from the Hells Angels. She had packed up, moved out, and gotten a quickie divorce, which I did not contest. But it turned out we really did love each other, and we missed each other. So we began dating again. I'd spend a few nights a week at my apartment above Big Joe's and a few nights with Kathy and Lisa in New Rochelle. Over time the scale tilted heavily toward Kathy's place, until eventually we were living like husband and wife all over again.

Not that Kathy ever accepted the Hells Angels. She did not like the club and she did not approve of my affiliation with the club. That never changed. But we came to an understanding because we loved each other and we loved our daughter and we wanted to be a family. Kathy never came to any Hells Angels parties, never wanted to be a part of that lifestyle, but she tolerated my involvement. She was polite and hospitable to my friends—she even cooked for them!—as long as they agreed not to wear their patches in our house. And my friends were courteous and respectful in return. More than that, really, especially where Lisa was concerned. My brothers in the Hells Angels loved Lisa like one of their own daughters, and they would have done anything for her.

To help keep peace with Kathy, I agreed not to ride my bike around the neighborhood late at night. She respected my wishes and I respected hers, and we managed to work things out. Although we never remarried, we were a family, in every sense of the word.

The Hells Angels helped me support that family, too. Sandy Alexander was a stuntman, and in 1979 he got me my first Hollywood job: as an extra in a motorcycle movie called *Dead Ringer*, starring Meat Loaf and Cher as an unlikely couple. Meat Loaf was huge at the time (literally and figuratively)—his album, *Bat Out of Hell*, had just sold millions of copies—so someone naturally got the idea of making him a movie star. His role was that of gang leader. Sandy recruited eighteen guys from the club to play bikers, and our job was simply to ride around behind Meat Loaf. It was kind of wild, because Meat Loaf actually knew nothing about riding a motorcycle, so they towed him along on a trailer, with the wheels up. On-screen you'd see a close-up of Meat Loaf, his long hair blowing in the breeze, a smile on his face, like he'd been born to ride a motorcycle. But he had no clue! All he did was sit there. When the director needed a long shot of Meat Loaf riding his bike on the highway, a stunt double would fill in. That role was played by a Hells Angel named Don Picard, more commonly known as Skeets.

I was fascinated by the whole moviemaking process, the way fantasy meshed with reality. It was my first experience with celebrities and movie stars, and I was struck by how "normal" most of them appeared to be. In fact, Cher and Meat Loaf seemed more intrigued by us—the Hells Angels—than we were by them. That was kind of cool, as was the 200 bucks a day I picked up for basically just being myself. There was potential here, I thought. I just wasn't sure how to exploit it.

I've always been conflicted about the reputation of the Hells Angels. A part of me certainly enjoyed having the reputation of a fighter—the patch alone is usually enough to compel most people to keep their distance. I thought of myself as a tough guy, and I didn't mind that others saw me that way, too. What I did not like was the idea that society in general viewed me as a hard-core criminal, and so I tried to think of ways to refute that image and some of the myths about the Hells Angels.

One way I attempted to accomplish that goal while prospecting for the Hells Angels was through motorcycle and automobile restoration. I entered a car show at the New York Coliseum with a 1923 Model T Ford that I had purchased in the early seventies while on vacation in Florida with my wife and daughter; I restored and painted the car to showroom quality. Pretty soon some of the other guys in the club took an interest in my hobby, and I began helping them fix up their bikes as well. We became regulars on the car-show circuit—mainly me, Bert,

Mike the Bike, and Diamond Danny Bifield. At first our presence was met with apprehension, if not downright fear. I guess promoters were worried about violence, as if we'd break the legs of the judges or something if our entries failed to win. But we were peaceful, respectful, and, I might add, pretty damn good at rebuilding vintage cars and motorcycles. After a while I think some

Diamond Danny Bifield and myself with my 1923 Model T Ford

people, at least in that corner of the world, began to look at the Hells Angels a little differently: *Maybe these guys aren't so bad after all.*

The following year, 1980, I was showing some of my bikes at a motorcycle show, again at the New York Coliseum, when my career as a bodyguard was born. Robert Conrad, the actor who had made a name for himself in the 1960s television show *The Wild Wild West* and who now was starring in the equally popular *Black Sheep Squadron*, was one of the featured guests at the show. As he was led through the crowd to a booth where he'd be signing autographs, the fans fell in on Conrad, surrounded him. His bodyguard, sensing trouble, saw me standing nearby and asked me to help out for a few minutes. So I jumped in—wearing my Hells Angels jacket—and the crowd suddenly parted like the Red Sea. They just got the hell out of my way, and I remember thinking, *Wow, that's pretty cool.*

Later I started talking with this guy about what it was like to be a bodyguard and whether it was possible to earn a living at it.

"Hell, yeah," he said. "It's profitable."

I was surprised . . . and intrigued. "What do I do?" I asked.

"Simple. Just get yourself some business cards saying you handle security and start passing them around. Believe me, you'll find work."

He was right. Although I wasn't really a big guy back then—I was about five-eleven, 165 pounds—I had a reputation for being able to handle myself. I was a Golden Gloves boxer, after all, and I had black belts in karate and jujitsu (I've since attained that level of expertise in six different martial arts), so I knew how to fight. And, obviously, being a member of the Hells Angels carried significant weight, too. There was one other thing I soon discovered: Most celebrities don't want a big monster of a bodyguard following them around, attracting attention. They just want to be accompanied and protected by someone who looks relatively normal but can take care of any "problems" that might arise.

That was me.

I went home that night and told Kathy of my idea. As usual, she was in my corner right away. We both pulled out pads and started taking notes. For the first time in many years, maybe the first time ever, I was excited about the prospect of work. But I needed a name, something catchy, something memorable. I jotted down dozens of ideas, discarded most of them, and then jotted down a few more. Nothing sounded right. Until . . .

Let's see, my name is Charles . . . Chuck . . . Charlie . . .

Yeah, Charlie. And I'm a member of the Hells Angels. That's it!

The next day I went to a printer and ordered a couple hundred business cards, advertising my telephone number and my full name, Charles Zito, Jr. In the center of the card, in big letters, was the name of my business. I was now, officially, a bodyguard-for-hire. I was an entrepreneur, the sole proprietor of, you guessed it . . .

Charlie's Angels Bodyguard Service.

12

Used to be the Hayden Planetarium boasted the most dazzling display of stars in Manhattan, but now there's competition across the street. At Café Central, the newest discovery on the West Side's suddenly chic Columbus Avenue, a nightly caravan of limos, taxis and cars deposits such luminaries as Matt Dillon, Harrison Ford, Penny Marshall and the Divine Miss M. The café now is the place for preening performers, models, business biggies and overpaid athletes to meet and eat.
                                    —People Weekly, January 30, 1984

IT'S TRUE THAT CAFÉ CENTRAL WAS TO THE 1980S WHAT STUDIO 54 HAD been to the '70s (although with far less cocaine): a hip and happening place for the rich and famous to party late into the night. When I was first introduced to the café, however, it was in a different location, a few blocks away, and still happily wallowing in wannabe status. It was, in fact, a gloriously tough and cool saloon that attracted an impressive array of gifted young actors and writers who were merely on the cusp of stardom. Many of them were trained stage actors putting in long hours honing their craft the old-fashioned way: on Broadway, or off-Broadway, or off-off-Broadway, or, in some cases, "so far from Broadway you couldn't see it with a telescope."

What they had in common was a willingness to roll with the punches, to audition all afternoon, perform in some shitty one-act play that no one had ever heard of in the evening, and knock back a few drinks late at night, all in the company of a similarly driven gang of friends. They supported one another and teased and taunted one another mercilessly. The camaraderie was not unlike that which I'd experienced in various motorcycle clubs, and I found it instantly ap-

131

pealing. It helped that Café Central, in those early days anyway, was also the kind of place where you never knew when a quiet night would erupt into violence. As at any good bar, there was always the potential for two people to drop their glasses and raise their fists. And, afterward, the winner was expected to buy the loser a drink.

Café Central was the brainchild of a former Catskills resort busboy named Peter Herrero. A Brooklyn native who dropped out of high school at the age of seventeen, Peter had joined the U.S. Marines in 1964 and ended up serving in Vietnam. Like a lot of men I know, he returned from Vietnam surprised to find that the country wasn't exactly opening its arms to veterans; so he moved to Spain for a few years, worked odd jobs, eventually returned to New York in 1972, and plowed through a succession of jobs in the New York restaurant industry. A self-made man, he obtained a contractor's license and drained his own life savings to build Café Central in the only place he could afford to put it: a neighborhood often patrolled by prostitutes and addicts.

Most young businessmen who open a club or restaurant, especially in New York, have their dreams crushed with a few short, ugly months. Not Peter. Café Central quickly became a second home to Manhattan's working-class theater crowd—serious, determined actors and actresses who aspired to movie stardom. And many of them would reach that goal. Peter Weller was a regular (and future business partner with Peter Herrero), back in the days before he made *RoboCop* or *Shoot the Moon*. Treat Williams was there a lot, right before he broke out with his starring role in *Prince of the City*. Other frequent patrons included *Animal House* alumni Peter Riegert and Bruce McGill, future *Home Alone* dad John Heard, and *Moonstruck* star Danny Aiello. Also John Goodman and Robin Williams. Oh, and behind the bar? Shaking martinis (and eventually whipping up egg creams for yours truly)? A young actor from New Jersey named Bruce Willis. This was pre–*Die Hard*, pre-*Moonlighting* . . . hell, it was pre-paycheck for Bruce. But he was there, working the bar and trying to make contacts . . . trying to build a career, just like everyone else.

My first trip to Café Central came in 1980, on the night of the first epic fight between two of the greatest boxers of all time: Roberto Duran and Sugar Ray Leonard. I was invited by John Belushi and Dan Aykroyd to watch the fight on closed-circuit television at the

Academy of Music on 14th Street. (John and Danny, both avid motorcyclists with a taste for the wild life, were good friends of the Hells
Angels back then.) After the fight ended, Danny said they were going
to stop by a place on 74th and Amsterdam. He asked me if I'd like to
join them.

"It's called Café Central," he said. "It's about to be the hottest place
in town."

If Danny and John were going there, then Café Central was indeed
about to hit the big time, for in 1980 there were few people in the
entertainment world who were hotter and hipper than Belushi and
Aykroyd: the Blues Brothers.

Nevertheless, I wasn't all that interested.

"You know what, guys?" I said. "Thanks for the offer, but I really
don't like to hang out in bars all that much. I mean I don't smoke
and I don't drink."

"That's cool," John said. Then he raised an eyebrow, just like Bluto
in *Animal House,* and smiled slyly. "But you might like it anyway. A
lot of models hang out there."

"Yeah?"

They both nodded.

"Ahhhhh . . . what the fuck," I said. "Let's go."

(Incidentally, the next time I visited the Academy of Music was to
watch Danny and John perform as the Blues Brothers. Really, though,
I went because I had heard through the grapevine that John had hired
a new bodyguard, and I thought maybe if I showed up and intimidated the guy a little bit, I could take his job. Boy, was I wrong. When
John came out of his dressing room after the show, I approached him
and said, "Hey, John," with my chest all puffed out, prepared to demonstrate that there was no better bodyguard in the business than
Chuck Zito. Then I looked behind John and saw his bodyguard: a
man named Bill Wallace, who was nothing less than a living legend
in the world of martial arts. Bill's nickname was "Superfoot" because
he had devastating kicking ability, which he had used to win numerous world championships. This was a man I respected and admired,
and there I was, about to make a fool of myself by getting in his face.
Instead, I smiled at him, put out my hand, and said, "Hello, Mr. Wallace. I'm Chuck Zito."

That was the beginning of a friendship that endures to this day. I began working out with Bill, John, and Danny in 1980; in fact, they were in my corner at my first karate tournament. We were regular training partners until John's tragic death in 1982.)

Café Central was precisely as advertised: loud, lively, and filled with great-looking women and intense young actors. I liked the place right away, but not more than ten minutes after we arrived I was approached by Peter Herrero. He seemed uncomfortable, and he invited me to sit down.

"Look," he said. "I love Dan and I love John. They're great friends, and if you're with them, you must be all right. So you're welcome to stay here and have a good time, but I'd like you to remove your jacket."

"Why?"

He pointed to the Hells Angels insignia. "That makes people nervous."

"Let me tell you a little bit about myself," I said. And then I repeated my mantra: "I don't smoke, I don't drink, I don't do drugs, I don't cause trouble . . . and I don't remove my jacket for anybody. This is a public place and I'm not doing anything wrong. I was invited here by a couple of friends, and when they leave, I'll leave."

There was a pause. "You're intimidating my friends," Peter finally said. Well, that wasn't what I wanted. Peter seemed like a nice-enough guy, and I didn't want to make his life any harder than it already was. At the same time, I wasn't about to remove my jacket. A little diplomacy was in order, so I spent the next fifteen minutes talking with Peter, explaining to him how he was misinformed, and by the end of our conversation he'd come around.

"You know what?" Peter said. "Don't worry about it. You're welcome here anytime you want."

Everything was fine for a few weeks. I became a semiregular at Café Central, as did some of my buddies from the club. No one bothered us, and we caused no trouble at all. I got the sense that in a strange way our appearance was appreciated, because it had a calming effect on many of the patrons. Who wants to fuck with the Hells Angels? Our mere presence will keep most people on the straight and narrow (of course, it'll send others fleeing for the door, but that's a price you pay). One night I was hanging out with one of my brothers, Bert Kittel, when we were approached by Paul Herman, the host of

Café Central. I'd quickly come to recognize Pauly as more than just a good-natured man who liked his work. He was a smart and loyal friend.

"Got a little problem," Pauly said. "I need your help."

"Anything at all."

Pauly pointed to a man across the room—he looked more like a kid, really. His name, Pauly said, was James Hayden. James was a talented and respected young actor who was then costarring with Al Pacino in a stage production of David Mamet's *American Buffalo*. Pacino was the big draw, obviously, but James, who played a junkie, was getting rave reviews. His career, it seemed, was about to take flight.

Now, though, he was having a bad night. Pauly explained that James had been taking a walk near Hells Kitchen (not a great idea, but I didn't question his judgment—maybe he was new to New York) when he was jumped by a couple of black guys. They took his wallet and gave him a pretty fair beating just for the sheer hell of it.

"He didn't do anything to provoke them?" I asked.

Pauly shook his head. "Not a damn thing. They just ripped him off."

"And he's a friend of yours?"

"A good friend."

"Okay, let me talk to him."

Pauly brought James to our table and we talked for a little while. He seemed like a genuinely decent kid, the kind of kid you'd want to befriend, and looking at the welts on his face, the cut over his eye, I couldn't help but feel for him. It wasn't long before the three—me, Bert, and James—were in a van, driving slowly through Hells' Kitchen, armed with baseball bats.

"If you see these scumbags, I want you to point them out," I said. "You stay in the van, and we'll take care of it."

"How so?"

In the back, Bert picked up one of the bats, gave it a little check swing (not as easy as it sounds when you consider that Bert had only one hand; he'd lost the other hand when a bomb, planted by a rival club member, exploded in his mailbox). "Crack a few skulls," he said.

James nodded. I could tell he was nervous, probably scared, but I figured that was only natural. I mean when you hit somebody in the head with a baseball bat, you're as likely as not to kill him. This was a serious mission we were on, one with serious, far-reaching repercussions . . . and James was in the middle of it.

"You Okay?" I asked. He looked a little green, almost as if he was going to be sick. "James?"

"Huh?"

"You all right with this?"

He rubbed his eyes and let out a little groan. "Oh, man . . ."

Something was wrong. I'd been around people who were anxious about the prospect of violence—hell, most people are that way—but this was different. James was stressing out in a way that made me apprehensive. Usually when someone's been robbed and beaten, he wants retribution. At the very least, he wants his money back. James looked like he just wanted out of the van. Immediately.

"Talk to me, kid," I said.

James let out a long sigh. "Okay . . . there's something I didn't tell you."

"Spit it out."

"I wasn't just walking around down here, minding my own business."

I slowed down. "No?"

"Uh-uh. I was trying to score some smack."

I hit the brakes and pulled the van off to the side of the street. "Are you shittin' me?"

James shook his head. "Sorry."

I punched the steering wheel. In the back, Bert chuckled. I didn't see anything funny about it. I mean I didn't know this kid from a hole in the wall. I was helping because Pauly vouched for him and because he seemed like a good guy who, through no fault of his own, had been abused by a couple of punks. Yeah, he was in the wrong neighborhood, but I'd been led to believe he was guilty of nothing more than stupidity.

"Man, this really changes things," I said. "As far as I'm concerned, if you came down here to buy drugs, you got what you deserved."

"I know," he said sheepishly.

"No, you don't know!" I was so angry I wanted to smack him myself. "You drag me into this thing, get me involved in some illegal bullshit? When I don't even condone drug use?" I put the van back

136

in gear and started to drive off. "Whatever happened, man . . . it's on you."

We drove in silence back to Café Central, where Pauly was waiting. I lit into him before he had a chance to say a word.

"Are you crazy, Pauly?"

"What are you talking about?"

"This guy went down there to cop heroin."

Pauly looked at James. "That true?"

James nodded.

Pauly, normally a pretty robust, lively guy, suddenly deflated. He'd been duped, too. "I'm sorry, Chuck. I didn't know."

James apologized again, and for some reason I couldn't help but want to forgive him. He didn't seem like a dirtbag; he seemed like a kid with a problem, and although I'm not normally sympathetic to junkies, I felt an urge to take care of this kid. At least he'd been smart enough and honorable enough to come clean before it was too late. Had we found the guys who beat him, we would have hurt them. We might have been caught and sent to jail, and it would have been on James's head. And, eventually, when the truth came out, his punishment would have been much more severe than the tongue-lashing he received from me.

My suspicions about James being essentially a good guy proved to be true, and in fact we spent a fair amount of time together over the next few months. He was cool, funny, and a terrific actor, which I'd only heard from others but finally witnessed for myself when I went to see *American Buffalo*. Jimmy, as his friends called him (and I was happy to count myself in that group), held his own next to Pacino, which is no small accomplishment for any actor, especially one so young and raw. You could see in Jimmy all this energy just trying to get out, and you knew that if he channeled it in the right direction, he could do almost anything.

If . . .

About six months after the night I went to Hells Kitchen with a baseball bat, I got a tearful call from Pauly. Jimmy Hayden was gone, he said. He'd died of a drug overdose.

Jesus Christ. . . .

Talk about life imitating art. The guy plays a junkie every night onstage, and it turns out he's not just acting after all. Bert and I rode our motorcycles to the funeral, where I was introduced to Jimmy's entire family by Jay Accavone, an actor who was a good friend of Jimmy's. These were wonderful people whose hearts had been shattered. It was tragic. They said Jimmy had talked about me, that he'd had only good things to say. Then, to my surprise, they asked me and Bert if we would like to be pallbearers. We agreed, of course. On the way out of the church, I saw Jimmy's mother crying and I wondered exactly what Jimmy had told her, if he'd mentioned how we had met. I wondered if he had told her about Hells Kitchen.

Probably not, I thought, and it really didn't matter.

It wasn't until my fourth or fifth trip to Café Central that the shit finally hit the fan. I was seated at a back table, near the bathroom, having a friendly chat with Pauly. The place was mobbed, as usual—Café Central was just beginning to get a reputation as a gathering place for actors, models, and wealthy young businessmen, and with that designation came increased traffic, including hordes of star fuckers and others who simply wanted to get a glimpse of someone famous. I was used to the noise and the commotion and even the occasional bump from some poor slob who had a little too much to drink. By staying in the back I could usually avoid the bigger crowds, but this was a Friday night and the club was filled to capacity . . . and then some. There was barely room to breathe. In my experience, it's in this type of atmosphere that a bar brawl is most likely to erupt. Guys are horny, hot, and filled with the false bravado that comes with having too much to drink. They all think they know how to fight when they've had a few beers. The truth is, most of them couldn't defend themselves if they were sober; drunk, they're just targets waiting to be hit.

Pauly and I were keeping to ourselves, having a nice conversation, when all of a sudden someone reached across my chest and picked up my glass of soda. At first I figured it was some kind of joke, that whoever had done this was probably a friend of mine and he was trying to get a laugh. But when I looked up, I realized it wasn't a joke. The man who had taken my soda looked completely unfamiliar to me. Standing with another man, talking as though nothing had happened, he raised the glass—the glass containing my Coca-Cola—and put it to his lips.

Okay, I thought, this wasn't a joke. Maybe it was a mistake. I wanted to give the guy the benefit of the doubt, for the only other explanation—that he was engaging in the type of moronic macho behavior that would inevitably leave him unconscious on the floor—was hard to fathom.

I pushed my chair back a few inches but remained seated. "Yo, buddy . . . what the fuck you doin'?"

He smiled in a drunken, punkish way, glanced at his friend, and responded with, "I was thirsty."

They both started laughing, and of course they were laughing at my expense, which did not make me happy. Pauly reached across the table, gave me a little pat on the arm, as if to say, *"Stay cool, brother."* Not wanting to offend Pauly or Peter, I gave the guy a chance to escape with his dignity, and his face, intact.

"You're thirsty, huh? Well then, why don't you take a walk over to the bar and get yourself a drink, pal?"

The guy didn't move. He just stood there, rocking on his heels, smiling like an idiot. A few moments passed before a third person appeared at the table. He threw an arm around the asshole's shoulder. "There a problem here?"

"Yeah," I said. "The problem is your friend is a jerk-off . . . and he was just leaving."

"I am?" said the asshole, taking another sip from my soda. "I don't think so."

Well, now I'd been pushed about as far as I was willing to be pushed. I stood up and put my nose in the guy's face. "Let's go, scumbag. Out the door."

"You first."

I looked at their group—a trio of men in their late twenties, early thirties, all over six feet tall, neatly groomed, well dressed, soft in the middle. I could tell right away that not one of them had been in a serious street fight in years . . . if ever.

Big mistake, boys . . . big mistake.

As I walked away from the table, I looked back over my shoulder at Pauly. He shrugged his shoulders and raised his glass, as if offering a toast. Then he got up out of his chair and followed us.

Well, at least he understands.

One thing led to another, as it usually does in these situations, and pretty soon the five of us were standing behind the club, right across the street from the Beacon Theater. Pauly was merely a spectator, and an enthusiastic one at that. He made no attempt to intervene. At this point he was willing to let nature take its course. Certainly he wasn't worried about me, despite the fact that I was outnumbered.

"Why do you want to fuck with us?" said the man who had lifted my drink. "There's three of us and one of you."

The others were right next to him, ready to jump in at the first sign of trouble. Their eyes were wide but glassy; it was a look I'd seen countless times before, in countless saloons. The look of a drunk who is in way over his head.

"Don't let that stop you, pal."

He didn't. For some reason, this guy wanted to fight with a Hells Angel. I've seen it dozens of times over the years—some loudmouth, or a group of loudmouths, challenges a representative of the most notorious motorcycle club in the land, usually because he's too drunk or stupid (or both) to know what he's getting into or because he wants to prove something to his girlfriend or his buddies. When you wear the death head, it's like being a top gunslinger in the Old West: most people are scared shitless of you, but some, the foolish, will seek you out and use you as a barometer of their own courage and manhood.

The asshole took a big, awkward step forward and threw a wild roundhouse hook in the general vicinity of my head. I didn't even have to slip the punch—it was off by a good two feet. I shifted my stance, lowered a shoulder, and came in with a tight, hard right hand. His weight did most of the work, carrying him straight into my fist. He was out before he hit the ground.

Incredibly, his friends were not dissuaded by what they'd seen. They charged in right behind him, yelling and cursing like soldiers going into battle. They flailed wildly, almost comically, and within a few seconds I'd knocked them both out. One punch for each.

So there I was, wearing my Hells Angels vest, standing over three prone drunks in the middle of the street, with Pauly on the curb, applauding politely, when the headlights of a car began bearing down on us. It came to a sharp stop just a few feet away, and as four doors swung open at once I was filled with a sense of dread.

"What the hell happened here?"

It was Peter Herrero, accompanied by Treat Williams and Peter

Weller, both of whom wore the silliest shit-eating grins. These were movie tough guys getting a glimpse of the real deal, and they seemed to find it hugely entertaining.

I held up my hands. "Peter, I did not start this."

I could only imagine what he was thinking. This was surely the type of problem he'd envisioned on the night that we'd met, when he had asked me to remove my patch. I had given Peter my word that I would cause him no trouble, that neither I nor my brothers would ever be a source of embarrassment to him. But here I was, tossing patrons of his café out into the street and kicking the living shit out of them. Don't misunderstand me. I'm not suggesting for a moment that what I did was wrong or unwarranted or even unavoidable. I'm just saying that it probably wasn't the kind of thing Peter wanted to see as he drove up to his club.

Thankfully, I had a witness, one whose opinion carried a lot of weight with Peter.

"Chuck's right," Pauly said. He gestured toward the street, where the three stooges were slowly returning to the land of consciousness. "They wanted a piece of him."

Peter Weller and Treat Williams laughed. Peter Herrero just nodded. "Well," he said. "I guess they got it."

As we walked back into the club, Peter Herrero shook my hand. "Chuck," he said. "How would you like a job?"

13

LIFE TAKES THE STRANGEST TWISTS AND TURNS. IF MY AFFILIATION WITH
the Hells Angels has gotten me into trouble from time to time, it's
also been responsible for countless opportunities. If not for my membership in the club, it's unlikely I would have been hired as a bouncer
at Café Central, no small irony considering Peter Herrero's initial response on the night we met. Now, though, my reputation as a fighter,
and a fighter with influential, potentially dangerous friends, was seen
not as a liability but as an advantage.

Not that I advertised my ties to the club. A stipulation of my hiring
at Café Central was that I agree to wear a suit and tie. I didn't have
a problem with that. Once I was an employee, the rules changed. The
club prohibits members from wearing their Hells Angels patches
when working. It's logical, really: a bouncer who wears a Hells Angels
jacket while on duty is either inviting confrontation or promoting the
club, neither of which is acceptable. And, to be perfectly candid, I
didn't really need the jacket. Word gets around, after all, and most of
the regulars at Café Central knew of my membership in the Hells
Angels. My job was to be visible, but in a subtle, nonthreatening way.
Intimidation was not the goal; security was the goal. Customers were
supposed to understand that if they caused any problems at Café
Central, there would be hell to pay (so to speak).

Although I did not promote the Hells Angels while working at Café
Central, I did occasionally take advantage of the opportunity to promote my own private endeavors. When I'd meet one of the many
celebrities who called Café Central home, I'd make it a point to slip
him or her a business card. Charlie's Angels Bodyguard Service was
slow to develop, but eventually it worked.

My good fortune began one night at Café Central when Paul Herman introduced me to Liza Minnelli. Liza, of course, was one of the biggest stars in the world at the time. A few years earlier she'd won an Academy Award for *Cabaret*, and more recently she'd starred alongside Dudley Moore in *Arthur*, in a huge box-office hit. Liza was a sensational singer, actress, and all-around performer at the peak of her career. It was a pleasure to meet her, and I told her as much. As often happens, though, she seemed more interested in meeting me. I could tell after just a few minutes that she had something serious on her mind.

"I have a job for you," she said. "If you're interested."

It turned out that Liza was recruiting me on behalf of her sister, Lorna Luft, who was also a talented (although less famous) actress. Lorna was performing in a play in New York at the time, and apparently she had been receiving threatening phone calls and letters from a deranged fan (or critic). In all likelihood, nothing would come of the threats, but Liza was taking no chances. She wanted to hire me as her sister's personal bodyguard for the duration of her performance in the show.

"Sounds good," I said. "Why don't I meet her, we'll talk, and if it seems like we'd get along, I'd be happy to do the job." (I was new at the job, but already I understood the importance of having a good relationship with a client; a bodyguard spends a lot of time in close proximity with the person he's paid to protect—it helps if they can at least have a cordial conversation.)

So I went to Lorna's play, and afterward I went backstage and we chatted for a while. Like Liza, she seemed to be a genuinely decent woman with a terrific attitude toward her work. I saw no reason to believe we'd have any problem getting along. And we didn't. I worked with Lorna for a couple months, without incident. Not more than a few days after Lorna finished the show, I got another call from Liza. She thanked me for keeping an eye on her sister and for behaving in a thoroughly professional manner.

"No problem," I said. "I'm available anytime."

"Well," Liza continued, "I'm glad you said that . . ."

"Oh?" I had a hunch about what was coming next, but I tried to play it cool.

"Yes," she continued. "I'm rehearsing a play called *The Rink*, at the

Martin Beck Theater, and when the show opens, in a couple weeks, I'm going to need a bodyguard."

There was a pause. Again, I played it very cool.

"And?"

"And . . . Lorna speaks very highly of you. So I'd like you to work for me, too—if you're available."

"Hold on," I said. "Let me check my calendar." (In any business, you want potential clients to think you're a hot commodity, right? Always in demand?) I stalled for a few seconds, then cleared my throat. "Should be okay."

"Great," Liza said. "I really appreciate it."

This assignment proved to be the break I'd been waiting for. I knew Liza was an A-list celebrity, a superstar in the truest sense of the word, but until I began working for her I didn't realize just what that meant. Not only did she sell out the Martin Beck, but she also attracted a seriously high-profile audience. The list of big-name actors and actresses and other celebrities who stopped backstage each night was endless: John Travolta, Robert De Niro, Andy Warhol, Al Pacino, Liberace, Elizabeth Taylor, Michael Jackson. Sylvester Stallone. These people, and many others, saw me with Liza, walking side by side with her, chatting with her, and they figured I knew what I was doing. From this single assignment word spread faster than I'd ever imagined possible.

It helped, obviously, that Liza gave me great recommendations. I found her to be a genuinely likable and decent woman with a great sense of humor, which made my job easier and more enjoyable. For instance: When Liza pulled up in front of the Martin Beck each day she was accustomed to seeing me waiting outside. One day, though, Chuck Zito wasn't there. Instead, Liza was greeted by a scraggly-looking bum who approached the car and began aggressively begging for money. The driver tried to chase the bum away, but the bum was persistent—and more than a little disgusting. When no money was forthcoming, he turned to the time-honored New York tradition of washing windows in exchange for a few bucks. Lacking any of the proper equipment—a squeegee or squirt bottle—the bum simply spit on the windshield and wiped the glass clean with his shirtsleeve.

"Get out of here!" the driver yelled.

In the backseat, Liza squirmed and wondered, *Where is Chuck?*

Finally, two doormen ran to the limo and grabbed the bum.

"Gimme some money!" the bum yelled, flailing his arms like a madman, tossing the doormen aside with ease. "I need money!"

"Wait a minute," one of the doorman said, no doubt wondering how a panhandler developed such tremendous upper-body strength. "This ain't no ordinary bum."

"You're right!" the bum yelled. "It ain't!" And with that I removed my mask and beard—the most vital parts of a disguise that had required me to sit still in a makeup chair for more than an hour. "It's me—Chuck!"

Liza jumped out of the car, laughing uncontrollably. "Are you nuts?!" she screamed.

"Nope . . . just having a little fun."

I liked Liza a lot, and I know she liked me, too. She even invited me to a party celebrating her fourth wedding anniversary.

"I'm just having a few friends over," she said. "I'd really like you to be there."

A few friends . . . I didn't realize what that meant until I arrived at Liza's apartment on the Upper East Side. I pulled up on my motorcycle, and it was obvious right away that the doorman wasn't accustomed to guests like me. I was dressed in an outfit that looked like something out of Elvis Presley's closet: white leather pants, white leather boots, a jacket with long, flowing red, white, and blue fringe (and a matching red, white, and blue headband); the whole outfit was studded with rhinestones. And, of course, I was wearing my signature Hells Angels vest.

"I'm here to see Liza," I told the doorman, who looked at me like I'd come from another planet.

"Who are you?" he asked.

"Just tell her Chuck Zito is here."

He picked up the phone, talked for less than ten seconds, then invited me in.

"Twelfth floor," he said.

"What apartment?"

"Twelfth floor," he repeated.

"Yeah, but what's the apartment number?"

He smiled. "The apartment is the whole floor, sir."

"You've gotta be shittin' me."

"No, sir."

Liza's place was the biggest apartment I'd ever seen, with an incredible view of the city and a living room bigger than my entire house. There were more than a hundred people there, including some of the biggest stars in show business: Liberace, Steve Rubell, Halston, Andy Warhol, and Truman Capote in one corner; Gregory Peck, Lucille Ball, James Mason, and Diana Ross in another corner; Robert De Niro, Al Pacino, Joe Pesci, Christopher Walken, and Danny Aiello in another. And me, the kid from New Rochelle . . . the Hells Angel dressed like Elvis . . . in the middle of them all.

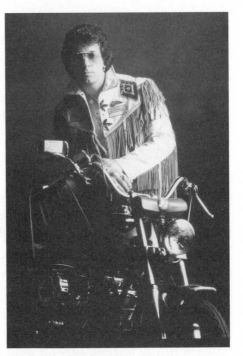

That's me impersonating Elvis.
Credit: Ken Nahoum

I didn't feel uncomfortable, though, especially since Liza came right over and welcomed me with open arms. Liza had a bit of an adventurous streak, and she loved the fact that I was a Hell's Angel. I once gave her a framed, matted poster of the 1983 movie *Hell's Angels Forever*, and she immediately hung it on the wall of her dressing room, which I thought was kind of touching. Sometimes I'd wear my jacket to the theater and at the end of the night, after signing autographs for hundreds of fans, she'd put on her helmet, hop on the back of my bike, and we'd take off together. For Liza, it was like a walk on the wild side—but a safe walk. Kind of like riding Space Mountain at Disney World.

Same with Cher. One night at Café Central she asked me for a ride, so we ducked out and hopped on my bike and cruised through the city with no helmets. The next day, of course, there were pictures in the *Post* and *News*, and pretty soon it became common for celebrities to be photographed with Chuck Zito . . . "Bodyguard to the Stars."

My life changed pretty quickly. One day I was just a guy from New Rochelle who happened to be a member of the Hells Angels—a guy struggling like everyone else to make his mortgage payments (Kathy and I had finally bought our first house together) and take care of his family—and the next day I was hanging out with some of the biggest stars in the entertainment business, making more money than I'd ever thought possible. How much? Well, when I was first starting out I'd charge $500 a day, because that's what I made as a stuntman. Pretty soon, though, that fee rose to $1,000 a day, or more—not bad for the early 1980s. Plus expenses, of course. I traveled all over the world, stayed in first-class hotels, ate in the best restaurants, and generally lived the pampered life of a movie star.

Unfortunately, I didn't save as much money as I should have. I'd grown up without much in the way of material possessions, so when I finally began making real money I was like a kid in a candy store. I pissed away a fair amount of money on vintage cars and, especially, jewelry. Sometimes, while bodyguarding, I'd wear a Hells Angels ring on each of my fingers: big, fat gold bands encrusted with diamonds and other gems. Gold death heads, gold skulls and wings. If someone shook my hand, he understood immediately that I was not just some low-rent leg breaker. I was being paid top dollar to protect valuable property, and I wanted that message to come across loud and clear.

It did, too. Dom DeLuise visited Liza's dressing room one evening, and when I met him at the door he took one look at my hand, dramatically fell to his knees, and began kissing my rings.

"I just had to do that," he said.

Dom was just joking, acting like the flamboyant clown he could be, and we all had a good laugh. But it still made me feel good. Maybe it was shallow on my part, but I didn't really care. After so many years of struggle, I felt as though I'd earned the right to spoil myself a bit.

When it came to rings, though, I was in the minor leagues compared to Liberace. We had a little contest one night, each of us showing off our respective rings, from the smallest to the largest. Finally, Liberace unveiled the biggest of his rings, in the shape of a piano. It was bigger than any other ring I'd ever seen. But that wasn't the only thing. He slowly lifted the top of the piano to reveal four one-carat diamonds rolling around inside. What could I do but smile?

"You got me," I said, admitting defeat.

It was while working for Liza that I learned the finer points of body-guarding, which was not so much about beating people up but rather about defusing potentially dangerous situations. The truth is this: a bodyguard should fight only as a last resort. His job is to protect his client, and that means avoiding trouble or shutting it down before it even begins. When you start throwing punches, you run the risk of losing control, and that's the last thing you want.

Knowing when to react and how forcefully to react—it's a more complicated job than you might think. Your antennae have to be up at all times. It's almost like being a Secret Service agent, whose responsibility, after all, is not limited to simply taking a bullet or firing a bullet but includes preventing violence in the first place and preparing for the consequences in the event that something terrible should happen. If I was traveling with a celebrity client, I'd scope out the hotel, the performance venue, the route between the two. I'd talk with local law enforcement agencies and get directions to the nearest hospital. I'd determine the quickest way into the concert hall or theater and the quickest way out, because that's when problems are most likely to arise, when fans are hanging out, waiting for a glimpse of their favorite stars, hoping for a meaningful exchange of words, a handshake, an autograph, whatever.

Liza was the type of performer who thrived on connecting with her fans in a personal way. She liked signing autographs, smiling, posing for pictures. But this made me, as a bodyguard, very nervous, because it was such an uncontrolled, unpredictable environment. A lot of times I'd collect fifty or sixty programs from the show and have Liza sign them. While she was getting changed, I'd go outside and distribute the programs, just to cut down on the crowd when we left. I never felt as though my concern was unjustified, but it was a while before I was experienced enough to be able to tell the difference between someone who presented a legitimate threat and someone who was merely an annoyance.

One night, for example, as we walked out the back door of the Martin Beck and into a crushing sea of humanity, I noticed a guy leaning off a fire escape, maybe four or five steps up from the ground. That was odd enough but even stranger, and of greater concern, was the fact that he was wearing a long oversize raincoat. As we got closer,

I saw him reach into his coat with one hand, and the first thought that leaped to mind was . . .

This is it—he's going for a gun!

Without hesitation I pushed Liza back toward the door and ran for the fire escape. Within seconds I had one hand around the guy's throat, squeezing his Adam's apple between my thumb and middle finger; with the other hand I reached inside his jacket and prepared to disarm him. I grabbed something hard, metallic, and yanked it out of his hand and into the open air.

"A camera? A fucking camera?! Are you out of your mind?"

Unable to breathe, his face rapidly turning purple, the man in the raincoat, obviously just a member of the paparazzi, gasped and writhed in my grip.

"Why aren't you down there, on the ground, like everybody else?" I asked, loosening my hold so that he could respond.

"I just wanted a good shot when she came out the door," the photographer said. "I'm not doing anything wrong."

As the air returned to his lungs and brain, he got feisty, started telling me I had no business accosting him when he was just taking photographs.

"Your job doesn't include hanging from a fire escape like a sniper," I explained.

"I don't even own a gun," he said. "Admit it—you fucked up. And I'm gonna sue your ass."

I had two options: punch his lights out, leave, and hope the whole thing blew over or . . . try to reason with him. I chose the latter option.

"Look," I said. "I didn't mean to hurt you, but let's be honest—you shouldn't be up here. And you know it. This fire escape belongs to the theater. It's private property. Now . . . what do we have to do to make all of this go away?"

The payoff was relatively painless: a photo of Liza and two free front-row seats for the next night's performance. Everyone has a price, and this guy, thankfully, came cheap. It was a valuable lesson. My hunch had been wrong, but my response was not unreasonable. It's always better to be safe than sorry.

*　　*　　*

Through Liza I made a lot of connections not just in the movie world but also in the music business. It was Liza who introduced me to the guys in the band Kiss (Liza was a big Kiss fan, believe it or not), and that led to my working as a personal bodyguard for Paul Stanley, the band's bass player. (Interesting stereotype-shattering footnote: I bought my first piece of upscale exercise equipment—a universal weight machine—from Paul, who worked out every day and actually was in terrific shape. There's more to the world of rock 'n' roll than sex and drugs.) I became friends with Bruce Springsteen, Billy Joel, the guys in the Grateful Dead, of course, who were longtime pals of the Hells Angels. If I wasn't working, I could get tickets for any show I wanted, although I never took them as freebies. If someone refused to accept payment, I'd present him with a gift in return. Ron Delsener, the legendary New York concert promoter, was an avid wine collector, so whenever he gave me tickets to a show I'd reciprocate with a bottle of vintage wine.

"Remember Altamont!" I'd say as I handed him a bottle of 1969 Château La'Fete, And Ron, who had a good sense of humor, would laugh and say, "Thanks."

(Explanation of inside joke: Altamont was the site of a famous concert in 1969, during which a fight broke out between an unruly spectator and several members of the Hells Angels. As the Rolling Stones sang "Sympathy for the Devil," the spectator was killed. The entire incident was captured on film in a documentary called *Gimme Shelter*)

Indirectly, my relationship with Liza also led to a job working for Sylvester Stallone. It began with a Monday night trip to a SoHo dance club called the Heartbreak. Liza liked this place, and once a week or so I'd accompany her there. On this particular night, not more than a few minutes after I walked through the door I was approached by a big, heavyset man who introduced himself as Tony Munafo.

"You know who you look like?" he said.

"No, who?"

"Sylvester Stallone."

I nodded. "Yeah, I get that a lot." Which was true. I was a little younger than Sly, but we had similar builds, similar coloring, and similar features. The resemblance was even stronger now that I'd gotten thicker, more muscular. Still, I didn't see what this guy was trying to get at.

"No, seriously, you guys could be brothers," he said. Then he paused, looked me up and down. "You know, I'm Sly's bodyguard, and he's coming into town in a couple weeks to start shooting a new movie. There might be some work for you."

I looked at Tony's belly and figured he hadn't seen the inside of a gym since high school. If this guy was Sylvester Stallone's bodyguard, then I was James fuckin' Bond. I thanked him for the compliment and walked away.

A few minutes later I ran into Paul Herman, who also liked to visit the Heartbreak once in a while. I told Pauly I'd just met a fat guy who was trying to pass himself off as Sylvester Stallone's bodyguard. I pointed the guy out, laughed, and poked Pauly in the ribs.

"You imagine that guy guarding anything except the buffet line?" I joked.

Pauly squinted. "Uhhh . . . Chuck?"

"Yeah?"

"He *is* Sylvester Stallone's bodyguard."

"You're shittin' me?"

"Afraid not."

I looked again across the room at Tony Munafo and cursed under my breath. I hadn't been disrespectful to him, hadn't said anything nasty or sarcastic. I just hadn't believed him. Still, I considered this to be a fairly significant mistake, for Sly Stallone was something of a hero to me, even though we'd never met. I thought he was a genius, a rare talent who could act and write and direct. Equally important, to me, was the fact that he had a big set of balls. This was a guy who wrote a brilliant screenplay, for *Rocky*, and refused to sell out, refused to take a few hundred grand to walk away and let someone else star in the movie, even though that would have been the easy and sensible thing to do. Instead, Sly stuck to his guns, made a great movie—a movie that redefined the underdog genre—and went on to became one of the most powerful men in Hollywood. How can you not admire that? It's every struggling young artist's dream. It's the American dream.

If Tony Munafo was a link to Sly, then I was a fool to walk away from him. There was only one thing to do: buy the man a drink and give him my card.

Tony turned out to be a pretty good guy, and by the end of the night we were getting along just fine. Before leaving, I said, "Tony, even if I don't get a chance to work for you, I'd like to meet Sly when he comes into town. He was a big inspiration to me."

"Absolutely," Tony said.

"You sure?"

He took a big drink. "Hey, when I say something, I mean it. No bullshit."

Several weeks went by without a word from Tony. In the meantime, Sylvester Stallone and his crew had already arrived in New York to begin filming *Staying Alive*, the sequel to *Saturday Night Fever*, the movie that had catapulted John Travolta to superstardom. This was a huge production featuring two of the biggest names in show business, so it was difficult, if not downright impossible, for work to proceed quietly. There were daily reports in the New York tabloids, sound bites on the evening news, videotape of hordes of screaming girls hoping for a chance to see the star (Travolta) or the director (Stallone) in person. Even if I wanted to, I couldn't escape the fact that I'd been blown off by Tony Munafo. Adding further insult was the fact that a large portion of the movie was being filmed at CBGB's, the landmark New York nightclub. CBGB's was located in the Bowery. The Hells Angels' clubhouse was right around the corner, on 3d Street, between First and Second Avenues. In other words . . . they were shooting in our backyard.

I steamed about this for a few days before finally saying to one of my brothers, "You know what? Fuck it! They're in my town, my 'hood. I'm going over there."

I wasn't worried about creating a scene. For one thing, it wasn't like I intended to provoke a fight with anyone; I simply wanted an explanation from Tony *"When I say something I mean it"* Munafo. Second, I anticipated no difficulty getting past whatever security there was on the set, for the owner of CBGB's, a man named Hilly Crystal, was a friend of mine and a friend of the Hells Angels. A normal night for many of the guys in our club involved several hours at a bar called Great Guildersleeves, followed by a stop at CBGB's on the way back to our clubhouse. CBGB's was one of our hangouts; there was no way anyone was going to tell me I wasn't welcome there.

So I pulled in front and parked my bike. I was decked out in full Hells Angels regalia—leather from neck to toe; a bright red bandana, tied at the side, with a tail hanging down, held my long black hair in place. No sooner had I gotten off my bike than Tony Munafo came walking out, a big smile on his face, his arms spread wide to greet me.

"Chuck, good to see you!"

I frowned. "Tony, Tony, Tony . . . You told me you were going to call when you got in town. What gives?"

He put his hands together. "I know. I'm sorry, but I've been real busy, what with the movie and all."

"No excuse, Tony. Our clubhouse is right around the corner. Don't tell me you couldn't take five minutes to stop in and say hello."

I wasn't about to cut him any slack. In my book, a man is only as good as his word; when you break a promise, you'd better have a damn good reason for doing it. Tony had nothing, which was why he was tap-dancing now.

"I meant to, Chuck, really. But—"

"Forget it, Tony. I'm here. What are we going to do now?"

Tony nodded. "Okay, I want you to meet Sly. But he's doing a scene right now, so you'll have to wait a few minutes."

"I've got all day."

We walked into the club and watched Sly work for the better part of a half hour. He seemed as intense and focused as I had anticipated. Eventually he yelled, "Cut!" and told everyone to relax for a little while. Then Tony led me over to his chair and introduced us.

"Sly," he said, "I want you to meet someone. This is Chuck Zito."

Sly turned, did a double take, and laughed out loud. "Whoa, man, it's like I'm looking in a mirror."

We shook hands and talked for a little while, and it was apparent from the get-go that we'd be good friends. We were both Italian guys who had grown up without a whole lot and who believed in fighting for what we felt was right. We both loved the sport of boxing, loved it like it was the only sport that really mattered. The chemistry was so good, in fact, that I started working for Sly the very next day. Actually, I reported to Tony, who was in charge of Sly's security team.

For the next several weeks, while the crew finished filming in New York, I was Sly's primary bodyguard. And it was a trip, I have to say. I'd gotten accustomed to hanging out with celebrities, but people reacted to Sly in a way that I'd not seen before—he had a real gut-level appeal. That's what happens when you create one of the most indelible characters in the history of American pop culture. To his fans, Sylvester Stallone *was* Rocky.

I remember one day walking through Times Square, with Sly sandwiched between me and Tony. We didn't have a crew. It was just the three of us out scouting locations, trying to be as inconspicuous as possible. Well, fat chance. There was no disguising Sly at that point in his career. Wherever he went, he was mobbed by fans, and occasionally challenged by morons who wanted a piece of the Italian Stallion, all of which he handled with remarkable style. The attention did, however, get a little overwhelming at times, this day being a good example. The crowd following us swelled with each passing block, until we were surrounded by scores of people, including women literally throwing themselves at Sly and supposed tough guys who kept lunging forward, getting in our faces, throwing jabs at the air, and shouting, "You ain't so tough!" or, "I'll kick your ass, Rocky!"

It quickly became the type of chaotic situation that can overwhelm a single bodyguard, or even a pair of bodyguards. Especially if one of the bodyguards or the person being guarded loses his cool and begins responding to the catcalls and insults. Sly was unflappable. He just kept walking and waving and smiling. But Tony and I knew something bad could happen at any moment, so we whisked Sly into a Dunkin' Donuts shop on 42d Street and stayed there until reinforcements arrived—in this case, roughly a half-dozen New York City cops on horseback. Once they cleared the street and set up barricades, we were able to return to the set. I realized then what it meant to be a superstar, to have no chance at anonymity . . . to be so famous that it was dangerous to leave your hotel without a police escort. I realized that success—at least success on a grand scale—came with a price.

Not that Sly seemed to mind. Day in and day out, regardless of the situation, he rolled with the punches . . . so to speak. By the time location filming on *Staying Alive* had been completed, I had come to think of Sly as a good friend and even a mentor. I knew that working for him would do wonders for my résumé, and I wanted to show my appreciation. So, on the day Sly left, I met him at the Regency Hotel on Park Avenue and I presented him with a gift: a beautiful piece of ivory hand-carved in the shape of a tiger. You know . . . like "Eye of the Tiger," the Survivor song that was used in *Rocky III*. Sly took one look at it, said, "You shouldn't have," and then told me that if I was ever in California, please give him a call. When he returned home, Sly had another gift waiting: a big trophy incorporating a pen and pencil set and a statue of a boxer—all set on a block of marble. The trophy was inscribed with these words:

TO SYLVESTER "ROCKY" STALLONE
LOVE AND RESPECT
CHUCK ZITO, HELLS ANGELS, NEW YORK CITY

I did in fact make it to California not long after that, and I did call Sly as he requested. True to his word, he invited me to his office, where we had lunch and another nice talk. While I was there, Sly thanked me again for the gifts and for my work in New York.

"Now I've got something for you," he added, and then he handed me a little box, the kind you'd get from a jewelry store.

Inside the box was a solid gold boxing glove, just like the one he wore in *Rocky III*. (Historic footnote: that glove was a duplicate of a gold cuff link that belonged to the great Rocky Marciano. Sly actually borrowed The cuff link from Marciano's mother so that he could have it copied for his character to wear on-screen.) The gold glove was a favorite gift of Sly's, one he said that he presented to the "special" people in his life. And now I was part of that inner circle. I've worn that glove ever since. It reminds me of how important it is to remember the good people, the ones who deserve trust and respect.

Oh . . . one other thing: I like to think that when Sly showed up in *Rambo*, wearing long hair and a red bandana, with a tail hanging off to the side, looking a whole lot like I looked the first day we met at CBGB's . . . that was a tribute to a friend.

Connecting with Sly led to more high-profile security assignments, more movie work, frequently alongside stars who have come to be regarded as . . . "difficult." Mickey Rourke, for example. Everyone thinks of Mickey as a tough guy, a badass, all that, and I guess I'm partially to blame, since I gave him his first Harley-Davidson. After I gave him that bike, it seemed like Mickey developed an identity crisis: he didn't know whether he wanted to be a biker, an actor, a wise guy, or what. Mickey's not really such a bad guy. He just has to remember where reel life ends and real life begins. As Sean Penn (with whom I've also worked) likes to say, "Mickey's problem is that he always wanted to be Chuck Zito." I was the biker, the boxer, the Hell's Angel. Mickey was a rich and famous actor, but I always got the impression he would have traded places with me in a second. Funny thing is, he never got in trouble when he was hanging with me. I kept him out of trouble. It's when he's surrounded by leeches, by his supposed friends, that Mickey has problems.

We met for the first time at Jimmy Hayden's funeral. Mickey was also a pallbearer. He was infatuated with motorcycles and outlaws and people who lived unconventional lives. I certainly fell into that category, and Mickey knew it. A lot of people are fascinated by the Hells Angels, but Mickey's interest ran deeper than most. When he was a struggling young actor in his late teens, early twenties, trying to break into movies, Mickey had a day job working as—I shit you not—a Good Humor man. He'd put on his little white outfit and cap and fill up his cart every morning at the Good Humor warehouse on lower 3d Street, right next door to the Hells Angels clubhouse. Then he'd push the cart all the way up to Central Park, to his station outside the Mayflower Hotel. Mickey would stand there all day, wilting in the summer heat, a grown man trying to sell ice-cream bars to the upper-class clientele of the Mayflower . . . and he'd dream about how things would soon be different.

When Mickey hit the big time and started making money, one of the first things he did was rent the penthouse apartment at the Mayflower—that was his way of saying, "Fuck you!" to everyone who had looked down on him while he was hawking ice cream. Mickey practically owned that place for a while. It became a hangout for his entourage—which sometimes included me—a place where all his friends could live and eat and party in style. Another thing Mickey did was indulge his fantasies, one of which was . . . playing the role of a badass, even when he was off-screen. Mickey spent a lot of time outside our clubhouse when he was a Good Humor man, and though

157

he never said a word to anyone in the club (a wise decision, given the likelihood of anyone in a Good Humor outfit getting ridiculed by a bunch of bikers), I know he often wondered what it was like inside.

When I first met Mickey, he was a seriously hot young actor. In the previous two years he'd strung together a succession of memorable performances, most notably, and first, practically stealing *Body Heat* with a brief flamboyant role as a scruffy low-rent arsonist who, in one of the movie's best scenes, tells William Hurt's gullible, pathetic lawyer, "You don't look like no genius to me, counselor." Mickey spent maybe five minutes on-screen, but it was an unforgettable five minutes, concluding with him cranking up the stereo and drowning out William Hurt with the sound of Bob Seger howling "Feel Like a Number!" Combine that performance, right out of the gate, with impressive roles in *Diner* and *The Pope of Greenwich Village* and you're looking at a guy who had every reason to believe the critics who told him he was going to be the next James Dean. And, in a sense, I guess that's what Mickey became: an actor who did his best work when he was still in his twenties and whose career never lived up to the promise of his debut.

Of course, there are differences, like the fact that despite his taste for wild times and fist-fights, Mickey has managed to stay alive. (He even quit acting for a while to become a professional boxer, and not a bad one at that. I mean, for an actor, he was good. It takes a lot of guts just to get into the ring. If you think it's easy, try moving around for three minutes and see how tired you get. And that's without someone throwing punches at you. For that, Mickey will always have my respect.) Of course, it's too bad he no longer shows up on the radar screen of most movie fans. Go back and watch *Body Heat*. Or, even better, *Barfly* ("Here's to all my friends!"), in which Mickey holds his own against the beautiful Faye Dunaway while getting his ass repeatedly kicked by Sly's little brother, Frank Stallone. It's a great performance in a great movie. Another fantastic performance is in *Angel Heart*, in which Mickey more than holds his own against the great Robert De Niro. Too bad not enough people saw either movie. But then, that's the story of Mickey's career: a string of bad movies and bad choices interrupted occasionally by good movies and good choices that unfortunately bombed at the box office. So, instead of commanding $20 million a movie and being on the same level as De

Niro or Pacino (which is where he should be), Mickey has become something of a caricature, a guy known more for his bad movies and bad behavior than he is for the legitimately good work he's done over the years.

Mickey has a reputation for being difficult to work with, but I never found that to be the case. He was always cool with me, probably because he respected me. That was always the most important thing to me as a bodyguard—that I had the respect of my client. When a celebrity respects you, it's much easier to keep him out of trouble. I think that's part of the appeal of hiring a Hells Angel: you know he can protect you; you also know he can hurt you. So, maybe, you're more likely to be on your best behavior. It's a theory, anyway.

The first time Mickey and I worked together was while he was shooting *Year of the Dragon* back in the early 1980s. We were together every day for the better part of four months while the crew worked on location in North Carolina and Vancouver, British Columbia. Mickey was great to me—not only was I his bodyguard, but he also hired me to be his personal assistant and trainer (as filming went on, I picked up some work in front of the camera, too, including bit parts as a cabdriver and a cop). We lifted weights together; we boxed; we ran. One morning, while running through Vancouver, we passed a gym, and all these people stopped their workouts and came running out into the street. They followed us for at least half a mile, and at first I thought it was because they all recognized Mickey. But then they started asking me for autographs and handshakes and patting me on the back. "Way to go, Rocky!" they shouted. Or, "Hey, Sly!"

As I've said, there was a similarity. And the fact that I used to wear a *ghee*—a type of robe favored by martial artists—surely added to the illusion. Mickey got a big kick out of it—until some guy came running up to me and said, with a nod toward Mickey, "Who's this, Rock, your bodyguard?"

"That's it!" Mickey shouted. "No more running with you!"

Another time, while we were in North Carolina, Mickey heard that Bruce Springsteen was playing a concert somewhere in Virginia, like six hours away. Mickey loved Springsteen, listened to his tapes all the time, especially while working out.

"We gotta go see him," Mickey said.

"Hey, Mick, you gotta be on the set at seven in the morning."

"I don't care. We're going."

So we hopped a flight to Virginia. Afterward, I took Mickey backstage and introduced him to Bruce. It turned out they were fans of each other's work. By the time we left, it was too late to get a flight out, so Mickey summoned his private bus—the Silverfish, we called it—all the way from North Carolina. We drove through the night and arrived just in time for Mickey to make it to the set; he was bleary-eyed but punctual.

That was Mickey, though, always pushing the envelope, always looking for a good time. We remain friends to this day. In fact, one of my three motorcycles actually belongs to Mickey. It's the original Black Death motorcycle that was used in the movie *Harley-Davidson & the Marlboro Man,* starring Mickey and Don Johnson. I was visiting Mickey one day at his house in Beverly Hills, the garage of which was full of bikes, a dozen in all, bikes that he had built or bought. Some of them were starting to rust by then—Mickey wasn't riding as much as he used to—so I said, "Why don't I take a couple back to New York and I'll restore them for you?" Mickey didn't mind; he was never one to be cheap. If he liked you, he'd give you the shirt off his back; in fact, whenever we finished working together on a movie, he usually gave me most of his wardrobe, including that awesome gray sharkskin suit he wore in *The Pope of Greenwich Village.* (Incidentally, I wore that suit to the movie's world premiere.)

Anyway, I had a friend who happened to be going to New York with some other bikes, so I put a couple of Mickey's bikes on the trailer, and off they went. Then I went back inside the house and Mickey asked me which bikes I took.

"The *Marlboro* bike and the bike from *Stone Cold,*" I said. (The 1991 movie *Stone Cold* featured a biker character played by an actor named Lance Henriksen, who was also a friend of Mickey's; Mickey had lent him the bike for that role. Like I said, Mickey gives everything to his friends.)

Back in New York, with the help of brothers John and Sal Petrazzi, I rebuilt the *Marlboro* bike to its original condition and changed the paint job on the *Stone Cold* bike—Mickey always liked black and purple, so I had my friend Jimmy Livecchi paint the tank and fenders black with purple flames, and another good friend, John DeVito, helped me put the finishing touches on the bike. It came out beau-

Me with my idol, Muhammad Ali

Bill "Superfoot" Wallace, myself, and John Belushi
after my first karate tournament

Myself and wife, Kathy, in St. Bart's

My daughter, Lisa, at age fourteen

Me on Mickey Rourke's motorcycle, Black Death, from the movie *Harley Davidson and the Marlboro Man*

Can't wait until I get out so I can ride again

Me with Pamela Anderson

Me with Joan Jett

Me and mom at Liza's opening

Me with Hulk Hogan and
The Disciple

Me with my arnis sticks

Me looking like Sylvester Stallone
in the movie *Nighthawks*

Me with my sisters, Cindy
and Rosanne

Rolf Moeller, myself, and Arnold Schwarzenager

Top: Lee Tergesen, me, Tom Fontana, Evan Seinfeld
Bottom: Chazz Melendez and J. D. Williams

Left to right: Bad Bart, me, Sonny Barger, and Brendan

Me wearing wolf coat made by Dirty Bill Hampton

Myself, Peter Bogdanovich, and Charlie Sheen

Son-in-law, Jonathan; daughter, Lisa; me; wife, Kathy; mom; and her
husband, Gene, celebrating Lisa's twenty-ninth birthday at Rao's
Restaurant on November 12, 1998

tiful, to say the least. As for the *Marlboro* bike . . . well, I borrowed it six years ago, and I still have it today. In fact, the inscription on the carburetor reads: "This is the original Black Death motorcycle used in the movie *Harley-Davidson & the Marlboro Man*. Owned by Mickey Rourke, operated by Chuck Zito, Hells Angels, Nomads, New York."

I've worked for so many celebrities, so many superstars, that I suppose it's no great shock to learn that I've been approached on numerous occasions to write some sleazy tell-all book about their indiscretions. You know, really dish the dirt. But I've never done that, and I never would do that, despite the fact that there's probably a big audience for it. To me, that's no different from being a rat. People hired me the first time because they knew I was good at the job, because they knew I could protect them effectively and quietly. They *rehired* me for other reasons, not the least of which was the fact that they knew they could trust me. As a bodyguard, I tried to live my life by the principles espoused in that old saying, the one you see paraphrased everywhere, from baseball clubhouses to fire stations: *"What you see here, what you hear here, what you say here . . . stays here when you leave here."*

I saw a lot of things when I was a bodyguard; I was privy to all sorts of information and, on occasion, witness to the type of behavior most stars would not want revealed to the public. A lot of my clients were married. After their husbands or wives, no one knew them better than I did. I traveled with these people. I shared airplanes, limousines, and hotel suites with them. I ate with them and worked out with them. I heard some of their deepest, darkest secrets, and I vowed never to betray them. More often than not, I considered these people to be not just clients, but close friends.

Rat them out? Please . . . I did six years in prison because I wouldn't rat. I'm sure as hell not going to screw the people I worked for just so I can make a few bucks. I'd like to think I have a little more dignity than that, a little more honor. In fact, I know that some of the people who hired me did so at least in part because they knew I would not only shield them from psychos and paparazzi, but also, under certain circumstances, I would do what few bodyguards are willing to do: protect the star from his own worst enemy—himself (or herself).

I'll give you an example. I remember a time in the 1980s when I was working for a very famous and successful young actress. She was talented, beautiful, smart. But she had a self-destructive streak. One night I accompanied her to a party at the Conservatory, a popular hangout in the Mayflower Hotel. It was a good night, filled with interesting conversation with the likes of Robert De Niro, Joe Pesci, and Paul Herman, all of whom were seated at our table . . . along with a young musician named Stevie Ray Vaughn. Hardly anyone knew Stevie Ray at the time—his star was just beginning to rise. But even that night, when he jumped onstage and began playing blues guitar (with Pesce joining him for a while), it was obvious the kid was something special.

Stevie Ray would also turn out to be a guy with serious problems, including a drug habit that would nearly cost him his life and his career and that already seemed to have its hooks in him. (Sadly, he died in a plane crash in 1990, shortly after finally getting clean and sober.) So, later, as the party moved upstairs, to my client's hotel suite, and she and Stevie Ray began whispering into each other's ears, I naturally became alarmed. After a while the two of them stood up and left, giggling and holding hands as they disappeared into an adjoining room, leaving me and Stevie Ray's brother behind, watching television.

This was precisely the type of situation that gives a bodyguard headaches. Under some circumstances, I'd merely turn a blind eye. But this was different. My client was married. She'd been drinking heavily, so I was reasonably sure that her judgment was cloudy; and, given the company she was keeping that night, I suspected it was only going to become even more impaired. About fifteen minutes went by, during which I tapped my foot nervously and fretted about whether or not to intervene. Finally, I stood up, turned to Stevie Ray's brother, who seemed not the least bit concerned, and said, "You know what? I don't care if they're fucking each other or if she's giving him a blow job. I'm going in there."

He smiled. "Whatever, man."

I took a deep breath and opened the door, strengthened by the knowledge that I wasn't just being a prude, that I was trying to keep a friend out of serious trouble. Once I was inside, my suspicions were confirmed. Although they were clothed, she straddled him like a drunken cowgirl. On the nightstand beside them was a veritable pharmacy of party favors. I walked to the bed and took her hand in mine.

"Get your coat," I said. "We're outta here."

Angrily she pulled away from me. "Leave me alone. You're not my husband."

"That's right," I said. "I care about you. Tomorrow morning you can fire me, but tonight we're leaving. So say good-bye."

Stevie Ray, a wisp of a man who probably would have known better had he not been so high, jumped across the bed and got in my face. "Hey, man," he drawled. "The lady asked you to leave. Now . . . get out!"

I hesitated for all of about two seconds before reaching out with one hand and lifting him off his feet and driving him against the wall. "Listen, you scrawny motherfucker. You ever disrespect me again . . . you ever give me another order . . . and I'll put you in a coma for the rest of your life."

So there I was, with one of the world's greatest guitar players turning blue in my hand, my client pounding me on the back. As I said, it was not the ideal situation for a bodyguard to find himself in. But, to me, it was the right thing to do. I loosened my grip and Stevie Ray slumped to the floor, gasping for breath, just as his brother ran into the room.

"Stay the fuck out of this," I said to him, "or you'll never play the drums again." Stevie Ray's brother froze in his tracks. Then I pulled my client out the door, still kicking and screaming, and, after driving around for a while, took her to a local diner for some coffee and quiet conversation. Slowly she calmed down and began to sober up. Before the night was out she gave me a little kiss on the cheek and thanked me for being so concerned.

14

IF CAFÉ CENTRAL ECLIPSED ALL OTHER NEW YORK NIGHTCLUBS AS THE PLACE
to see and be seen in the early 1980s, Studio 54 nevertheless remained
a popular destination. Like most people, I had trouble getting past
the front door for a while. I remember prom night, for example. I
was with my girl, Kathy, and Sally and Jimmy and Dougie and Carol.
After a great dinner at the Hawaii Ki Restaurant in Times Square,
the six of us went to Studio 54, pulled right up to the front door in
a limo. We stood there with dozens of other people, trying to gain
entry. But no such luck. Studio 54 was like a gated community, and
I did not have a key—until I joined the Hells Angels, and suddenly I
was welcomed with open arms. Go figure.

One night in 1982 I walked into the office of Mark Fleischman, the
club's owner, and found him chatting with a group of people.

"Chuck," he said, "I want to introduce you to someone." A big guy
with long hair, a beard, and a cowboy hat stood up and extended his
hand. "This is Hank Williams, Jr.," Mark said.

Now, I didn't know a whole lot about the world of country-western
music. Johnny Cash, Waylon Jennings, Willie Nelson—those guys I
knew. And I'd worked for Tanya Tucker. But that's about as far as my
interest and understanding went. I'd heard of Hank Williams, Jr., but
I wasn't familiar with his music and had no idea what he looked like.
I couldn't have picked him out of a lineup, to tell you the truth.

He did look the part, I'll give him that, but his demeanor was
strange, to say the least. I said, "Nice to meet you," and shook his
hand, and right away he seemed fidgety, nervous, not at all what you'd
expect from a big star.

"Hey, you're a Hells Angel, huh?"

"That's what the jacket reads," I said.

He dropped into an awkward little boxer's stance and raised his hands. "You know, I'm a fighter, so . . . uh . . . I hope we don't ever have a problem, you and me."

I looked at Mark, who shrugged—I guess he'd seen so much bizarre celebrity behavior over the years that nothing surprised him. Me? I was offended. And confused.

"Listen, pal, I don't know what you're talking about. We just met. Why would there be any problems?"

He sniffed. "I'm just saying, man. We both like to fight, so I hope everything stays cool between us."

"Yeah, whatever."

Out of respect for Mark, I let it go at that and drifted away from the guy. He seemed like nothing but trouble. Later that night I rode my bike to the Hells Angels clubhouse, where I hooked up with Sandy Alexander, whose taste for country music was well known. I thought he'd like hearing that I had just met Hank Williams, Jr., and of course I was right. What I didn't know was that Sandy had run into Hank, too, and had even secured a promise from him to perform a benefit concert for the New York City Hells Angels.

Cool, I thought. *Maybe he's not such a bad guy after all.*

Two nights later, on another trip to Studio 54, I asked Mark Fleischman if Hank was around. I wanted to give the guy another chance—after all, if he was a friend of the club, how bad could he be?

"Oh, man, don't even mention that guy's name," Mark said. "He's a fraud."

"What do you mean?"

"I mean he isn't Hank Williams, Jr. He's a fake. A lookalike. A nutcase. Been running all around town ripping people off."

"You're kidding?"

"I wish," Mark said.

The next day I went into a record store and looked at an album by Hank Williams, Jr., and damned if there wasn't an uncanny resemblance between the real Hank and the fake Hank. In fact, they looked like twin brothers. The guy I'd met was an impostor who'd been living the good life for a while and charging all the bills to Hank Williams, Jr. Why? I have no idea. Seems like a stupid crime to me. You're

166

bound to get caught. It's just a matter of who gets to you first: the cops or the people you're ripping off. This guy committed the potentially fatal mistake of choosing the Hells Angels as one of his targets.

"You mean he lied to us?" Sandy said when I broke the news.

"Yeah, I'm afraid so."

"So there's no benefit concert?"

"Uh-uh."

Sandy's eyes narrowed. I'd seen that look before.

"Hey, brother," I said. "I'll take care of it."

I put word on the street that night to friends and acquaintances who owned bars, restaurants, nightclubs. The message was simple: If you see this guy, give me a call. Immediately!

It didn't take long, maybe a few more days at the most. A friend who owned a tavern on the Upper East Side of Manhattan called and said that a man claiming to be Hank Williams, Jr., was at that very moment hosting a party at his establishment.

"Keep him busy," I said.

"No problem—they just ordered dinner. They'll be here awhile."

Accompanied by two prospects from the New York City chapter, I drove to the bar in a station wagon. No bikes for this trip. No patches, either. You see, sometimes, when we take care of business, we don't advertise who we are.

I instructed the prospects to wait outside while I went inside and had a little meeting with "Hank." He was in the back of the room, holding court at a big table, surrounded by close to a dozen people, none of whom had any idea that they weren't partying with a country music star. I marched right up to the table and took a seat next to Hank.

"Hey, Chuck," he said. "How's it going?"

I said nothing. He looked me up and down. "Where's the jacket, man?"

I leaned in close, so that only he could hear me.

"Don't need it tonight, pal. Say good-bye to your friends. We're taking a walk."

The color drained from his face. "What do you mean?"

I put my mouth within an inch of his ear. "You phony motherfucker. Who do you think you are, trying to get over on people like that?"

He leaned back a bit and put a finger to his mouth. "Keep it down, man. These people are paying the bill."

"Fine," I said. "Then excuse yourself and we'll finish this outside."

On the way out I put an arm around his shoulder, as if we were buddies, and told him not to try anything stupid.

"If you think you're going to run, think again." I opened my coat enough to give him a glimpse of the gun I was carrying. He blanched. "Because I *will* shoot you in the back."

With Hank sandwiched between me and one of the prospects, I pulled out onto the street and steered the station wagon toward the FDR Drive.

"See that over there?" I said, looking out the window. "That's the East River. Ever hear any stories about that?"

Fake Hank lowered his head. His face was ashen. He looked like he was going to be sick.

"Yeah," he mumbled.

"Yeah? What do you hear?"

"A lot of bodies have been found there."

"That's right," I said. "Something to think about, huh?"

He dropped his head into his hands and moaned. "You're gonna kill me, aren't you? Aw, fucking Christ. . . ."

"Oh, shut the fuck up," I said. "No one's going to kill you. But going around ripping people off, lying to them, pretending you're someone you're not . . . that's bullshit. It's wrong, and before this night is over, you're going to realize just how wrong it is."

We took him to Big Joe's Tattoo Shop in Mount Vernon, the perfect setting for teaching someone a memorable lesson. I steered the car through a set of gates and into the backyard. I cut the engine, and then the three of us led Hank down a set of stairs to the basement. This was, I have to admit, a truly frightening place, cold, dark, and dank, the concrete walls illuminated only by a single bare forty-watt lightbulb. It looked and smelled and felt like a dungeon.

"What are we doing here?" Hank asked.

I handed him a folding chair, then took one for myself. The prospects stood close by. "Just having a little talk, that's all."

Hank seemed not to believe this. Actually, he seemed scared shitless, which, of course, was precisely the point of the whole exercise. I proceeded to give him a lecture on the stupidity of lying and stealing, especially to Hells Angels. I told him he'd made some very serious mistakes.

"You screwed around with a lot of people I know. You promised Sandy you'd do a concert for the Hells Angels. Bad move. Bad fucking move." Hank closed his eyes, nodded. "What I'm going to do now is make sure that every time you wake up, you realize you fucked with the wrong people."

I told one of the prospects to run upstairs and get a razor and a pair of scissors, both tools readily available in any tattoo shop, since tattoos can only be sketched on smooth, hairless skin. The thing is, when you shave someone for a tattoo, you don't use a little plastic Bic or a Gillette Trac II. You use a straight razor.

"Holy shit!" Hank said when I held up the blade. "What are you going to do with that?"

"Me? I'm not doing anything." I held the razor out to him, handle first. "You're going to do it."

So he used the razor and the scissors to cut his own hair and shave his own beard. But it was all a bit too neat for my satisfaction. He gave himself a little Buster Brown bowl cut, which, while humiliating, wasn't quite what I had in mind.

"Give me the blade!" I said.

I proceeded to shave the guy's head. No shaving cream, no soap, no hot water . . . nothing! Just a rough, dry shave, the kind that invariably leaves the victim with welts and cuts and oozing red razor burns all over his skin. By the time I'd finished, Hank's head looked like a bad golf course: a bare patch here, a clump of hair there . . .

I threw down the razor and told him to get up out of the chair. Then I dragged him over to a mirror and told him to take a good, hard look at himself. I wanted him to see what I saw: not Hank Williams, Jr., but just some lowlife prick who tried to use people.

"Now we're going to go down to Studio 54, and you're going to apologize to Mark Fleischman," I said. "And then we're going to my clubhouse, and you're going to apologize to Sandy Alexander. You hear me?"

He whimpered, nodded.

"Good. That's your punishment. Now let's go."

As we walked toward the door, I stopped and turned to face Hank. "Oh, and one other thing."

"What?"

"Remember when we first met, and you said you were a fighter?"

"Uh-huh."

BAM! I hit him with a hard right hand to the chin. He went down and out. The prospects threw some water on him, lifted him to his feet.

"You're a tough guy, huh? A real cowboy?"

BAM! I hit him again. And again the prospects roused him with buckets of cold water.

With his nose broken, his eyes blackened, and his head all hacked up, Fake Hank was escorted downtown. Mark Fleischman refused to see him or hear his apology. Sandy took one look at him, practically died laughing, and told Hank he'd gotten off easy. Then the prospects took him to the Bowery and dumped him on the street somewhere.

I never saw the guy again. I never met the real Hank Williams, Jr., either, although I presume he'd be grateful if he heard about what happened. I'd like to think so, anyway.

By the way, if there's one thing worse than impersonating a celebrity, it's impersonating a Hell's Angel. This, I must tell you, is a very, very bad idea. So bad, in fact, that I've seen it happen only twice during my tenure with the club. The first time was the early 1980s, around the same time Fake Hank showed up. I was looking for some parts at a motorcycle shop in the Bronx when a guy walked in off the street, looked at my patch, and said, "Hey, I just saw one of your brothers riding around. Some guy from South Carolina."

I was there with two other club members. They seemed as clueless as I was. You have to understand—when a lone Hells Angel visits another region, he typically makes his presence known as soon as he arrives (in fact, he usually reveals his plans in advance). We'd heard nothing about anyone from South Carolina coming to New York. Something about this sounded fishy.

"South Carolina?" I repeated. "Are you sure?"

The guy nodded. "That's what his jacket said."

So I went back to the clubhouse, called someone from the South Carolina charter, and asked if anyone was missing. The answer was no. Everyone was present and accounted for.

"That's funny," I said. "Because somebody up here is riding around with one of your patches."

There was a long pause.

"You're shittin' me?" Some five years earlier, he explained, luggage belonging to one of their members had been stolen during a trip to New York. The guy had lost just about every piece of clothing he owned—including his Hells Angels patch! It had never been recovered.

I hung up the phone and jumped into my car. Accompanied by two of the biggest, scariest guys in the club, I began driving around the streets of the Bronx, looking for a Hells Angels wannabe. The search didn't last long, maybe an hour or so. Not far from the motorcycle shop where the impostor had been spotted earlier, we found a half-dozen guys hanging out by the side of the road, leaning on their bikes, bullshitting. We parked the car and walked right up to them. The fact that we were outnumbered two to one didn't matter in the least. Honor was at stake. Anyway, they seemed nervous, which only reinforced my suspicions. As we drew near, it became apparent that one of them had something folded up under his arm.

"What's that?" one of my brothers asked, pointing at the object, which was obviously an article of clothing.

The guy glanced down. "It's a leather vest. Why?"

"Let's see it."

"Fuck you!" the guy said, and instantly he took a crushing blow to the chin from the biggest of my brothers. The punch sent him reeling, but he managed to stay on his feet. As he regained his balance, he turned and ran.

"Son of a bitch!" I shouted.

We took off after him. Unfortunately, while I was no more than 165 pounds soaking wet and still in good shape thanks to my boxing and martial arts training, neither of my two brothers, who weighed a combined 600 pounds, was fit for flight. Consequently, in less time than it took to cover a single block, I was the only one in pursuit, and I was getting pretty tired myself. Thankfully, so was the impostor. He dropped the vest to lighten his load, and as I ran by I snatched it up and took a quick look. The letters were clear: HELLS ANGELS, SOUTH CAROLINA.

I knew it. . . .

Finally, exhausted from the chase, he stopped and turned to face me, but not before pulling a knife. Unarmed, I quickly wrapped the patch around my arm and moved in on him.

"Come on, motherfucker! Let's see what you got!"

As I suspected, he had no idea how to use a knife. He lunged at me and I used a crescent kick—a sweeping motion that takes the attacker away from the body, so that he has no target other than your leg—to knock the knife out of his hand. Then I dropped him with a left hook and pounced on him.

"Come on, scumbag! You want to be a Hells Angel? Prove it!"

He was nearly unconscious, his face shattered, by the time my two brothers drove up (they'd abandoned the chase in favor of retrieving the car). They pulled me off him and dragged me into the car. A few days later the patch was returned to its rightful owner in South Carolina. As far as I know, the impostor left town, which was a very good idea.

The only other person I've ever seen impersonate a Hells Angel, believe it or not, was Rudolph Giuliani. It happened a few years later, while I was doing time. Rudy, who then worked for the U.S. Attorney's Office, took a patch that had been confiscated as evidence during a federal investigation of the Hells Angels (much more on that to come). Then, remarkable as it may sound. He and New York senator Alphonse D'Amato drove up to Washington Heights (with scores of undercover police doing surveillance) to show how easy it was to buy drugs. Later that day, they were all over the news, looking like a couple of clowns: D'Amato in army fatigues and Rudy in the Hells Angels jacket he took from the evidence safe in his office. I suppose it made for good publicity, and I have to admit that I admire what Rudy later did for New York, the way he cleaned up the city and all. I respect him as a mayor. But I have no respect for him as a man. And I'll tell you this: if I hadn't been locked up at the time, I would have treated Rudy exactly as I treated the guy from South Carolina. An impostor, after all, is an impostor.

15

EVEN AS MY BODYGUARD BUSINESS GREW, PROVIDING ME AND MY FAMILY
with a nice income, I continued to be an active member of the Hells
Angels. Well, *active* doesn't really do it justice. By the fall of 1983 I
was vice president of the New York City chapter, and with that position came a certain level of responsibility and expectation. I had no
problem with that because first, as I've said, my affiliation with the
Hells Angels was never a detriment to obtaining security work—if
anything, it was seen by potential clients as a valuable job skill. Second, I loved the club and the guys in it.

We did have enemies, other clubs that wanted to infringe on our
territory, engage in warfare of one type or another, or simply disrespect us by talking trash. None of which was deemed acceptable by
the Hells Angels. When this type of behavior was encountered, it was
met with swift and ferocious retaliation. Crude, perhaps, but that's
the way it worked. I accepted that code of honor the day I became a
member, and as an officer of the club I upheld it with all of my emotional and physical strength.

Simply put, I was an enforcer.

Traditionally, the sergeant at arms is considered the true muscle of
any motorcycle club. He is the most formidable, and often the cra-
ziest, officer in the club. But I took my membership seriously, and I
expected others to do the same. When provoked, I was more than
willing to fight; although I rarely tried to initiate a physical confrontation, neither did I ever walk away or back down. It simply wasn't
my nature. I don't mean to imply that I never took the first big step
that would lead inevitably to battle; I did . . . many times. Usually,
though, that action was preceded by something, some type of behav-

173

ior, that I deemed unacceptable. In short, I always had a reason for fighting. Maybe, in some people's eyes, the reason was insufficient; and certainly there have been times that, in the eyes of the law, I overstepped my bounds. Too bad. I did what I felt was right given the circumstances.

A writer once asked me during an interview if I've ever felt any remorse about hurting someone in a street fight. My answer: Not in the least . . . because that person was trying to hurt me, too. It's either hit or get hit, so I try to do the hitting. There's nothing wrong with trying to talk your way out of a fight—once in a while. Sometimes, though, there's only so much talking you can do before you fight. I look at it this way: if I know I'm going to get it on with a guy, I might as well hit him first.

It's not the most enlightened attitude, I suppose, but enlightenment is overrated. Life can be brutal, unforgiving, uncompromising. Sometimes the most primitive philosophy is the best. It's all some people understand.

Take the assholes from a rival New York club (which shall remain nameless here; it deserves no publicity) with which we had an ongoing problem in the early to mid-1980s. Representatives of this club had not only brazenly cruised our streets but also insulted our name and reputation to anyone who would listen (which wasn't many, by the way).

My personal interaction with this club began in November of 1983 while attending a car and motorcycle show at the New York Coliseum. I was upstairs, looking around, minding my own business, when a friend named Steve, who later became a member of the Hells Angels, came running up to me, all excited and out of breath.

"They're here," he said. "A bunch of them. They're downstairs."

"Who's here?"

"Those pricks you've been looking for. Or, at least, guys from their club anyway."

"They wearing patches?" I asked.

Steve frowned. "Hell, no. They ain't stupid."

"Then how do you know? I'm not going to go kick the shit out of some poor bastard who hasn't done anything to deserve it."

"Trust me," Steve said. "It's them."

There was reason to believe Steve knew exactly what he was talking

174

about, for he lived in a neighborhood that was basically ruled by this other club. He knew what they looked like, how they dressed, how they behaved. Patch or no patch, he might be capable of picking them out. It was worth investigating, anyway.

"Downstairs, huh?"

"Yeah, come on."

So we went downstairs and Steve quickly pointed out a group of three guys, all big and wide, with long, shaggy hair, beards, and army jackets. Standard biker types—there were probably a few hundred people in the Coliseum who fit that description. I turned to Steve.

"You're sure about this?"

"Uh-huh."

As I got closer, I could see they were also carrying cameras. Christ! They looked like tourists! How could they possibly be the same guys who had the balls to challenge the Hells Angels? It seemed a ludicrous notion, but I investigated anyway. Well, maybe *investigate* isn't exactly the right word. I simply walked up to the biggest guy, told him who I was, and asked him, straight out, if he belonged to this other club.

"Why do you want to know?"

"Because I hate them, that's why," I said. "They're scumbags."

The big guy stuffed his hands into his pockets and nodded approvingly. "I know what you mean," he said. "We have problems with them, too. They're assholes, no doubt about it."

"Yeah," added one of his friends with a laugh. "Assholes."

Something about the way they acted was disconcerting, but there wasn't a whole lot I could do under the circumstances. If they were willing to piss on their own club and weren't even brave enough or proud enough to display their own colors, then maybe they weren't worth our time. More likely, it seemed, they were telling the truth.

I left them standing there, taking pictures, and returned to where Steve was waiting.

"What's up?" he asked. "Aren't you going to do anything?"

"It's not them," I said.

"The fuck it ain't! I recognize at least a couple of them."

"Steve, what do you want from me? I asked them, they said no . . . that's it."

Steve was pissed, and his anger made me wonder if perhaps I'd been too willing to accept their explanation, especially when I looked

175

up and noticed the entire group walking hurriedly toward the front door of the Coliseum.

"See?" Steve said. "They're leaving. They're scared."

He had a point. I summoned two of our prospects, Giuseppe and Butch, and we followed them to the front door, where I once again confronted the biggest member of their group. He was about six-foot-five and a good 230 pounds—in other words, substantially bigger than me—but I could tell he was scared, nervous.

"Hey, man," I said. "We have a little problem. You just told me you weren't part of this club, but my friend over there insists that you are."

"Yeah, well, your friend is lying."

"Well, we'll see if he is." I scanned the group, looking for some sign that would connect them to the rival club. "Why are you leaving all of a sudden, anyway?"

"Time to go," he said.

A crowd was beginning to gather, which seemed to make these guys even more apprehensive. They knew who we were (we were wearing our patches) and they knew we meant business.

"You boys have any tattoos?" I asked.

They all nodded.

"Let's see them."

The big guy began to roll up his sleeve.

"Uh-uh," I said. Take off your jacket; take off your shirt; strip down to your waist. I want to see your tattoos—every one of them."

He put his hands on his hips. "You're kiddin' me. It's gotta be thirty degrees out here."

I stepped closer, put my nose against his chin, just to let him know I meant business. "Take off your shirt. Now."

While cursing and mumbling under his breath, he opened his jacket, revealing an assortment of knives and razors, all capable of considerable mayhem. He threw the coat angrily on the ground and began to unbutton his shirt as I instructed Butch to remove the blades. "The rest of you, too," I said. The others followed his lead until, within a few minutes, they all stood shirtless and quivering in the fading afternoon sun, a crowd of a few dozen onlookers laughing at their expense.

To my surprise, not one of them wore the mark of this club. There were tattoos dedicated to Mom and Dad, to various girlfriends, to their children and wives. But nothing that stamped them as members of an outlaw motorcycle club. Nevertheless, I was convinced of their culpability. Everything about their behavior said "guilty."

"Let me tell you something," I said to their leader. "I'm going to give you the benefit of the doubt, just because I don't see any tattoos. But if I find out you're lying, I will track you down and knock you the fuck out." I got right in his face again. "And if you don't think I can do it, then let's get it on right now, big guy."

He took a step back and picked up his shirt. "We're not looking for any trouble, okay? We just want to get out of here."

"Okay," I said, motioning to Giuseppe and Butch. "Give them their knives back." They finished dressing and waited for permission to leave, which we granted. As they disappeared into the crowd outside, I went back into the Coliseum, to check out the girls and the cars and the bikes, which, after all, was why I had come there in the first place.

Fast-forward . . . two months later . . . the Nassau Coliseum
I was there with one of my brothers, a guy named Bill, watching a Willie Nelson concert (one of Willie's bodyguards was also a Hells Angels from San Jose named Larry Gorham—we call him LG—so it was natural for us to show up, as we did whenever the Grateful Dead came to town). Now, in the interest of full disclosure, I must admit that we had more on our minds than merely taking in a good show. The Coliseum was located smack in the middle of territory dominated by this same rival motorcycle club. Bill and I wore our jackets not simply because we were proud of our membership but also because we were trolling for trouble. Maybe by advertising our affiliation with the Angels we could draw some of these guys out of the crowd, provoke a reaction that would lead to either a discussion and perhaps a reasonable resolution or, more likely, a fight. Either way, the issue would be settled once and for all.

As the road crew prepared the stage for Willie's show, Bill and I wandered around the Coliseum, looking for anyone who might belong to this club. At the top of a set of stairs, near a concession stand,

I spotted a security guy I recognized. He was a biker, too, and I thought there was a chance he might know some of the people in this club.

"Yeah, I know who they are," he said. "And you don't have to look far."

"Why's that?"

He looked down the hallway. "Because two of their guys are right over there by the phone."

Sure enough, there were two men standing near a bank of phones, each wearing a T-shirt bearing the logo of this rival club. I thanked the security guard and walked right over to the phones.

"Hey, fellas," I said. "I'd like a word with you—in the bathroom."

They looked at our jackets, then at each other. "We're not going anywhere," one of them said.

"Oh, no?"

"No. We're staying right here."

I was getting pissed now. "What's with you guys, anyway? Nobody in this club has any balls. You're always running around, talking shit about us, saying the Angels don't have any presence on the Island. Well, here we are . . . right in your fucking backyard. What are you going to do about it?"

He started whining, complaining that we wouldn't let them wear their colors in New York City, but here we were, on Long Island, wearing our colors.

"That's right," I said, sticking a finger in his face. "We're Hells Angels, and we wear our patches anywhere and everywhere in the world."

As we bantered back and forth, I glanced out the window and saw a large group of motorcycles, maybe twenty of them, all pulling up together, and as soon as they planted their kickstands they were surrounded by cops. The usual hassling ensued—I'm sure the cops were telling them to be on their best behavior, or maybe they'd been tipped off about the presence of a couple of Hells Angels and were merely trying to avert a small war from erupting. I didn't really care, for I was too busy scanning the faces of the bikers, looking for anyone I might recognize. Sure enough, there in the middle was the big man from the New York Coliseum car and bike show, the leader of the group I'd forced to strip.

178

Son of a bitch!

Like the others, he wore the colors of this club. But there was more. As I looked closer, I could see a tag dangling from his patch, a tag that could only mean one thing.

This cowardly, lying motherfucker was not only a member of the club . . . he was the president! I stepped closer to the window, put my face right up against the glass, and stared until my eyes hurt. All I wanted was for this prick to see me, to know that I'd busted his ass and that soon he'd have to pay. Suddenly, as if he'd read my mind, the guy looked up, saw me standing there, and, with a big smile on his face, began to wave. A dainty little feminine wave, using only his fingers. Next to him was another man, shorter but much more muscular, pounding a fist into his hand, talking to himself. I couldn't hear him, of course, but it looked like his mouth formed the words, *I'll beat your ass!*

"They're mocking me!" I said out loud. "Oh, man . . . I'm gonna fuck these guys up."

I turned and walked back to the phones.

"That piece of shit swore to me that he wasn't part of your club," I said to the first two guys we'd cornered.

One of them shrugged. "I guess he lied."

"You think I'm joking?" I pointed toward the window. "That cocksucker is going to get you hurt. Because before they walk in here, I'm going to knock you both out."

He held up his hands. "What do you want from me?"

"I want to settle this bullshit—right now! Your whole club has been acting like a bunch of punks, and if it doesn't stop, a lot of people are going to get hurt."

"Hey, I'm no boss," he said. "I'm nothing. I'm not even supposed to talk to you."

"Fine, I'll give you my number, you go talk to that president of yours, and then you can give me a call."

He took my card and walked away. I knew there was no chance I'd hear from him.

By the summer of 1984, the dispute had still not been settled; in fact, things had only gotten uglier. For example, our club used to give T-shirts to people—friends and relatives, mostly—bearing the inscription: "Support Your Local Hells Angels." We no longer do that. Unless you are a member of the Hells Angels, you're not allowed to wear the colors of the club or anything bearing the name of the club. To do so is to risk great bodily harm. In 1984, however, the rules were different. If you were given one of these shirts by a club member, you were considered a supporter, an ally. Unfortunately, you were also an easy target for enemies of the Hells Angels.

We discovered that representatives of this rival club were attacking and beating anyone who wore these shirts, which just infuriated me. After all, these were civilians, innocent people who were doing nothing more than showing support for their friends. To drag them into a conflict with another club, a conflict that had nothing to do with them . . . well, that was unforgivable. Oh, and one more thing: after administering these beatings, our rivals would invariably steal the shirts off their victims' backs, leaving them bloody and half-naked in the street.

This kind of thuggery so disturbed me that I decided not to attend USA Run, an annual gathering of all the Hells Angels in the United States. USA Run was scheduled to be held in the Midwest that summer, and it promised to be a terrific time. But I wasn't interested in throwing a big party. Friends of mine had been beaten. Our club had been insulted. Our honor was at stake.

"This is bullshit," I said at one of our annual parties. "I'm going to Laconia instead."

Laconia was (and still is) the site of the oldest motorcycle rally in the country, a massive multiday party that annually attracted more than a half-million bikers to a resort town on the coast of New Hampshire. Anyone who owned a motorcycle was welcome at Laconia; unlike USA Run, this rally was not a private affair, so at the party, about sixty Hells Angels decided we were going to ride to Laconia.

We agreed to meet at the Sheraton Hotel near the main intersection in Laconia, at noon.

Shortly after I arrived, I was hanging out in the Sheraton parking lot, talking with a few of my brothers, when two guys from this club rode by on their way to Weir's Beach.

"What are we supposed to do, chase them?" one of my brothers said.

"They have to come back sometime," I said. "Let's just wait right here."

Everyone hung out for a little while before eventually finding their way to their rooms, except for Flash and Pinball, who stayed behind to work on their bikes in the parking lot. Myself, I wanted to make sure these guys didn't get away, so I grabbed a beach chair, walked from the parking lot to the corner of the intersection, and sat right down, so close to traffic that I could feel the breeze and smell the exhaust of each car and bike that went past. I had no plan, no strategy; I just figured if I saw someone from this club, I'd stop him and initiate an impromptu summit meeting.

I didn't have to wait long. Within perhaps fifteen minutes, just as I was about to doze off, I heard the rumble of motorcycles off in the distance. There was a big pack headed my way, eighteen to twenty bikes, all wearing the colors of a single club.

Bingo!

I looked around for my brothers and saw only two of them, Flash and Pinball, who were tinkering with their bikes in the parking lot. As far as I could tell, they hadn't even heard the approaching bikes. For now, at least, I was on my own.

I jumped out of my chair and stepped out into the middle of the intersection, like a crazy man, and just stood there with my arms held high, waving slowly. I made no attempt to ambush anyone or to disguise my identity. I wore my jacket. They knew exactly who I was.

"Pull over!" I shouted. "Pull over!"

The entire group came to a stop at the intersection and let their bikes idle loudly. I walked right up to the leader of the pack and grabbed his handlebars.

"What do you want?" he shouted over the noise.

"Same thing I wanted a month ago—I want to talk to you."

"Yeah?" he said. "Well, I don't want to talk to you." With that he leaned into the accelerator and jumped off the line. A few others started to follow, but there were so many of them that it took a while for the whole pack to clear the intersection. That gave me time to look them over, to see if there was anyone I recognized. Sure enough, coming right at me, slowly enough for me to see his face clearly, was one of the guys I had cornered at the phone booths in Nassau Coliseum a few months earlier. He was riding a chopper with big ape hangers, his hands held high and wide. As he tried to go by, our eyes locked, and I reached out and grabbed his arm. Nearly losing control of the bike, he stopped in traffic and shouted, "Let me go!"

I kept a tight grip on his arm. "Remember me, asshole? You think I was kidding around?"

He dropped his feet to the ground and straddled the bike, and I could see now that he was wearing the patch of a sergeant at arms. For an enforcer, I thought, this guy was a real wimp. But then, out of the corner of my eye, I noticed him shift his weight just a bit, a signal to anyone who has ever been in a fight that one of two things is about to happen: either a punch is going to be thrown or he's going to retreat. Well, there was no place for this guy to run, so I wasn't surprised when he balled his free hand into a fist and threw a wild roundhouse left at my temple. I saw it coming and was able to side-step just in time. The punch merely grazed the side of my head, and the force of it threw him off balance. I countered with an open right hand, which knocked him off his seat. He hit the ground first, fol-lowed by his bike . . .

And then by me.

There was no backing out at that point, no room for détente or apologies or cease-fires. The battle had been joined. I jumped on top of the sergeant at arms and began pummeling him with all my strength. Within seconds I felt the weight of a half-dozen men piling on top of me, brothers of the sergeant at arms. I threw a couple of them off, only to find them replaced by others. I kept kicking and punching, doing whatever I could to inflict damage. They did the same. I had a knife in my back pocket, and I was prepared to use it if necessary, if the rumble reached a point where I felt my life was in danger. It was while contemplating that option and the weight of its consequences that I looked through a tangle of arms and legs and saw the cavalry coming to my rescue.

It was Pinball and Flash, running through the intersection, yelling like madmen. Flash jumped in and started pulling people off me, throwing punches all over the place. Pinball's efforts were more dam-aging. He'd been changing the kickstand on his motorcycle when he noticed the melee, and now he was swinging the kickstand like a blackjack, knocking out one biker after another with each blow.

Bam! Bam! Bam!

While all this was going on, I later discovered, Lightfoot was back up in his hotel room, talking on the phone with some of our brothers at USA Run, giving them an update on the events in Laconia. Everything was quiet, Lightfoot reported. No sign of trouble. Then he heard something, looked out the window, and saw three Hells Angels brawling with nearly twenty rival bikers.

"Holy shit!" he yelled into the phone. "It's on!"

Then he dropped the receiver and ran out into the street. Well, he didn't exactly run. You see, Lightfoot was known as Lightfoot for a reason: Some years earlier he'd been so badly hurt in a motorcycle accident that doctors had been forced to amputate his leg below the knee. So the best Lightfoot could manage was a quick shuffle. Oh, and one other thing: he'd also lost an eye in a bar fight. What Lightfoot didn't lack was spirit . . . courage. So there he was—one-eyed, one-footed Lightfoot, hobbling out the front door of the Sheraton, galloping across the street, screaming at the top of his lungs, and leaping into the fray. Behind him were several other Hells Angels, including one who went by the name of Hoppy. Bodies were flying all over the place, and suddenly, instead of having five or six guys on my back, I was fighting only one. I rolled the guy over, put a knee in his chest, and began hitting him in the face . . . over and over, until I felt his cheekbone collapse beneath my hand. I heard someone say, "Yeah, Chuck," and when I looked up, there was Hoppy, bouncing around (as always), laughing, a camera pressed against his face.

Fucking Hoppy! We're in a rumble here and he's taking pictures.

Finally there was the inevitable wail of sirens and the arrival of more than a dozen police cars. Two cops pounced on top of me and applied a choke hold with a nightstick. I was too tired by then to put up much of a fight, especially since the result would have been a loss of consciousness and incarceration was inevitable anyway. Why make it worse? You beat down a rival biker, and the cops really don't give a shit; you beat down one of their own, however, and it's a whole different story.

So the brawl was over. We'd made our point. The numbers favored our side by a wide margin: ten people arrested, only two of whom were Hells Angels; we also sent a good half-dozen of the other club's members to the hospital. Considering how severely we'd been out-manned, it was an impressive display of muscle and might. To commemorate the event, when we returned to New York we decided to make special tags for everyone who took part in that fight. So if you ever see a Hells Angel wearing a "Rumble Squad" tag, you won't have to ask him for an explanation (not a good idea, anyway)—it means he was in Laconia, New Hampshire, in the summer of 1984, kicking ass in the middle of an intersection.

Not long after the Laconia incident, I traveled to Florida with Bert Kittel and John the Baptist, ostensibly to support a Hells Angel named Kevin Cleary, who was competing in a big motorcycle race in Fort Lauderdale, just minutes away from another rival club with which we were having some problems. Bert, John, and I decided that before Kevin raced his bike we would ride over to the Fort Lauderdale airport and hire a pilot to fly one of those little single-engine planes over the racetrack, with a banner trailing behind him. The message we chose was this: "Kevin Cleary, Hells Angels—No. 1." Our goal was just to let everyone know we were there, and it worked beautifully. The plane flew overhead just moments before Kevin raced down the track.

We were so pleased with the pilot's performance, in fact, that we went right back and hired him to tow another banner. This one was of a more general nature, and the target was, well . . . not just our rivals but also the law enforcement agencies that typically gave us a hard time at any big motorcycle event. You see, we had made a decision shortly after the races that we would ride up the coast to Daytona, where, in just a few days, one of the world's biggest motorcycle rallies would begin. The Daytona rally was an annual event but one that had always been ignored by the Hells Angels. But we decided it was time to make our debut, so Bert, John, and I recruited six other Hells Angels to join us, and together we invaded Daytona Beach. But not before commissioning another flyover, this time with a banner that would read: "Daytona Welcomes the Hells Angels!"

After arriving in Daytona, we went into town to walk around and shop and kill time while waiting for the plane to fly overhead. We just wanted to see what type of reaction it would provoke. We were browsing in Dirty Bill's, a leather shop run by a true craftsman from

Tennessee, when eight brass from the Daytona Beach Police Department came strolling in. These were not foot soldiers. These were captains, lieutenants, commanders. After hanging in the doorway for a minute or so, one of them removed his sunglasses and said, "Which one of you guys is Chuck Zito?"

Obviously, these guys had done their homework. Not only did they know the Hells Angels were in town, but they knew our names.

"I am," I said. I turned and smiled. "What can I do for you, Officer?"

He casually approached me and said, without a trace of anger or hostility in his voice, "You know, fellas, we don't let any other outlaw motorcycle clubs wear their patches in Daytona Beach. It just causes trouble. And we don't want any of that, now, do we?"

"No, sir."

"Good," he added. "Then I'm sure you'll understand why I'm going to have to ask you all to remove your patches, too."

I looked at Bert and John. They both smiled. "Officer," I said. "No disrespect to you or any of your men here—I know you have a job to do—but we don't take off our patches for anyone." He sighed, scuffed the floor with the toe of his shoe. "Now, if that means you're going to have to arrest us, well, then you do what you have to do. And we'll do what we have to do."

The cop looked up. He seemed more amused than anything else. "Look at the balls on this guy," he said, and with that the tension broke and we all started to laugh. "Welcome to Daytona," he said. "You boys have a good time."

The cop turned and started to leave but stopped before he got to the door.

"Oh, one other thing," he said.

"Yeah?"

"That banner you were planning to fly over the city?" He winked. "That ain't happening."

Whoa . . . these guys are good.

"How did you know about that?" I asked.

"This isn't that big a town," he said. "We know everything. Keep that in mind."

"I'll do that."

A few minutes later, when we walked out of Dirty Bill's, the cops were waiting. They put us up against a wall, spread-eagle, and patted us down. After finding nothing, they let us go.

"What's with this?" I said before leaving. "Five minutes ago you said, 'Welcome to Daytona,' and now you're jacking us up."

The cop shrugged, smiled. "Comes with the territory, Chuck. You know how it goes."

Indeed I did. We went back to the airport and made a new deal with the pilot. For the rest of the week he towed a banner that read: "Support Your Local Hells Angels."

It didn't have quite the same ring to it, but it was sweet nonetheless.

I've frequently used the word *brother* to describe my fellow Hells Angels, and we do consider ourselves to be an extended family, with all that the word implies. As in any family, though, there are times when people simply do not get along. We protect and support one another without question. But if one of my brothers tries to hurt me or disrespects me, I'll react just as swiftly and righteously as I would if such a transgression occurred on the street with a complete stranger. I think it's important to make that clear, so you understand that the Hells Angels are not just a collection of thugs who tolerate almost anything. It doesn't work that way.

Maybe this story will illustrate my point.

The New York City chapter of the Hells Angels traditionally held a big party every year on the Fourth of July. We'd close off the block around the clubhouse, have a band, fireworks, lots of food and beer. As many as a thousand people would attend, the great majority of whom were not members of the club. We'd invite friends, relatives, celebrities . . . all kinds of people. And everyone had a good time. I usually helped prepare for the party by obtaining the fireworks (let's just say I had connections and leave it at that) and doing a little decorating, including hanging a thirty-foot flag in the middle of the block, between two buildings.

We'd never had a problem with the party, and I sure expected none when I walked into the fourth-floor apartment of another member on July 4, 1984, wanting nothing more than access to his window and fire escape so that I could drape the flag, as I did every year. The apartment belonged to one of our wilder members, a six-foot-four, 400-pound monster known for his savage fighting ability and, unfortunately, his fondness for drugs. He was sitting on the floor when I walked in, his eyes wide and red, staring off into space.

"Just using the fire escape," I said, showing him the flag.

To my amazement, he leaped up off the floor and charged at me. "What do you want?!" he screamed.

I tried to remain calm. It was obvious the guy had been up all night and was completely zooed out on crank or speed. At the time, I wasn't even sure he recognized me. If he did, he didn't care.

"Take it easy, man," I said.

He paused, then grabbed a foot-long bowie knife that had been resting on the coffee table. He took a couple big, lumbering steps forward and put the blade to my throat. He didn't just show it to me, and he didn't just touch the tip lightly to my skin. He pressed the full edge against my skin, hard enough that I could feel a small trickle of blood.

"Get the fuck out of my house!" he screamed.

Now, there isn't a lot that scares me, but this guy, in this altered state, was about as frightening a creature as you'd ever want to encounter. I'd seen him at work, seen the damage he could do. I'd seen him seriously hurt a lot of people in street fights and not feel even slightly bad about it afterward. I knew that with this guy on the other end of a twelve-inch knife, the smartest thing I could do was get the fuck out of his apartment—fast! I had no doubt that the slightest provocation—the wrong word, a punch . . . a *sneeze*—would have resulted in that knife disappearing into my neck. So I started backpedaling. When I reached the hallway he gave me a shove in the chest, growled something inaudible, and slammed the door in my face.

For a few seconds I was relieved. Then the anger set in.

You motherfucker! Pull a knife on me . . .

Furious, I ran down the stairs to Casey's house, where I found Sandy Alexander. I explained what had happened, not because I wanted Sandy to do anything about it but simply to give him fair warning.

"I'm telling you right now," I said. "I'm going to beat that scumbag out of the club."

Sandy tried to calm me down, suggested that the other guy (who will remain nameless here) probably thought I was a burglar trying to break into his apartment.

"Bullshit," I said. "I told him exactly what I was doing. For Christ's sake . . . I was carrying a thirty-foot flag."

Sandy was a good and reasonable man, and he didn't want to see the situation get out of control. Part of his role as president of the club was to serve as mediator in disputes between members.

"Come on," he said. "Let's go up together. We'll see if we can straighten this out."

So we went back upstairs and knocked on the door.

"Who is it?" he growled.

"It's me: Sandy."

There was a pause. "Oh, okay, Chief. I'll let you in."

Another pause as he fumbled with the dead bolt. Then the door swung open and there stood this bear of a man, half-naked, covered with tattoos, fire in his eyes . . . and a nine-millimeter pistol in his hand. He started to smile when he saw Sandy, but the moment his eyes locked on me, he became enraged again.

"Chuck!" he howled, killing any doubt that the drugs had rendered him incapable of recognizing the difference between a stranger and a fellow Hells Angel. I knew what was coming, but there was no room for evasive action. This was a shitty tenement with three-foot hall-ways. I was a sitting duck. "You motherfucker!" He raised the gun and put the barrel within a few inches of my face. I lunged to the side just as he pulled the trigger. There was a flash of light, a deafening explosion, and then I felt something warm flowing down my cheek.

Am I dead? Did this cranked-up son of a bitch just kill me? Un-fucking-believable!

I stumbled back down the hallway as Sandy tried to wrestle the gun away from him. *Bam! Bam! Bam!* Three more shots were fired. I staggered down the stairs and out into the street, where Bert, John the Baptist, and Lightfoot were hanging out.

"Jesus," Bert said. "Are you okay, Chuck?"

I looked at my reflection in a first-floor window. The bullet had missed my head, but I'd been so close to the gun when it discharged that I'd sustained some pretty severe flash burns on my face, which now looked like a roasted red pepper.

"Do I look all right?" I answered. "That crazy motherfucker just tried to shoot me."

"Why?"

"How the hell should I know? I was just trying to hang the flag and he went nuts."

That was all John the Baptist needed to hear. "That motherfucker!" he said. "Let's go upstairs."

So I went back with John. We got to the apartment, and the door was open. We saw Sandy standing there with the gun in his back pocket. Just as Sandy turned to face us, the other member spotted me and John. "Get the fuck out of my house!" he screamed, and again he picked up the bowie knife.

John had known this guy longer than I had and knew what a dangerous man he could be, especially with a twelve-inch knife in his hand. John and I looked at each other and then bolted for the exit, getting stuck in the doorway for a second before stumbling outside. Once there, however, we were both pissed.

Sandy followed us out and tried to play the role of peacemaker: "Let him sleep it off. He promised to stay in his room all night."

I decided, at least for the moment, to let go of the anger I was feeling. It was the Fourth of July, after all. A day of celebration.

"All right," I said. "But this ain't over yet. And if he shows his face at this party, I'm going to hurt him."

So I went inside and cleaned up. Then I resumed preparations for the party. Everything seemed to be cool for a while. We had a big crowd, a great barbecue, lots of good music. Around nine o'clock I took a stroll over to an empty parking lot that had been transformed into a barbecue pit. We called this area, which was used by the club, the O.K. Corral, because it was where brothers went to settle their disagreements. If you had a beef with someone and you couldn't come to an agreement with words, then you went outside to the O.K. Corral and ended the dispute with your fists. Just like in the Old West.

The Corral on this night, though, was a happy, festive place, at the center of which was a giant roasted pig. I was standing near the barbecue pit, talking with a few friends, when, out of the corner of my eye, guess who I saw? Bingo! The guy who had tried to blow my head off. I was furious. This asshole was supposed to be locked up for the night, and here he was, a few feet away from me, acting like nothing had happened. There was no way I could let him get away with it. I didn't care that he was nearly twice my size. And I didn't care that we were supposed to be brothers. He had tried to kill me, and he didn't seem the least bit sorry about it. So I walked over and asked him what he thought he was doing. With a stupid grin he said, "Getting something to eat. What's it to you?"

Okay . . . that's the way it's going to be.

Within five minutes the O.K. Corral had been cleared of all civilians. Only a handful of club members remained, along with a nasty rottweiler that belonged to an Angel named Ginzo. The dog ran loose within the confines of the Corral at night, to guard and protect our clubhouse. Right now, though, he sat quietly at Ginzo's side, just another spectator waiting for blood. He was going to get it, too. It was just a matter of whose blood would be spilled. To an outsider, I suppose, I seemed the most likely candidate to sustain serious injuries. My opponent was much bigger, stronger, and, well . . . crazier. But I knew how to fight.

"Let's get it on!" he growled, pointing a meaty finger at me.

"Wait a minute, man," I said. He stopped, confused. "You got a gun on you?"

"No!"

"You got a knife on you?"

"No!"

Before he could take another breath, I hit him with the hardest right hand I could muster. The force of the blow drove him several feet backward. I hit him again before he could regain his balance, sending him crashing to the ground. There was no way I was going to take a chance on letting this guy get up, so I jumped on top of him and began flailing away, crushing his face with a series of punches.

"Pull a gun on me, huh? You motherfucker!"

I was still throwing punches when I felt something tearing at the back of my leg, ripping my pants. Then I heard barking and snarling and realized what it was.

"Jesus, Ginzo! Get that fucking dog off me!"

Ginzo and the others jumped in and pulled the dog away (he didn't ordinarily attack anyone in the club—he'd been trained to recognize us—but I guess he smelled blood and just couldn't help himself). Then they pulled me away. As my opponent was lifted to his feet, bloodied and dazed, I let him know this was just the beginning.

"You come back here tomorrow and we'll do it again," I said. "And we'll do it every day until you're gone."

As it turned out, he did come back the next day, if only to hear the verdict of a hastily arranged meeting of our membership. Much to my chagrin, it was decided that he would not be dismissed from the club but rather merely suspended for an indefinite period of time. He surrendered his patch in front of everyone and then asked for my forgiveness. It was the drugs, he said. They'd made him behave like an animal. Under normal circumstances, he would never have pulled a gun or a knife on me, and he regretted everything that had happened.

My response?

"Bullshit," I said. "Every man is responsible for his own actions, including taking drugs."

He offered me his hand and I pushed it away, even as he promised not to return to the club or to accept his patch until I found it in my heart to forgive him.

A few weeks later I went out to San Jose, California, to take part in that charter's ten-year anniversary celebration. While there I got into a conversation with the legendary Big Albert, one of the original members of the Oakland Hells Angels. Word of my fight with a fellow New York Hells Angel had spread quickly (and not entirely accurately), and Albert wanted to know exactly what had happened.

"The guy tells you to get out of his house and you beat him up?" Albert asked. "Kind of harsh, don't you think?"

"Is that what you heard?" I responded. "Man, he pulled a gun on me. He tried to kill me."

"What? I didn't hear that part of it," Albert said. "Then fuck that piece of shit. He's never welcome in the Oakland clubhouse again."

You have to understand that such a proclamation, coming from one of the most respected men in the history of the Hells Angels, carried tremendous weight. If Albert said you weren't welcome in Oakland, well, then you really weren't welcome in the club.

Ironically, just a few minutes later, as we were still sitting around talking, the telephone rang. Albert answered.

"Yeah, San Jose clubhouse." There was a pause. Albert rolled his eyes. "Hold on, man. He's right here. You'd better tell him yourself."

I took the phone. On the other end was Brendan, a New York City Hells Angel.

"We just voted him back in. I thought you should know."

"Oh, really? Well, tell him I'm taking the first plane out in the morning and, when I get back, he and I are going to dance again."

The scene was set for a nasty turf war. I was determined to drive this guy out of the club, to hold him accountable for what he'd done. I couldn't imagine seeing him every day at our clubhouse. One of us had to go.

When I returned to New York, I went straight to the clubhouse, where I made my feelings known to everyone who was there, including the guy who had gotten his patch back.

"You punk motherfucker," I said. "You promised me you'd wait until I gave the okay before you even thought about taking back your patch."

He stammered something about forgiveness, about just wanting to put everything behind us.

"You ain't a Hells Angel to me," I said. "I have no respect for you. You say one word to me and we're fighting again."

But you know what? It never came to that. Albert and the boys from Oakland intervened. They made it clear that this person was no longer welcome in Oakland and that he should not be welcome anywhere else. By the end of the week he had turned in his patch and quit the club. I felt vindicated by his departure. Unfortunately, though I would never lay eyes on him again, he would resurface about a year later. And he would indeed hurt me, without even throwing a punch.

16

100 Hells Angels Members Arrested in Drug Sweep
—Headline in *The New York Times*, May 3, 1985

MAYBE I SHOULD HAVE SEEN IT COMING. I'VE ALWAYS BEEN A LITTLE SUS-
picious of happiness, and my life, in the spring of 1985, was almost
too good to be true. Certainly it was better than I'd ever imagined it
might be when I was a kid growing up without a father in New Rochelle.

Although we were still legally divorced Kathy and I had done a
commendable job of patching up our relationship. She'd bought a
house on Davenport Avenue (a modest wood-frame ranch that I'd
spend many years and tens of thousands of dollars transforming into
a showcase . . . with a stone-and-brick facade and marble throughout), and we were in the process of making a home there. A traditional home, with a mom and dad and a beautiful daughter. I suppose
I was somewhat naive. I thought I could have all that despite my
affiliation—which had now become prominent—with the Hells Angels.

I'd left the New York chapter in November of 1984 to start the New
York Nomads chapter of the Hells Angels. There was no animosity
involved, just a desire to start something new and to be the person
in charge. Five others had joined me, including Bert, Lightfoot, and
John the Baptist, my closest friends in the club. This wasn't as difficult a thing as you might imagine. I was a respected officer of the
club, and so all I had to do was make a few courtesy calls. I contacted
the head of the first (and only) Nomads chapter in the world, the
California Nomads; I talked with the president of the New York chap-

ter, Sandy Alexander, and with representatives of the other charters in New York State (Binghamton, Troy, and Rochester). There was little or no resistance. Starting a new charter isn't such a big deal and in fact is encouraged because it allows the club to grow, provided the people initiating the move are already members of the club.

As it happened, the New York Nomads were born without incident, and I knew right away it was a good decision. I liked the idea of not being tied to a specific region, of being able to wander and do what I wanted (within the parameters of the Hells Angels bylaws, of course).

It really never occurred to me that raising my profile within the Hells Angels might not be the smartest thing to do, that by starting our own charter and assuming the role of an officer I'd likely be the target of considerable interest should the proverbial shit hit the fan. I never looked at it that way, never considered all the ramifications. Sure, I liked to fight once in a while and I'd been arrested. But that hadn't hurt my career any. In fact, my bodyguard business was booming. I was getting calls to do more stunt work. I was making a good living. I was happy.

In late April of 1985 I traveled to Tokyo with Bert and eighteen other Hells Angels on what amounted to a recruiting trip. For years a thriving motorcycle club there had repeatedly expressed an interest in starting a Japanese chapter of the Hells Angels, so the purpose of our mission was to check these guys out, meet with them, talk with them, see if they were up to our standards. If we liked what we saw, we had the power to grant them a charter, right on the spot. I knew before we even left that it wasn't likely to work out, that the cultural differences would probably be insurmountable. There had long been Hells Angels chapters in other parts of the world—in Australia, Europe, even Africa—but there were none in Asia. Our hope was that this Japanese club would be the first.

Unfortunately, it didn't work out. Not that they were bad guys or anything. It's just that they had a way of looking at the world that didn't exactly mesh with the typical perspective of the Hells Angels. I realized the venture was doomed the first time I saw two men in Tokyo holding hands as they walked down a street. In Japanese culture, we were told, that sort of display of affection is perfectly normal, acceptable behavior and is not seen as a reflection on one's sexuality. Well, that may be, but I have to tell you: there is absolutely no chance that any Hells Angel is ever going to prance hand in hand with another guy. Call it homophobic; call it narrow-minded; call it whatever the hell you want to call it. It simply is not going to happen. Case closed. End of story. No Hells Angels chapter in Japan.

I had planned to return to the United States within a week or so, but those plans changed on May 2, as Bert and I sat in our hotel room and watched a remarkable scene unfold on television. There, flickering on the screen, was videotape of a massive federal assault on the Hells Angels' 3d Street clubhouse. There were nearly 200 FBI agents with automatic weapons, drug-sniffing dogs, tanks . . . everything needed to fight a war. We stared wide-eyed as they broke the door down, barged in, and began tearing the clubhouse apart. The reporter's narration explained that this raid was the culmination of a three-year investigation (dubbed "Rough Rider") into the Hells Angels and "associates" allegedly involved in the manufacturing, sale, and distribution of drugs, most notably methamphetamine and cocaine.

It was an astounding revelation to me, and not merely because I'd personally done nothing wrong. You see, no undercover law enforcement official had ever infiltrated the ranks of the Hells Angels—the bond is simply too tight, the organization too vigilant, for that ever to happen. Strangers are not welcome and certainly not trusted. There are, however, other motorcycle clubs whose members occasionally get in trouble and quickly turn to the easiest way out: by working as informants. Apparently, we later discovered, some of the Hells Angels had befriended a guy from a club down south, obviously without knowing that he was a rat for the feds. This guy would go to different places, meet with members or friends from different chapters, arrange various deals involving the sale of narcotics, and each party would say to the other, "Don't tell anyone about this." Meanwhile, anyone who was stupid enough to cut a deal with this rat quickly found himself under a heavy blanket of suspicion. Phones were tapped; homes were placed under surveillance. For three years this went on and nobody associated with the Hells Angels had the slightest idea it was happening.

Now, I'm not going to insult you and suggest that out of the thousands of Hells Angels around the world there aren't some people who, for their own personal gain and profit, sell drugs on the side. There may be. But, as I've said, it's not something that is organized or endorsed by the club. As for the guilt or innocence of others swept up in the Rough Rider sting, I'll offer no opinion one way or the other. I'll speak only of my own situation. I did nothing wrong, nothing illegal. In fact, even as I watched the raid on CNN from my hotel room in Tokyo I wasn't terribly concerned. I mean I felt bad that it was happening and I was worried about some of my brothers, but I didn't expect that I'd be personally targeted by the investigation.

It wasn't until I called home that night to speak with Kathy that I discovered just how deeply I was involved.

"Your friends just left," Kathy said, her voice shaking. "They tore the place apart."

Here's what happened: Within minutes after the raid on the 3d Street clubhouse, more than two dozen armed law enforcement officers, representing the FBI, local police, and the Drug Enforcement Agency, descended on my family's home in New Rochelle. They blocked the driveway and nearby intersections and launched an assault that was so forceful, so intimidating, that you'd have thought Manuel Noriega was holed up inside. They went through every room, every dresser and cabinet. Worst of all, they cornered my daughter in an upstairs bedroom and filled her head with lies: *Your father isn't the man you think he is. He's a bad man who sells drugs and hurts people.* Then they forcibly moved Kathy and Lisa around the house at gunpoint, as if they were criminals, which of course they weren't.

The sadness I felt at that moment, listening to Kathy cry over the phone, was almost more than I could bear. Here I was, in a hotel room half a world away, and my family was taking the heat for something that had nothing to do with them. I envisioned Lisa, only fourteen years old, with a gun to the back of her head, and I wanted to cry.

I told Kathy there had been some sort of mistake, that I hadn't broken any laws, and that I'd certainly never been involved in the trafficking of narcotics. She believed me, too. Kathy knew how I felt about drugs, and she knew I hadn't been stockpiling weapons around the house, which is the sort of thing you'd expect from a major drug dealer. The cops found nothing at our home. Absolutely nothing. And yet . . .

"I knew something like this would happen," Kathy said. "I just knew it."

True enough. Although Kathy believed I'd never have anything to do with the use or sale of drugs, she had long expressed concern that my involvement with the Hells Angels would eventually get me in trouble. That's why we'd gotten divorced in the first place, and even now, when we were in the process of reconciling, she fretted incessantly that somehow the club would hurt me. And if it hurt me, it would hurt her. I'd repeatedly promised her that nothing would ever happen, that she'd never be touched or affected by the club in any way. But I was wrong. Kathy's prediction came true. To this very day I feel bad about that. I embarrassed her, I embarrassed Lisa. . . . I embarrassed my entire neighborhood. My family's privacy was invaded, their world turned upside down.

Don't confuse what I'm saying with an admission of guilt. I'm simply saying that I was responsible for hurting the people I loved the most. I should have realized that as an officer of the New York Nomads chapter of the Hells Angels I would be the focus of almost any major criminal investigation into the club's activities. Not because I was directly involved, necessarily, but simply because the cops would figure that, at the very least, I'd have information to offer.

And that's precisely what they were after.

It was all just a game. Think about it—when the feds broke into my home, armed for World War III, they supposedly were looking for me, but they'd had my phones tapped for months, so they knew I wasn't there. They knew exactly where I was. They just wanted to harass my family and piss me off, which they did. The cops also claimed to have a tape of a telephone conversation that allegedly reflected my involvement in the sale of a pound of methamphetamine. Where this information came from I had no idea (and I still don't), because I was never involved in any such conversation. It never happened. Somehow, though, I was charged with conspiracy, and a warrant was issued for my arrest. (All told, the Rough Rider investigation resulted in more than 150 people being indicted, 33 of whom were members of the Hells Angels Motorcycle Club.)

Bert Kittel also had been charged. In fact, I quickly learned, Bert was the person with whom I supposedly had this dubious telephone conversation. For the sake of clarity, I'll reiterate my stance on this subject: I don't know if anyone tried to sell a pound of methamphetamine. If so, it was his private business, his risk to take. I know only that I never talked to anyone about any such venture. Moreover, at the time I supposedly was up to my neck in this big drug deal I was in Vancouver, British Columbia, working for Mickey Rourke while he filmed *Year of the Dragon.* There were no phone records from my hotel room corroborating these charges, no records from my home or any other source. It was a sham, an attempt to extort information. I guess the feds figured they'd threaten me with prison time on a trumped-up conspiracy charge and I'd cave in and give them whatever they wanted, despite the fact that I was innocent.

My first concern, however, was Kathy and Lisa.

"We're still legally divorced," I told Kathy. "They have no business searching the house. It's in your name."

That was true enough. Kathy had bought the house in February, and I had yet to move in with her. Before leaving for Japan, however, I had moved most of my stuff out of my apartment and into the garage of Kathy's house, in anticipation of residing there when I returned. As far as the cops were concerned, the presence of my belongings in that house was sufficient evidence that Kathy and I lived together; therefore, they were justified in searching the premises.

"Sit tight," I told Kathy. "Let me talk to a lawyer."

Easier said than done. After all, I didn't know any lawyers in Japan. I didn't speak the language, and I didn't understand the culture. With Kathy's help, I hired a private attorney back in the States and began the long and complicated process of trying to figure out my options.

There weren't many. Of the twenty Hells Angels in our group, eighteen returned to the United States within a week or two of the initial raid. Only Bert and I remained in Japan. We wanted to figure out exactly what charges we'd be facing if and when we returned and what the consequences might be. That, of course, turned out to be another mistake. We were both indicted in absentia, and pretty soon we became the targets of a nationwide manhunt in Japan. And let me tell you, it ain't easy for a couple of American Hells Angels to go unnoticed in Japan. Bert and I couldn't very well remain at our hotel, so we had to turn to some of our new Japanese biker friends for help. I was overwhelmed, frankly, by the generosity and kindness extended to us by some of these people. After all, we had as much as told them that they weren't Hells Angels material, and yet they weren't resentful in the least. They knew we were in trouble and they wanted to offer assistance—no questions asked. They gave us food, shelter, clothing. I stayed with one family; Bert stayed with another. It was a wild and fascinating time.

Bert and I would meet every few days, maybe once a week, to pool our resources and call our lawyers and families back in the United States. This (in the dark days before cell phones) was an expensive and complicated process. There were a limited number of public places that allowed international phone calls, and all of these required prepayment with either a credit card, cash, or a certified check. We'd be allotted a certain number of minutes, and when the time was up the line simply went dead.

To avoid being conspicuous, we tried to keep the calls short. Bert once even tried to disguise the fact that he was an American fugitive—with hilarious results. I was standing on the corner of a busy Tokyo intersection when I saw someone who looked vaguely like Bert on the other side of the street. Except this guy was wearing thick black glasses, a white button-down-collar shirt, a tie, and a crisp pair of trousers. His hair was cut short and parted on the side; a dab of gel held every lock in place. I couldn't help but smile. There I was, in a guinea T-shirt and jeans, a head taller than everyone else, and Bert was dressed up like Clark Kent!

He scurried nervously across the street and tried to walk right past me, but I quickly caught up with him.

"What's the problem, man?"

"Jesus Christ," he said. "I spotted you a mile away. You're going to get us caught."

"Yeah, Bert," I said, laughing out loud. "No one's going to figure you for a guy on the run."

The longer we stayed in Japan, the more difficult it became to resolve our situation. We wanted to simply get on a plane, go home, and surrender to American authorities after we landed. But we were fugitives now, so there was little chance of our getting out of the country without being captured and detained, and God only knew how long we might rot in some Japanese prison. We were running out of options. Our visas had expired and warrants had been issued for our arrest. I was homesick as hell and tired of acting like a fugitive. Kathy was pleading with me to surrender and come home. My lawyer, too. I even went so far as to talk with a few of my friends back home who were cops. They also urged me to turn myself in.

"Just give up," they said. "You're only making it worse."

"But I didn't do anything."

"Well, you're sure acting like you're guilty."

They had a point. Eventually, after nearly two months in Japan, Bert and I decided to turn ourselves in. But we had a very specific plan. We would conduct an interview with a reporter from CNN, during which we would explain our side of the story, and then we would surrender to authorities at the U.S. Embassy in Tokyo. Our goal— our hope—was that by turning ourselves in to American authorities we would quickly be extradited back to the United States, where we would then be granted bail. If there was any jail time at all, it would be minimal.

The interview was conducted at a hotel. The reporter walked in with a cameraman, set up his equipment, and began reviewing his notes. I'm sure he felt it was some sort of a professional coup, getting this exclusive interview with two American desperadoes. Before asking a single question, though, the reporter looked at me, then at Bert, then at his clipboard. He seemed confused.

"There's some kind of misinformation here," he said. "The police report identifies one of you as being an amputee." He wiggled his fingers. "You know . . . missing a hand."

Back in the States, Bert's prosthetic preference was a hook attached to his stump. Like some relic from the days when pirates sailed the high seas. He wasn't stupid, though. Bert figured that as a fugitive, he couldn't just wander around Tokyo with a hook on his hand without attracting a fair amount of attention. So, shortly after arrest warrants had been issued, we went to a novelty store, like a Halloween place, and bought one of those fake rubber hands, the kind with artificial dried blood and cuts all over it. Once we removed the blood with nail polish remover, it actually looked like a real hand. It had fingernails, pores, hair . . . everything. Then we cut off the end of the hand, slipped it over Bert's stump, and held it in place with electrical tape.

Now, as Bert sat on the couch, his fake hand rested neatly and comfortably on his lap, fingers intertwined with the fingers of his real hand. I could see why the reporter was perplexed.

"Is the information wrong?" the reporter asked.

Bert smiled. "Nah . . . that's me." He grasped the rubber hand with his good hand and removed it in a single swift motion.

As the fake hand jumped out of Bert's sleeve with a *pop!* the reporter practically fell off his chair. "Holy shit!" he yelled.

"Sorry," said Bert, tucking the fake hand back into his sleeve.

"That's okay," the reporter said, laughing nervously. "Can we get started now?"

So we did the interview, presented what we believed to be the truth (we denied the accusations), and then asked the crew from CNN to accompany us to the U.S. Embassy. We wanted irrefutable proof that we were surrendering of our own free will. We didn't want anyone to be able to say that we had been captured. But officials at the embassy wanted no part of us. After discussing the matter for more than an hour, they told us we were free to leave.

"Wait a minute," I said to one of them. "Did you call the Japanese police?"

"Yes," he said. "We did."

"Fine. Then I want you to turn us over."

And they did. Our own embassy officials walked us out, handed us over to the Japanese authorities, and immediately we were hand-cuffed, thrown into two separate vans (to make sure we didn't corroborate stories, I presume), and brought to a local precinct station somewhere in Tokyo. I was put in one interview room; Bert was placed in another. I sat in a chair, my hands and legs shackled, as a Japanese cop interrogated me for the better part of three hours. He kept circling the room slowly, occasionally stopping to bark out a question, which would then be translated into English by an interpreter.

"How long have you been in the country?"

"Where have you been hiding?"

"Who helped you?"

Some of the questions I answered; others I ignored. The interpreter wrote everything down. At the end of the session, the cop took a seat, looked over the interpreter's pad, turned it to face me, and growled a few more words.

"Sign it," the interpreter said.

I looked at the pad, which was covered with Japanese symbols, and laughed. Then I slid it back across the table.

"No thanks."

The cop's face immediately flushed red. He barked at me again.

"You said these things," the interpreter said. "So you must sign."

"I don't care what I said. I'm not signing anything. I can't even read this."

"These are your words," the cop explained through the interpreter. "Sign. Now!"

"No chance. I want a lawyer."

The interpreter said something to the cop, who scowled and walked out of the room. They let me sit there a while longer before a handful of armed guards came in and led me out of the building and into another van, where Bert was already waiting.

"What happened?" he asked.

"They asked me a bunch of questions."

Bert nodded. "Me, too. They try to get you to sign something?"

"Uh-huh."

"Me, too." He paused. "You do it?"

"No way, brother."

Bert smiled. "Me, neither. Fuck 'em."

Handcuffed together, we rode through the crowded streets of Tokyo for nearly an hour before finally arriving at our destination: the Tokyo Correctional Facility. We'd been told at the precinct house that we were going to be detained only overnight and that the next day we'd be flying home to the United States. But as we shuffled into this place, with its thirty-foot gray walls and bare bulbs and 400-pound sumo wrestler guards, I began to have my doubts.

"Jesus," I said to Bert. "What did we get ourselves into?" Before the words had even escaped my mouth one of the guards got right in my face and yelled, "Quiet! No talking!"

For some reason this seemed funny to me, and I started laughing.

"No laughing!" the guard screamed.

But I couldn't help it. The whole situation was ludicrous. I was in jail for something I hadn't done, in a country where I didn't speak the language. It seemed like a practical joke.

They took my fingerprints without incident. Bert, however, was a different story. As a guard grabbed Bert's wrist and tried to roll his fingers over the ink pad, the prosthesis began to leak air. A high-pitched whine filled the room as the hand deflated into a lifeless lump of rubber, prompting the guard to leap back in fear.

"Oh, it's no big deal," said Bert, removing the hand. "See?"

The guard just stared in amazement.

They gave us khaki jumpsuits. They bagged our clothes and meager possessions. Then they took Bert in one direction and me in another. As they led us away, I looked back at Bert.

"See you tomorrow, brother."

"Okay," he said.

We had no idea how wrong we were.

17

I DIDN'T SEE BERT THE NEXT DAY. OR THE NEXT WEEK, FOR THAT MATTER. IN fact, I spent four months in that prison and not once did I lay eyes on Bert Kittel. We were the only Americans in the entire prison, and they made a point of separating us—I think this was less a matter of preventing us from rehearsing our story than simply a way to make our incarceration more unpleasant. And it worked.

I was taken to the fourth floor (Bert, I later discovered, was on the third floor) and placed in a tiny concrete cell. All around me, on both sides of the corridor, were Japanese inmates, some crammed four to a cell. But I had a cell to myself. The cell had a concrete bunk (covered with a two-inch mattress) and a toilet. Nothing else. A single small window, covered with bars, looked out onto the prison yard, above which rose four massive concrete walls. The entire complex was a giant square.

We stood outside the cell for a moment, and then one of the guards motioned for me to go inside. The other inmates, their faces visible through small windows in their cell doors, stared at me but said nothing. I nodded at the guard and walked into the cell. Instantly the door, made entirely of steel, slid behind me and closed with a tremendous *thud!*

I paced a tight circle around my cell and looked out the window. Other than a few overnights in county jail, I'd never done any time before, and certainly I'd never been in a place like this. This was *prison*. And it was more than a little intimidating.

Man, I'm glad I'm only going to be here a day or so.

The fact that I was still under the impression that my stay at the Tokyo Correctional Facility would be brief helped me avoid the panic and anger that often overwhelms a first-time convict. I was disoriented, yes, but I was confident that the disorientation would be brief and that soon I'd be back in New York, talking with my lawyers, arranging bail, preparing to beat the charges that had been unfairly leveled at me. By this time it was evening, so I took my prison-issue bedroll, spread it out on the bunk, and went to sleep.

Just one night . . . just one night.

I woke to the sound of a breakfast tray being slid through a small door into my cell. That was the first indication of trouble. I wouldn't be taking my meals with the general population. As a matter of fact, I'd be spending almost every moment in my cell.

After five days of this routine I was ready to explode. I'd press my face against the door and yell for Bert, just to see if he was nearby, but he never answered. Only the guards responded, and they weren't happy. Twice in that first week I was allowed to meet with an interpreter.

"I want to speak to my lawyer," I said. "I want to get the fuck out of this place and go home."

He just smiled and nodded. "Yes, yes. But not yet. It takes time, Mr. Charles."

Toward the end of the week they brought me to the prison barbershop, for another step in the indoctrination process. Unlike American convicts, who generally are allowed to wear their hair any way they like while incarcerated, Japanese inmates are subjected to a military-style shearing. Part of the rationale is hygienic, I'm sure, but mostly it's about degradation and control. The most active and notorious gang in Japanese culture is the *Yakuza*, which, for lack of a better term, can be likened to the American Mafia. Members of the *Yakuza* are identifiable by their long permed hair, tattoos, and, most notably, their hands. You see, part of the initiation process involves the self-amputation of a pinkie finger. There's not much prison officials can do about the hands of the *Yakuza*, but in every other way the gang members are robbed of their identity. Their heads are shaved; their tattoos are covered at all times with long sleeves and long pants. In a Japanese prison, everyone looks the same and is treated the same: like shit.

I wore a pompadour at the time, and I wasn't about to have it cut off by some Japanese butcher. So when they brought me to the barbershop, I refused to get into the chair.

"Haircut!" the guard shouted in butchered English.

I gestured toward the barber, who was grinning like an idiot. "You're out of your fucking mind if you think I'm going to let that guy put a hand on me."

"Haircut!"

"No!"

"Haircut!"

"Fuck you!"

"Haircut!"

Soon there were more guards, but since they didn't try to overpower me and force me to get a haircut, I had an idea that their options were limited. Maybe, I thought, the rules were different for foreign prisoners. As it turned out, I was right. An interpreter was brought in to resolve the dispute, and he handled it masterfully. He asked me, politely, to take a seat in the barber's chair.

"I ain't getting no fuckin' baldie," I said. "I'll fight every guy here if I have to."

He laughed. "Oh, no. Just a little."

So we compromised. I sat in the chair and let the barber do some minor work. In that way, the guards were allowed to save face and I was allowed to save most of my hair.

In the middle of the second week I received a visit from a woman representing the American embassy. She did not have good news. Because of a post–World War II treaty between the United States and Japan, she explained, extradition was a slow and convoluted process.

"Meaning what?" I asked.

"Meaning . . . you're going to be here for a while."

"How long?"

She sighed. "At least a month. Maybe more."

"You've gotta be kidding?!"

"I'm sorry," she said. "I know this is difficult, but we're doing everything we can. We'll send you magazines, books, newspapers . . . anything to help you pass the time."

"I don't care about that. Just do me a favor and let my wife know where I am."

I gave her Kathy's phone number and address (I wasn't allowed to make any phone calls myself), and sure enough, the next week I got a letter in the mail. It was from Kathy. She urged me to be strong, to think often of her and Lisa. Most important of all, she said, "Don't do anything stupid." That letter, and subsequent letters, kept me going, because I'll tell you, it's easy to go nuts in prison—especially a Japanese prison. There's no messing around over there. Japanese prison time is serious, hard, lonely time.

The worst prison in the United States is like a hotel compared to the best prison in Japan. When you're a convict in Japan, you get away with nothing. There's no television, no radio, no games. The guards have complete control, and they humiliate you at every opportunity. There is no freedom at all, no individuality. There's a foot-wide rubber path that runs throughout the prison, and every inmate who leaves his cell is expected to follow it precisely. (The path also serves another purpose: because it's made of rubber, it allows the guards to patrol stealthily, twenty-fours a day, seven days a week.) While moving from one place to another there is no talking whatsoever among inmates. Unlike in American prisons, the guards' control is absolute and unquestioned. Prison is meant to be a frightening prospect, something to be avoided at all costs. It must work pretty well, too, because they don't have much crime in Japan. And they don't have many guns. At least, not compared to the United States.

Because I was an American, my situation was even worse. I was locked down twenty-three hours a day. For one hour each day I was taken out of my cell and placed in an outdoor cage—like a kennel—where I could do sit-ups, push-ups, shadowbox, walk in a small circle. Even then I was segregated from the general population. The Japanese prisoners would be in huge caged areas, thirty of them together, playing baseball, soccer, whatever. But I'd be all alone. While I'd go through my own little fitness routine, the other prisoners would point and stare. Some would shout, "Rocky!" and the others would all laugh.

And then there was the music. Every day we woke to the same song played through the prison sound system: "Over the Rainbow," by Judy Garland. Every day, the same fucking song! I later told Liza Minnelli that her mother's voice woke me each morning, which we both thought was kind of funny, although it didn't seem it at the time.

Once a week we were allowed to bathe; the first time was quite an experience for me. They brought me into an area divided into three rooms. In the center room was a giant bathtub filled with water, along with a bucket and stool (I couldn't see what was in the other three rooms—not yet, anyway). I'm not that big a guy, but compared to the Japanese prisoners I was huge, and I found myself wondering, *How the fuck are those little guys going to get into this tub?*

But I really didn't care. I undressed, climbed in, and started soaping up. I was having a good old time until I looked out through the window of the gates, to where some of the other prisoners were waiting their turn, and noticed they were all staring, pointing, murmuring something to one another. Then a guard came by, did a double take when he saw me, and went absolutely crazy. He rumbled into the room, started screaming at me in Japanese, and pulled me out of the tub. I didn't know what was happening until the guard led me into one of the other rooms, where I saw two naked Japanese inmates sitting together on their stools, soaping each other's backs, and carefully rinsing with water from their buckets.

Suddenly it hit me: The water in the tub was communal water, intended to be shared by the entire prison population. I was supposed to fill my bucket from the tub and go into one of the other rooms. Instead, I had treated it as my personal Jacuzzi! No wonder everyone was so upset. But what could they do? Punish me? I was already in solitary confinement, locked up twenty-three hours a day. How much worse could it get?

The answer to that question depended on your situation and your ability to cope with stress and loneliness. I'll give you two examples. I remember one night waking up to the sound of breaking glass and screaming guards and inmates. People were in a panic, running around, yelling Japanese shit, and I had no idea what was happening. Then my bunk started shaking and banging and bouncing around the floor, like that scene at the end of *The Exorcist*, and suddenly I realized what was happening: We were in the middle of an earthquake!

Oh, great. We're gonna die like dogs trapped in a cage. . . .

I stood there in my cell, shitting pickles, thinking the whole place was about to collapse around us and that I was as good as dead. But then, as quickly as it had started, the quake stopped and everything went back to normal. The next day I found out that hundreds of people had died in the towns surrounding the prison. We'd been lucky.

The other example occurred early in my stay, about three weeks after I arrived, when the guards put a new inmate in the cell next to mine. I saw them bring him in, a lanky white man with thick blond hair, and instantly my spirits soared. I'd been something of a wreck up to that point, to be perfectly honest, and the isolation and boredom were really starting to get to me. The sight of another Anglo, someone who might perhaps speak English, prompted a flood of emotion. I'd never even met this man, but suddenly he seemed like the answer to a prayer.

We whispered to each other through our doors, and I soon found out we had a few things in common. Yes, he did speak English (better than most Americans, in fact). He was from Switzerland and, like me, had been imprisoned on drug charges. I told him I was a member of the Hells Angels, and that needed no further explanation. The Hells Angels were very active in Switzerland, he said: "They seem like good guys."

At first, I thought this guy would be okay, that he had the temperament to do hard, solitary time. He seemed calm, almost tranquil. But that was hardly the case. The second night he was there, he started to crack. He'd never been to prison, he said, and now he was looking at a twenty-year sentence. He missed his home, his friends, and his family.

"Me, too, buddy," I said. "Hang in there."

The next morning I woke up to the sound of people running. A half-dozen guards suddenly stopped at the cell next to mine. One of them pulled out a key and opened the door, and the others followed him in. I didn't know what was happening, but I had a bad feeling. Maybe, I thought, my neighbor had done something wrong, broken some ridiculous rule, and now he was about to receive a beat-down, But there were no sounds of a struggle emanating from his cell. No yelling, no screaming. Just the muffled conversations of Japanese guards and an occasional *thump*—the sound of too many people in too small a space.

After about five minutes, the guards backed out of the cell, dragging behind them the limp and pallid form of my Swiss neighbor. His eyes were closed, his face bloated. His neck appeared to be covered with a severe red rash. A couple of the guards worked on him for a few minutes. They pumped his chest, tried to breathe life back into him, but he was clearly long gone. One of the guards eventually gave the signal to stop. With no emotion whatsoever, two of the other guards picked up the body and dragged it back into the cell. I heard it hit the floor, and then I saw the guards walk out, talking casually. The last one pulled the door shut behind him.

A good three hours passed before anyone returned. Three hours . . . during which this poor bastard's body lay on the floor of his cell. The interpreter later explained that he'd hung himself with his sheet. How he did this I'm not exactly sure. It took some work to kill yourself in a Japanese prison. He must have tied one end around his throat and the other end around one of the higher bars on his cell. And since that bar wasn't really very high at all, he must have then slumped to the floor and allowed the noose to tighten, somehow ignoring his body's instinct to survive. He had to have done all this in one of the fifteen-minute windows between the guards' rounds.

Yup . . . this was a guy who was serious about taking himself out. And as far as I could tell, he'd be missed by nobody in this prison. He was a statistic. Nothing more.

Not that the place was populated and controlled by nothing but heartless pricks. I don't think that was the case. In any prison there are compassionate guards and sadistic guards. Granted, the sadists usually seem to be in the majority, but in my experience you can find pockets of humanity in even the foulest of dungeons. For example, I'd wake each morning at six to the sound of a knock at my cell. Then the door would be thrown open and two guards would enter the cell. One person was clearly in charge. He would do the talking. The other guard held a book and a pen. This was their way of taking morning roll. You were expected to get on your knees and state your number (never your name). Then your number would be checked off in the logbook and the guards would move on to the next cell.

I was completely ignorant of this routine the first time they came to my cell. I was doing push-ups at the time—I'd crank out at least a thousand every day—and as they entered my cell I jumped up off the floor. I can only imagine what they thought when they saw me— wearing only my gym shorts, breathing like a freight train, my chest puffed out, my face and arms flushed and covered with sweat. The first guard jumped back into the doorway and began screaming in Japanese. He was obviously scared.

"Sorry," I said, being very careful to keep my hands low, so as not to prompt an attack.

With the two guards was an interpreter. "Mr. Charles," he said politely. "No stand . . . kneel. And wear your uniform."

The next day I was wearing my uniform, but I forgot the part about kneeling. They just shook their heads. And as for saying my number . . . well, that was hopeless. After a few days, though, another interpreter, with whom I developed a pretty good rapport, began teaching me how to recite my number in Japanese.

"It's easy, Mr. Charles: *Sunjuniban.*"

"*Sun* . . . what?"

He sighed, then walked to the window, pointed outside. "Sun," he said.

"Okay . . . sun," I repeated.

"You," he said, pointing at my chest. "You."

I nodded. "You."

He smiled. "Good. Sun . . . you . . ." He tapped his leg lightly. "Knee."

"Knee," I repeated. "Got it."

"Sun-you-knee . . ." he said. Then he added, *"Bon."* (Guess he couldn't think of an image for the final syllable.) He paused. *"Sun-juniban."*

I hesitated, ran the word and images through my mind, and gave it a try: *"Sunjuniban."*

"Very good, Mr. Charles."

I messed it up badly on the fourth day, but on the fifth day, when the two guards entered my cell, I was on my knees, hands at my side, as mandated by prison rules.

"Sunjuniban," I said.

The first guard's eyes lit up and a huge smile crossed his face. Then he did something I thought was extraordinary: he bowed. *"Sunjuniban,"* he said again.

And I bowed in return.

There was another guard who tried to teach me Japanese, and I tried to teach him English. Not formally, of course. It was just a matter of trying to communicate. Some guards knew I couldn't speak Japanese and didn't even bother trying to talk with me. Others did. This particular guard wondered why I was in prison. He looked at me quizzically, then made a motion with his hand, as if injecting something into his arms.

"Oh . . . you think I'm a drug dealer, huh?" I shook my head.

The guard then put an invisible cigarette to his mouth and pretended to take a long drag. "Weed?" he asked in fractured English.

"Uh-uh," I said. And then I tried to explain to him who I was and what had happened, how I'd been set up because of my affiliation with a prominent motorcycle club. He just started at me blankly, as if he had no idea what I was talking about. So I unbuttoned my shirt and showed him my Hells Angels tattoo.

"American Yakuza," I said, pointing to my chest.

"Ohhhhhh," the guard said with a smile. Then he raised his hand, thumb up, forefinger extended, like a child playing cops and robbers with an imaginary gun. "Bang-bang!"

"Yeah . . . bang-bang. That's me."

I wrote to Kathy and Lisa every day, even though I was allowed to mail only three envelopes a week. I'd take my time, compose long, rambling letters, then stuff them all into a single package (on the envelope I'd draw pictures of my bike, my car, my family, my house— on one I even drew a picture of me busting through the prison walls on my motorcycle). They did the same in return. Mail meant everything to me—I corresponded not only with my wife and daughter but also with my mother, my sisters, and several of the clients I'd befriended through my bodyguard service: Mickey Rourke, Sean Penn, Liza, Cher. Communicating with my codefendant proved interesting. I asked the interpreter one day if he could hand-deliver a letter to Bert: "Just walk it down to the third floor," I said.

But the interpreter shook his head. "I can't accept that," he explained. "You must mail."

"Mail? He's right here in this building."

Crazy as it sounds, the only way I could communicate with Bert was to write a letter, mail it, and wait for it to come back to the prison. Weeks passed before we finally exchanged letters and I was encouraged to see that Bert was faring no worse than I was.

"Brother, this place is crazy," he wrote. "Maybe we should have just gone home."

No doubt. But hindsight is twenty-twenty, right? For the most part Bert and I avoided self-pity in our letters. We shared jokes and stories—I told him all about my experience in the bathing area, which he thought was a scream—and generally just tried to elevate each other's spirits. We knew we had to stay strong, for there was no telling how long we might be there.

The answer came with no advance notice. One day the interpreter walked into my cell, clapped his hands, and said, "You go home today, Mr. Charles."

I wasted no time gathering my bedroll and a few articles of clothing. I stuffed everything into a bag and said, "Let's go!"

When I reached the discharge area, I was amused (not surprised) to discover that I'd received many articles in the mail that never made their way upstairs to my cell, including a metal container of chocolate chip cookies and a life-size inflatable doll—a sex toy with an open mouth and everything—both courtesy of Mickey Rourke. There was a short note stuffed into the box. I read it while shedding my prison uniform and dressing in my old, familiar clothes:

Hey, Chuck. You don't have to do anything with her if you don't want to. But maybe you can at least share a cup of tea. Love and respect, Mickey.

The guards seemed amused by the doll, so I stuffed it back into the box and gave it to them. "Here . . . have a party, fellas."

After I'd finished changing and signing my discharge papers, I was led into another room, where six U.S. federal marshals were waiting.

"Hey, isn't this a surprise," I said sarcastically. "I thought there would be more of you."

Most of the marshals seemed pretty cool. They'd been through this sort of thing before, and it was merely their job. Some even laughed at my little joke. But there was one guy who had a real attitude. He marched right up to me, looked at my T-shirt, emblazoned with the American flag, and scowled. "Take that off," he said. "You don't deserve to wear it."

"Oh, there's always one in the group, isn't there?" I said.

One of the other marshals stepped between us and led me away. "Be cool, Chuck," he said. "We don't want any trouble. This is a long trip."

They offered me another shirt and I agreed to wear it. I was tired and I wanted only to get home. I had neither the energy nor the inclination to fight with some egotistical federal agent over something as trivial as my shirt. Anyway, it wasn't like I had much of a choice. My wrists were handcuffed and shackled to my waist; my ankles were shackled, too. So, before getting in the van and driving to the airport, they pulled a sweatshirt over my T-shirt.

It was a commercial flight, completely packed. We sat in first class, which was kind of nice, considering it was a fourteen-hour trip. I tried to be on my best behavior, but some things proved irresistible. Like when the flight attendant stopped at our row and said, in a sweet and perky tone, "Can I get you gentlemen anything?"

I smiled and pulled back my sweatshirt, revealing the handcuffs and shackles.

"Yeah, honey . . . how about a hacksaw?"

As the flight attendant's eyes bugged out, one of the marshals reached over and pulled the hem of my sweatshirt back down. "Knock it off, tough guy."

In general, I was treated like John Dillinger or the most dangerous man alive. Each time I went to the bathroom, I was accompanied by no fewer than three marshals. "Jesus," I said. "What am I going to do—jump out the window?" I peed with only one hand free and my wrists still shackled to my waist. Try that sometime. It's quite a challenge, especially when the plane hits a pocket of turbulence.

When we landed at Kennedy Airport, the plane stopped out on the tarmac and was quickly surrounded by police cruisers and ominous black federal vans. I was led out the door and down a flight of stairs and pushed into one of the cars. As we pulled away, two helicopters joined the escort. Sirens wailed and lights flashed. Through the windows I could see the plane taxiing back to the terminal, carrying hundreds of people to the waiting arms of their friends and families. Soon enough, I thought, that would be me.

Soon enough.

18

ONCE ON U.S. SOIL I THOUGHT MY SITUATION WOULD BE RESOLVED WITH
relative ease. I couldn't have been more wrong. I was immediately
labeled a danger to the community . . . a risk of flight . . . and re-
manded to Metropolitan Correctional Center in New York without
bail.

If I was Dillinger, Bert must have been Hannibal Lecter, for he was
brought to MCC practically in a state of immobility. In addition to
being handcuffed and shackled, Bert had been wrapped in duct tape.
He could walk only by taking the tiniest of baby steps, and even then
he kept losing his balance and falling, not that anyone cared, I'm sure.
I saw Bert for the first time in four months while I was being finger-
printed—unbeknownst to me, he'd flown out of Tokyo the very same
day.

"Yo, brother," he said. "It's been a long time."

"Good to see you, Bert."

It was the strangest thing—after so many months of being isolated,
prevented from even speaking to each other or passing notes without
using the postal system, Bert and I were now allowed almost unres-
tricted contact. In fact, since we were codefendants, they assigned us
to the same floor, and within a couple days we had become cellmates.

My first reaction to MCC was one of quiet relief. I was processed
and put in the general population. A lot of inmates, especially those
making their first visit to MCC, nearly faint from horror when the
doors to the central portion of the jail are thrown open. It's a vast
canyon of a place, with six giant tiers rising from a common area.
The smell, the noise—it's enough to overwhelm almost anyone. But
after what I'd just been through . . . sitting in a quiet cell twenty-three

hours a day, speaking and hearing almost nothing but Japanese . . . wondering if I'd ever get home again . . . well, suddenly being surrounded by several hundred men didn't seem like such a terrible thing. I saw people watching television, shooting pool, playing cards. I hadn't been there five minutes before I ran into half a dozen of my brothers (there were, as it turned out, more than two dozen Hells Angels scattered around the jail, almost all of them awaiting trial and sentencing for alleged crimes uncovered during the Rough Rider sting). I couldn't help but think, *Man, this is going to be a piece of cake.* That was naive, of course. In time I'd come to hate MCC as much as any other jail.

I called Kathy as soon as I could, and she naturally started to cry on the phone. She'd known exactly when I was arriving and had been waiting to hear from me. She'd already contacted an attorney and said he'd be at MCC first thing in the morning.

"Don't worry," I told her. "We'll get this thing cleared up and I'll be home in no time."

Three days later Bert and I finally met with representatives from the U.S. Attorney's Office. Predictably, deals were flying all over the place. I expected that I'd have to compromise in order to secure bail, if not outright release, but I did not anticipate having to bend over and take it up the ass.

"Look," they said. "We want to know all about the Hells Angels, and we want to know all about the celebrities you work for. Where do they get their drugs from?"

None of this had anything to do with my case. I'd been indicted for making a phone call—a phone call that never took place—and now I was supposed to rat out the guys in my club and everyone who had ever given me a job in Hollywood.

"You know what?" I said. "I don't go home to the Hells Angels at night, and I don't go home with the celebrities I work for. I go home to my family. And I have nothing to say about anyone."

They didn't like that.

"You sure you know what you're doing, Mr. Zito?" one of them said. "We can give you a new identity, a new place to live, a new life. We'll put you in the witness protection program."

"No chance," I said. "I already have a home and a family, and I intend to go back to them as soon as possible."

There was a pause. One of the prosecutors stroked his chin. "And when do you think that will be?" He smiled. "We can keep you here a long time, Chuck. You won't get bail, and it'll be at least another year, maybe more, before your case goes to trial. Are you sure you want to spend that much time in here?"

They had my nuts to the fire, no doubt about it. But the heat only made me more determined, more hostile.

"Go to hell."

They shuffled their papers and called for the guards. "Have it your way," one of the prosecutors said. "Let us know if you change your mind."

Who blinked first? Well, they did. Two weeks after turning down their oh-so-generous offer of a new life in some godforsaken town in the middle of nowhere, I was summoned to a second meeting with prosecutors. This time they had a better offer. All I had to do was plead guilty to conspiracy and they'd give me a year (Bert was offered a three-year sentence). I'd already done four months in Japan, which would have counted toward my sentence. With time off for good behavior, I'd be out in four or five more months. I considered the offer for all of about five seconds.

"Fuck you! I'm not pleading to anything."

The offer remained on the table for a while, and I let it sit there, despite loud and emotional protests from friends and family.

"It's a good offer," my lawyer said. "Take it."

"Please," said Kathy. "Come home."

I know they felt as though they were looking out for my best interests, but they didn't understand. I hadn't done anything wrong. Taking a plea would have been a tacit admission of guilt; I would have been willingly accepting the label of "felon," without even having earned it. The very thought of it made me sick to my stomach.

"The hell with them," I told Kathy one day. "They can't force me to take a plea when I didn't commit a crime. I'll go to trial and beat them. They don't have a goddamn thing on me."

Weeks went by, then months. I was denied bail a second time. Then a third. I grew angrier, more determined to fight back. But then there was a new development. The feds decided to attack on a different front, by appealing to our sense of brotherhood. The two members of the Hells Angels facing the stiffest penalties were Sandy Alexander and Howie Weisbrod, each of whom was looking at as much as forty years—in other words, a life sentence. After a few months, though, the prosecutors came up with a new and intriguing offer, a package deal that would result in shorter sentences for everyone, including Howie and Sandy (who would probably receive twenty-year sentences—no small punishment, but at least they'd have a chance to see the outside world again). But there was a significant catch: the offer was, in essence . . . *everyone or no one*. If we started to break off into factions—some of us accepting the plea, others rejecting it—the whole deal would fall apart. Obviously this wasn't exactly an ethical way for the feds to conduct business; nevertheless, that was the offer they made. Their goal was clear: to validate the Rough Rider sting by convicting everyone involved. If we all accepted guilty pleas, the prosecutors could easily validate the time and money they had spent, not to mention the questionable methods they employed. For them, this offer represented a way to end the Rough Rider story with an exclamation point.

It was brilliant, really. If I didn't plead guilty, then I'd feel guilty for denying some of my brothers the chance for an early release. That was a heavy cross to bear. So, after much hand-wringing and consultation, I acquiesced. And everyone else soon followed. I would take my year and Bert would take his three years, and so on down the line. There were twenty of us, and we all agreed to plead out. I didn't like it one bit. I felt like I had a shotgun to my head. But I was ready to take one for the team, so to speak, so that Howie and Sandy wouldn't spend the rest of their lives in prison.

On the day that the papers were supposed to be signed and agreements made, we all gathered in a room to meet with our lawyers. All of us, that is, except Pinball, the lone member of our club who had been granted bail. Pinball's home life was harder than most—his daughter had cerebral palsy and his wife wasn't emotionally up to the task of caring for the girl alone. So, in a surprising display of compassion, the judge had granted Pinball bail and set him free while he was awaiting trial. To our complete surprise, just as were getting ready to accept the package deal, one of our lawyers walked into the room.

"Hold everything," he said. "We've got a little problem."

Pinball was outside, the lawyer said, and wanted to meet with us.

When Pinball came in, he seemed anxious, conflicted. It was obvious something was bothering him.

"I can't do it," he said. "I can't take the plea."

I was shocked but not altogether displeased.

"Why not?" I asked.

"Because it's like somebody is forcing me to lie," Pinball said. "I've fought against shit like this my whole life. I can't give up now."

A few guys rolled their eyes and groaned. Others nodded their approval. I gave Pinball a slap on the back and said, "I'm with you, brother. Fuck these people. I'm not going to be held hostage."

Not everyone agreed, and there was, for a few minutes, some pretty heated discussion. But when Howie chimed in, the debate ended. "Fuck them and their plea," he said. "Whatever happens . . . happens."

With a life sentence on the line, Howie was the high roller of our group. By comparison, the rest of us were playing dollar slot machines. It seemed ludicrous for anyone to argue with him.

Shortly after we had come to our collective decision, however, the case took another wild turn. When we appeared in front of the judge, we let it be known that we felt as though we were being blackmailed, that the prosecutor's office had made an unethical offer, the details of which we explained.

The judge was not amused.

"Oh, really?" he said. "Fine. Anyone who wants to plead in front of me today, feel free to do so. No strings attached."

That made it easier. Howie and Sandy pled out and received twenty-year sentences. A few others, maybe five in all, also entered guilty pleas. I did not. Neither did Bert. Was I upset that some of my brothers jumped ship? A little, I suppose. But each man had to make his own decision. It wasn't until a week later that I discovered Pinball had changed his mind. The guy who had been beating his chest, encouraging everyone to fight . . . to stand up for what they believed . . . had pled guilty and quit the club. Not only that, but he received no jail time. The judge sentenced him to time served, which had been almost nothing. *Unbelievable!* And there I was, imprisoned for more than a year for a crime I did not commit.

After fourteen months at MCC, I met with the prosecutors again. This time they seemed not only frustrated but almost sympathetic.

"Look," one of them said. "We know you didn't make that phone call, and we know you don't want to take a plea. But you have to understand . . . this is our game, and we aren't going to lose. Why don't you just take the plea and we'll make sure you get bail and we'll recommend the judge sentence you to time served. Then this whole nightmare will be over."

"I don't know, man."

"Chuck," the prosecutor said, "you're gonna get old in here."

I believed him. After being denied bail three times, I knew I had no chance of getting out before my case went to trial. And I didn't even have a trial date yet. I was looking at perhaps another year at MCC. I thought about everything I'd been through, about how long it had been since I'd slept in my own bed and held my wife and daughter. I just wanted to get home.

"Okay," I said. "I'll take the deal."

Officially, I pled guilty to conspiracy. I admitted making a phone call to a man who sold a pound of methamphetamine. But let me be clear about this: It never happened. I made no such phone call. I wasn't involved in any drug deal. I know what you're probably think-ing: *Everyone in prison says they're innocent.* Well, I really was inno-cent. But I was tired of fighting a battle that couldn't be won. I consider myself to be a fairly patriotic man, but what I learned from this experience is this: If the cops want to get you, especially the feds, they're going to get you. They'll do whatever they have to do: plant stuff on you, set you up, invent allegations . . . anything to make their case. If it hadn't happened to me, I never would have believed it.

Guess what happened the day after I entered a guilty plea? I made bail. Suddenly, after fourteen months, I was no longer a risk of flight and a danger to the community. Within a week I went to work for Liza Minnelli, who was on a national tour. I spent the better part of two months traveling all over the country. Liza, by the way, was great. Not only did she offer me a job, no questions asked, but she stood up for me when she was subpoenaed to testify in my case.

"I've never even seen this man drink a cup of coffee, let alone do any drugs," she said.

Sylvester Stallone and Mickey Rourke also were subpoenaed. Sly said only that I was a good guy; Mickey told them, in not so many words, "Go fuck yourselves."

By the time the sentencing hearing rolled around, I'd gotten on with my life. I knew it would be painful to stand before a judge and formally admit guilt for something I hadn't done but it was a necessary part of the process. To take some of the sting off, I arranged a big party at Lanza's restaurant on First Avenue in Manhattan. I had reservations for thirty people. I figured we'd go there, have a nice meal, celebrate my freedom, and then try to forget the whole thing ever happened.

The courtroom was filled with my friends and relatives. Among the people who showed up in court were some of the celebrities I'd worked with, including Danny Aiello, Chita Rivera, and Liza Minnelli. Imagine my amazement when the judge sentenced me to ten years in a federal penitentiary.

"Your honor, excuse me . . . but I think you have me confused with somebody else. I'm supposed to get time served."

The judge looked at me and said, "Mr. Zito, who told you that?"

"The prosecuting attorney."

"Do you have that in writing?"

"No, sir, I don't."

Bam! He slammed his gavel and said, "Ten years. Now get out of my courtroom."

And that was that. With my wife and daughter crying (my mother and sisters, too) . . . my friends in shock . . . I was handcuffed and shackled. I gave Kathy a quick kiss before they led me away.

"I'm sorry," I said. "Better cancel that reservation."

They're out there in the yard again, where they are almost every day, holding hands, kissing, making out in front of everyone. The guards see them and pretend they don't notice, or they laugh and keep right on walking, amused at the sight of this oddest of couples: a big, buff black man, skin pulled tight across his muscles, veins popping at the surface, like he just stepped off the cover of Anabolic Steroid Weekly, *and his bitch, a frail little man with long eyelashes and milky white skin, all points and angles, except for the soft mounds that rise from his chest, surgically implanted gifts to his partner and protector.*

They move slowly toward a wall, into the shadows, away from the other inmates, and now the little man who is almost (but not quite) a woman falls to his knees. He fumbles with the bigger man's waist, and then his head begins to bob. The bigger man stands over him, flexed, proud, lost in a lustful dream. This is the deal for the little man. This is his life inside prison walls, an endless series of degrading, dehumanizing encounters. All he has to do to stay alive is agree to be a punk, to service the bigger man anywhere, anytime. No one else will touch him; no one will hurt him. I guess, for him, it isn't such a bad deal. But as I see them together now, rhythmically rocking, I can't help but wonder, What the fuck am I doing in here?

ARE YOU THINKING ABOUT BREAKING THE LAW? ARE YOU LEADING A LIFE-style that might result in a trip to the county jail or, worse, a state or federal prison? Looking for advice on how to get by once you're inside? How to negotiate safely with pimps and predators and prostitutes? Well, here's tip number one:

Don't get arrested.

All other suggestions pale in importance, because once you're arrested, once you begin that long descent into hell, you're on your own.

I'd like to tell you that prison really isn't all that bad. I'd like to tell you that my initial reaction when I walked into MCC was correct: *American time is easy time.* But that would be a lie. Life in a Japanese prison is lonely, boring, rigid. Life in an American prison is barbaric. It is, in fact, just as horrible as you might imagine: no privacy, rancid food, the strong preying on the weak at every opportunity. It's like junior high school all over again—only a whole lot more violent. To tell you the truth, I wouldn't wish it on my worst enemy.

But let's say you're stupid enough to disregard tip number one. Let's say you get arrested and sent to jail. I'm talking about a real jail, not some minimum-security white-collar work farm. I'm talking about a big municipal lockup, like MCC, or a maximum-security state or federal penitentiary. Any one of these is pretty much indistinguishable from another, and if you're sent to one, consider yourself fucked. You may hear some uninformed asshole suggest that federal prisons aren't as bad and that federal time is better time. Bullshit. There is no "better" time. Prison is prison. You're locked up twenty-four hours a day: in your cell, with the door bolted shut; in a courtyard, surrounded by thirty-foot walls and guard towers manned by sharpshooters who would love nothing more than to use your sorry ass for target practice; in a putrid, overcrowded cafeteria, where the smell is so bad you want to puke and where the slightest mistake in decorum can get you shanked.

Believe me, I spent nearly six years in prison and I can assure you that there is no shortage of violent offenders in the federal system. It ain't all crooked accountants and high-powered drug lords. There are rapists, murderers, and pedophiles. And, of course, in any jail you'll find plenty of twisted corrections officers who take great pleasure in beating inmates or, even better, watching inmates beat each other. I experienced and witnessed all kinds of bestial behavior, so please don't tell me federal time is preferable to state time. When you're doing state time, at least you're eligible for conjugal visits. You can sleep with your wife or girlfriend, which not only allows you to connect emotionally and physically with the person you love but also performs the very basic and essential function of giving you an outlet for a lot of pent-up testosterone. There are no conjugal visits in federal prisons, which is why so many men remove their underwear and cut holes in their pockets before marching off to the visiting room. A quick and sneaky hand job under the table is about as good as it gets.

You'll hate every moment in prison; you'll feel lower than whale shit. Somehow, though, if you want to survive, you'll have to be strong. I'm not talking merely about hitting the weights and pumping up (although that's not a bad idea); I'm talking about inner strength. Some people have it; some people don't. And it has nothing to do with the size of your biceps. I've seen little guys who were willing to fight for themselves, who seemed to fear nothing, and I've seen bigger guys crumble as soon as the door slammed behind them. I remember one poor slob at MCC who was arrested for his involvement in a drug ring. He was brought in one night looking scared and lost; the next morning, while standing on chow line, he collapsed and died of a heart attack. Not an especially little guy, not an old guy. Just a guy who was scared to death.

And understandably so. When I was a holdover in Lewisburg, Pennsylvania, it seemed like at least once a month someone got killed or beaten so badly he wished he were dead. There was a big room where movies would be shown a couple times a week, and every so often, after the lights went down, you'd hear someone moan or scream and then the movie would stop and the corrections officers would rush in, and there would be someone sprawled on the floor, all alone, convulsing and bleeding.

Now, you might think this guy had it coming, that he was probably just a lowlife scumbag who was brutal on the outside and brutal behind bars and finally it all caught up to him. Not necessarily so. Most fights in jail are about simple things—protocol and turf and money. People get shanked for using the pool table when it isn't their turn, for cutting in line at the telephone. It's a fucked-up world.

How do you learn to live in such a dangerous and violent environment? It's easier for some than others, of course. I knew how to fight. I could defend myself. And, as I was a prominent member of the Hells Angels, my reputation preceded me. But I still managed to have maybe ten really good brawls during my time in jail. Most people, even hardened criminals, don't want to mess with the Hells Angels. But there are other factions in prison, too, and there are always power struggles. So it wasn't like I was able to rise above the ugliness. I just had the admittedly significant advantage of being part of a strong team.

What about you? Let's say you knock over a liquor store or get pulled over for a third DWI. Let's say you "forget" to pay your income taxes for a few years. What can you, little fish, expect to find when you get to prison?

Well, if you're a white guy, like I am, you can expect to find that most people don't look much like you. Welcome to life as a minority! Ain't it a bitch? Most prison populations are roughly 60 percent black, 35 percent Hispanic, and 5 percent Caucasian. What you will find, almost from the moment you arrive, is that for the first time in your life, being white is no longer an advantage. In fact, it's a liability. White prisoners are more likely to be challenged, shaken down, and generally abused. And, I'm sorry to say, they're more likely to be the target of sexual assault. Any inmate who doesn't stand up for himself, who doesn't "hold his mud," has the potential to be turned out. But a young, thin white man? He's especially prized, and the chances are reasonably good that within a few days of orientation he'll find himself, almost incomprehensibly, bent over a bunk with another man's dick playing "Wipe Out" against the walls of his rectum.

You think this is merely the stuff of drama? That TV shows like *Oz* simply make this stuff up? Uh-uh. No one much likes to talk about prison rape—not the corrections officers, not the inmates, not the administrators. I know there was a book called *Newjack* that was published a couple years ago in which the author, who worked as a prison guard at Sing Sing for a year, argued that stories of prison rape are greatly exaggerated and that most sexual encounters between inmates are consensual. With all due respect, I can respond to that suggestion with only a single word: *Bullshit*. The truth is, men do get taken in prison. They do get raped. It doesn't happen every day, but it does happen. For those who are small or weak, it's a very real and persistent danger.

Look in the mirror. Are you fragile? Are you white? Are you young? Do you have money? If you answered yes to any of these questions, you might as well paint a bull's-eye on your ass and hang a sign from your neck saying: PLEASE FUCK ME. If you look like you're not capable of protecting yourself or if other inmates suspect you have something of value (and they'll find out as soon as you arrive), you'll be a target. Expect someone to latch onto you, someone bigger, tougher, someone who will act like he's your buddy. He'll throw an arm over your shoulder, volunteer to show you the ropes, introduce you to the right people. You should politely, but forcefully, decline this offer, for to accept it is to make a deal with the devil. Before you know it you'll be giving him your commissary money (remember what I said about junior high—there's extortion in prison, too). Then you'll be in his cell, performing sex acts you never imagined in your worst nightmares. And then, maybe, since you're his punk, you'll find yourself being loaned out to other inmates, as payment for debts or simply as a "thank-you."

For some guys this is the only way to survive prison. I saw a lot of them in my time, and I always felt sorry for them. These are the types of relationships prison officials point to when they use the term *consensual sex*. Well, sure, it's consensual. The weaker man figures he has two choices: get raped . . . or get beaten *and* raped. He's scared, he doesn't want to get hurt, and he sure as hell doesn't want to get killed. So he gives in, figuring, *This is the way I'll do my time. And when I'm out, I'll put it all behind me.*

It's gruesome, it's animalistic, but that's the way it is. For a lot of people in prison, the only way to survive is to become a punk . . . *a bitch*. Theirs is a wretched, pathetic existence, but at least they're alive. Personally, I'd rather be dead. But that's just me.

Generally speaking, you'll get nothing but contempt for adopting this punk attitude. Prison is an angry, macho world, and those who can't defend themselves are usually the object of scorn and ridicule. Sure, the punk avoids beatdowns and assaults, but he's reviled by his fellow inmates. There are exceptions, of course. I tried to help a couple guys when I was at MCC. I was new to the system and not quite jaded enough to turn my back on the weak. I'd see these scrawny guys who were obviously decent human beings, who had no hope of surviving in a cesspool like MCC, and I'd want to help them. There was one little Jewish guy, for example. I don't even know what law he had broken—some type of white-collar crime, I presume. Everyone picked on this poor bastard. One day I watched as he tried repeatedly, unsuccessfully, to make a phone call. Now, what you have to understand is that phone time is cherished time in prison and certain cliques run certain phones. The blacks, the Italians, the Latinos, in some cases the bikers—they all lay claim to certain phones. It's all a big game, although a very serious game with strict rules. If you want to use the phone, you have to ask permission or pay a certain fee. It goes without saying that if you're not part of one of the controlling factions, you're going to have a hard time getting access to a phone, as this Jewish man discovered. He waited and waited . . . and then he waited some more. No one would let him use the phone. I presume he had paid, too, but that didn't seem to make a difference. Finally, after a couple hours, I decided to intercede.

I took the guy up to the top tier of MCC, to the Latino section. By this time I already had a reputation as something of a tough guy. I respected each group and I knew they respected me, but still I knew I was asking for trouble. We walked together to the phone, which was being used by one Puerto Rican inmate and guarded by another.

"Look," I said. "This guy has been waiting all day to use the phone."

The man guarding the phone scowled as his friend kept talking.

"You hear me?" I said.

"Yeah, I heard you." He paused and looked down the tier. "Hey, Luis!" he yelled.

I didn't know Luis, but I had a hunch we were about to be introduced. He emerged from his cell like a bear leaving its cave, shambling and grunting as though he'd just been shaken from hibernation. Luis was new to MCC, but apparently he'd already been elevated to a position of prominence among the Latinos, probably because he weighed close to 400 pounds. I mean this mother was *huge!*

"Is there a problem here?" Luis growled.

The man who had summoned Luis nodded. "Yeah. This guy's trying to take the phone, man."

Luis inched closer to me. "Is that true, motherfucker?"

In prison you have to know when it's time to talk and when it's time to take action. I had stepped on their turf and demanded use of their phone. I had instigated the confrontation. There was no point in trying to be diplomatic. So, almost before the word "motherfucker" had escaped from Luis's lips I reared back and hit him with everything I had, a solid right hook to the chin. His eyes rolled back in his head and he dropped to the floor like a four-hundred-pound bag of bricks. Out cold.

Within seconds the other Latinos had backed off and the phone was free. I handed the receiver to the little Jewish guy.

"There, make your call," I said.

He thanked me and began to dial. I stood there for the next ten minutes, until he was finished, because I know they would have jumped him the minute I left. And then I walked him back to his cell. I could have easily used the phones in the Italian section, but I woke up with a bad attitude that day.

A few hours later I was in the gym, working out. There were no free weights at MCC, so we used buckets of water attached to a broomstick to do bicep curls and bench presses. We also had a chin-up bar. It was a primitive setup but effective enough. I was hanging from the chin-up bar when I noticed Luis walking into the gym. Assuming he was pissed and eager for a second chance at me, I jumped off the bar and got right into his face. This guy was too big and dangerous to give him any room. If we were going to fight, I wasn't about to let him throw the first punch. Before I could say or do anything, though, Luis held up his hands submissively.

"Easy, brother," he said. "I just want to introduce myself."

"Yeah?"

He extended his hand. "I'm Luis, and I gotta tell you . . . no one's ever hit me that hard in my life. Anytime you need me, I'm right there for you."

"Okay," I said, and we shook hands. From that moment, Luis and I were friends. You never know how these things are going to turn out in jail. Sometimes you hit someone and he comes back at you with a blade. And you end up starting a gang war. Other times you make a new friend. Like I said, it's crazy.

If there is one word to keep in mind while you're in prison, it's this: *respect*. Respect for yourself, respect for others. There are different factions, different cliques, and sometimes problems do arise and eventually erupt into violence. But generally speaking, people try to respect one another, because if you disrespect someone—if you disrespect his space or his property—you're going to have a serious problem. Here's an example. When you get up in the morning and you brush your teeth and shave, you'd better clean that sink and wipe it down for the next guy who comes in. Simple as that. You don't leave your spittle there, your toothpaste, your shaving cream. That sink better sparkle, because there are a couple hundred guys who have to use it and not one of them wants to lean into a bowl covered with someone else's gunk. That's simple respect. Maybe it was no big deal when you were in the dorm at college, but it's a big deal in jail. Forget to clean the sink and you're going to get dumped. That's just the way it is.

If you want to find trouble in prison, you won't have to look far. Very few people take any shit at all. So if you disrespect somebody, you'd better be prepared to get punched, stabbed, or hit over the head with a pipe.

Respect, obviously, is a commodity that's earned. Those who exhibit no respect for themselves will have a hard time getting the respect of others. This brings us to the only piece of advice that really matters after you've been arrested, printed, convicted, and thrown behind bars: stand up for yourself. Only by demonstrating that you are not afraid and that you won't be easily intimidated can you do time on your own. You can't let anyone shit all over you, because others will pick up on it . . . they'll sniff it out, like sharks drawn to blood in the water, and they'll make your life miserable.

On my first day after being transferred to Petersburg, Virginia, I walked into the television room and took a seat in one of the back rows. There were only two other people in the room at the time, a couple of black guys sitting several rows in front of me. I chose a seat far behind them specifically to avoid a confrontation—I was the new kid in town and I knew it was only a matter of time before I'd be tested, challenged, but I was in no hurry to provoke the matter. In fact, when one of them turned around, stared at me, and said icily, "Yo, man, that's our chair," I let it go. *Ok, these guys have probably been here awhile, so I'm not gonna fuck with them. I'll be cool.* I stood up, moved to another row even father from the TV, and sat down.

Well, damned if the guy didn't turn around again and say, "Yo, that one's mine, too."

Son of a bitch . . .

Enough was enough. I had given him his space, I had respected his seniority, but he clearly wasn't going to be satisfied until he either kicked my ass or got his own ass kicked. So I wasted no more time. I picked up the chair, flipped it over to look at the bottom, and said, "Oh, yeah? I don't see your fucking name on it."

With that, both of the black men jumped up and sauntered toward me. I took two big steps, met them halfway, and clocked the first one in the head with the chair. *WHAM!* He dropped like a dead man, leaving the second one exposed. Wide-eyed, he put up his hands to protect himself, but it was too late. I swung again, with all of my strength, and he, too, fell to the floor. Then I dropped the chair and walked away. A consequence of fighting is that you get thrown into "the hole" (solitary confinement, twenty-three hour lockdown). If you get caught, that is. Some guys are natural rats, and they'll spill their guts to the nearest guard. But a lot of inmates know enough to keep their mouths shut. It's part of the prison code. These particular guys said nothing, because they knew they were wrong. They were fucking with me, testing me, and you just can't let anyone do that to you when you're new in prison.

So, if somebody comes at you in jail—and rest assured, somebody *will* eventually come at you—you'd better be prepared to defend yourself. If someone tries to steal from you or humiliate you . . . if someone tries to make you his bitch . . . just punch him in the face. That's all there is to it. You want to be quiet? You want to do your own time and just be left alone? Fine. But the minute someone threatens you or disrespects you in any way, you'd better go to war. And I mean *instantly!* Fight like a crazy man. Use your fists, fingernails, teeth . . . whatever you have at your disposal. Your first fight will be the one that everyone remembers and talks about. Make it a good one.

20

HERE'S WHAT HAPPENED: MY SENTENCING MEMORANDUM, SIGNED BY RU-
dolph Giuliani, included testimony from an informant who swore
that not only had I been involved in a conspiracy to traffic methamphetamine but I also was, supposedly, one of the hardest criminals
in the Hells Angels. My rise to the rank of vice president in the New
York chapter, the informant said, was facilitated by my willingness to
engage in the most brutal illegal activities. He told the cops that I'd
planted a bomb on the undercarriage of a mobster's car, supposedly
in retribution for the shooting of a fellow Hell's Angel one week earlier. He described me as the drug lord of Westchester County, a man
who, like Al Pacino's Scarface, buried his head in a pile of powder
whenever a new shipment arrived.

Who was this informant? Well, take a wild guess? That's right—
the guy who had pulled a gun on me one year earlier. He'd left the
club, but not before getting caught up in the Rough Rider sting. And,
unlike the rest of us, he'd taken the easy way out: by turning rat. Last
I heard he was in the federal witness protection program, probably
pumping gas at a 7-Eleven, leading a quiet, shitty life, praying to God
that I never catch up with him. His lies, his bullshit, his self-serving
attitude . . . they cost me almost six years of my life.

To make my sentence especially miserable, the feds kept moving
me around. I served time in New York, Pennsylvania, Virginia, Louisiana, Alabama, Oklahoma, Missouri . . . I was all over the system.
Every time you're shipped out, it's like you're the new kid on the
block, and you have to prove yourself all over again. Maybe the feds
were hoping I'd get stabbed or I'd stab someone else. It really didn't

matter. Either I'd be dead or I'd get another twenty years tacked onto my sentence, and they'd have their revenge.

But I managed to avoid anything that horrible. Oh, I got in fights. I had my hand broken; I got hit over the head with a steel pipe; I got smacked in the face with a cue ball. Fighting is a way of life in prison, and I adapted to it better than most.

Of course, you have to accept the consequences of your actions. Shortly after I broke my hand in a fight at MCC with two Colombian drug dealers (over phone usage—and, yes, I knocked them both unconscious), I was sent to the hole, where you're locked down twenty-three hours a day. A couple days later, I was in my cell, completing the last of my push-ups, when I heard the rattling of the guards' keys. I jumped up to see two guards escorting a middle-aged man with thick gray hair, and as he got closer I realized who he was: the boss of all bosses, John Gotti.

Nobody had any idea that John had been brought in. And now here he was, coming my way, getting closer . . . closer . . . closer . . . until he was standing right in front of my cell, looking at me through the glass door.

Holy shit! John Gotti is going to be my cellmate! Cool!

We stared at each other for a moment. I said, "Hello, Mr. Gotti," and he said, "Hey, Bo." (That's what he called a lot of people—he didn't know me from Adam.) Just as the door was about to open, another guard yelled, "Hey! Don't put him in with Zito. Put him in another cell until tomorrow. Then we'll shuffle him around somewhere."

Damn!

I'm not sure why the guards didn't want John bunking with me. I guess they figured it wouldn't be a good idea to put the boss of the Gambino family and one of the leaders of the Hells Angels together in a cell. Maybe they were afraid we'd be playing gin rummy and, instead of talking about how much we missed our families and how we couldn't wait to get home, we'd be talking about our lives of crime with two of the most powerful organizations around. Who knows?

Anyway, John spent that night on my tier, directly across from my cell, and the next day they moved him to another cell with somebody else. When we got out for breakfast, we saw each other and I walked right up to him and said, "Mr. Gotti, I'm Chuck Zito. It's a pleasure to meet you." I took a deep breath, extended my swollen, fractured hand, and placed it in his, knowing full well that the man probably had a vice grip of a handshake.

And he did. But I couldn't let him see that he was hurting me. John said, "Hey, how are you?"

And I was, like, gritting my teeth, wincing, barely able to speak. *"Okaaaaay."*

In a sense, I was lucky. Some thirty members of the Hells Angels served prison time for charges stemming from the same case in which I was involved, and we all were sent to federal facilities. So everywhere I went, I had at least one brother, and we took care of one another. It's also a fact that inmates affiliated with motorcycle clubs, even rival clubs, tend to band together and form cliques (it's understood, of course, that the Hells Angels are at the top of the food chain). But there are limits to how much you can and will tolerate when forming these alliances.

When I was in El Reno, Oklahoma, during the fourth year of my bid, it seemed to be the hub of all outlaw motorcycle clubs. There were dozens of bikers there, including three of my brothers from the Hells Angels: Skeeter, Red Dog, and Hammer. On my very first day, we were walking in the yard when Skeeter told me that

Left to right: Skeeter, myself, and Red Dog in front of the gym at El Reno prison, Oklahoma

another club, with which we had experienced a long-standing (and sometimes violent) rivalry, was well represented within the walls of El Reno.

"So what?" I said. "Fuck them. We'll do our thing, let them do their thing. We're all just doing time."

Skeeter seemed agitated. "It's not that simple."

"What do you mean?"

"One of them has a tattoo on his arm that says: 'Kill all Hells Angels.' "

I stopped, put a hand on Skeeter's shoulder. "You're kidding."

"Uh-uh. But I told him to cover it."

"When did you tell him?" I asked.

"Six—" Skeeter began, and I thought sure the next word out of his mouth would be "days" or "hours," maybe even "minutes." Nope. The next word out of Skeeter's mouth was "months."

"Six months?" I was flabbergasted. "You gave this scumbag six months to cover a tattoo and he hasn't done it yet?"

All three of them nodded.

"And he's still eating solid food?"

It was an awkward situation for all of us. While Red Dog, Hammer, and Skeeter were inmates at El Reno, I was simply a holdover, awaiting designation to another federal facility. Protocol dictated that I keep a low profile, because if I were involved in an altercation with a rival faction, my brothers would be left behind to clean up the mess. In other words, I'd be starting something I couldn't finish, and that was generally regarded as selfish and inconsiderate, not to mention dangerous.

Nevertheless . . .

"You know," I said, "this is bullshit. I don't care if I am just a holdover; I'm going to have a talk with this guy."

As I said, respect is an important thing in prison, maybe the most important thing. Anyone who wears a tattoo defaming the Hells Angels in my presence might just as well spit in my face. Because my response will be the same.

Two days later I ran into this guy in the gym. He was a formidable-looking guy, maybe six-foot-one, 210 pounds (I was about 180 pounds at the time), with long, flowing hair. Real biker hair.

"Hey, man, I want to talk to you," I said.

"Yeah, sure . . . after I get a drink."

He seemed to have an attitude, which kind of annoyed me, but since I was new to El Reno I was willing to give him the benefit of the doubt. Maybe, I thought, he'd be reasonable.

We met in the bathroom a few minutes later. (A lot of fights in prison take place in the bathroom or shower area. You go there for privacy, to talk, but often it escalates into something more.)

"What's that all about?" I said, gesturing to his arm.

"Hey, man. We got no problems, you and me. We're all neutral in here."

"The fuck we are. Who told you that shit? If I don't like you on the street, I don't like you in here."

He took a step back. "I don't want any trouble."

"Yeah? Well, you sure look like you want trouble when you walk around with that shit on your arm. So the best thing you can do is cover it up. And then we won't have any trouble at all."

He sighed. "I'm gonna have to ask my boss."

Now I was getting pissed. "Wait a minute. I'm talking to you man to man, eyeball to eyeball. Did you ask your boss for permission to put that tattoo on your arm?"

"Well . . . that's different."

"The hell it is."

"Look," he said. "I don't want to argue politics with you. I can't do anything until I talk—"

I cut him off. "Shut the fuck up. You're an asshole, and that tattoo is an insult to me and my brothers. End of story."

BAM!

I hit him flush on the chin, and he went down. Rather than jumping on him, I took a step back and went into my boxer's stance. I was willing to give this guy a chance to fight, to defend himself and his honor, but he turned out to be a gutless weasel. He scrambled to his feet, put his hands up for an instant, as if he were going to fight, and then turned and bolted for the exit.

You punk-ass bitch . . .

I lunged after him and grabbed a fistful of hair, tried to yank him back into the bathroom. But he kept right on going, even as his scalp surrendered a huge divot into my hand and I fell to the floor.

"Yaaah!" he screamed before disappearing. "I'm gonna get you, you motherfucker! I'm gonna get you!"

The cop shop, where the corrections officers were stationed, was located right outside the bathroom, so I figured I wouldn't be alone for long. The guards would hear his squealing and come running to find out what had happened. So I ducked into one of the stalls, flushed his hair down the toilet, and took a seat on the shitter. I just sat there hanging out, looking like any other con loosening his bowels after another bad prison meal, and waited for the guards to show up. But they never did.

I don't mean to brag when I talk about the fights I've had, and I hope I don't sound like a lunatic or a sadist. The truth is, despite my ability and willingness to fight, I was hardly one of the more violent types you're likely to encounter in a typical maximum-security prison. Even behind bars, where tempers flare in a heartbeat and where some people kick ass just to break the boredom, I tried to be reasonable and understanding. But when a man tells me he has to ask for permission to remove a tattoo, even though he hadn't asked for permission to get the tattoo in the first place . . . well, that's just plain stupid. If I'd seen this guy in a bar, I would not even have given him the courtesy of a conversation. I simply would have turned his lights out. But I wanted to do things the right way, the diplomatic way, because I was in jail, and when you get caught fighting in jail you go straight to the hole. I wasn't trying to be a tough guy or a wise guy. I merely wanted to let him know that the prudent thing to do was cover his ridiculous tattoo. But he didn't want to hear it, so I had no choice but to take matters into my own hands. That's prison justice, which ain't a whole lot different from street justice.

Of course, by decking this guy I touched off a minor problem. There were only four Hells Angels in El Reno and eight representatives of this other motorcycle club. "Eyes open," I told my brothers. "Be prepared for anything."

The next day, while Skeeter and I were training in the gym, we saw all eight of them approaching at once. And they had some big, nasty-looking guys. Rather than brawl right there in the gym, where we might have been hit with pipes and weights and where guards surely would have witnessed every moment—resulting in each of us being sent to the hole—Skeeter and I decided to walk outside to meet them. Out in the yard, one member of their group stepped forward, his hands across his chest. This, I knew from experience, was not an attack but rather a negotiation. He addressed his remarks to Skeeter, because Skeeter had been at El Reno the longest.

"We want to meet this guy"—he tilted his chin at me—"Sunday night . . . leisure time."

"Hey . . . fuck you!" I said. "Let's get it on right now. Eight of you against two of us. That should be fair."

He looked around the yard. It was a typical Thursday afternoon: lots of inmates hanging out, some playing ball, others just talking, wasting time. Guards in the towers, guards on the ground.

"No way, man," he said. "It's too light. Too many cops."

"Fine, then. Sunday night."

It was a bad idea, really. Leisure time was conducted in a big, open room, where inmates worked on various hobbies or read books. It was a dangerous, uncontrolled environment, and any fight that took place there was likely to involve shanks, pipes, and other weapons. The more Skeeter and I talked, the more reluctant we were to engage in that type of battle, especially when we were outnumbered two to one. An ambush was certain. Murder was a legitimate possibility.

So, Skeeter set up another meeting, the outcome of which was an agreement that I would fight the man I'd already beaten once. Skeeter bunked right next door to one of their guys, so we decided to use that area as an arena: one cell would serve as the boxing ring, and the other cell would be for private viewing. No one from either club would be allowed to interfere in any capacity. This would be a one-on-one fight. Bare hands. No weapons.

You ever see that movie *Hard Times*, in which Charles Bronson stars as a street fighter? There's a scene in which Bronson and his opponent step into a cage to do battle and each of them walks in a slow circle, holding his hands up, turning them around, fingers spread wide, to show nothing is hidden—no brass knuckles, no coins . . . nothing. Well, that's what I did when the door closed and the two of us were locked in that six-by-eight-foot cage. I held up my hands, showed him my palms, and said, "It's just me and you, kid."

I'll give him credit—he didn't seem scared. Despite what had happened in the bathroom a couple days earlier, he wanted to fight. As I showed him my hands, in fact, he raised his foot and tried to kick me in the balls! But I intercepted the blow with my right hand (which hurt my thumb and made me even angrier). Then I stepped in and dropped him with a left hook to the chin. Again, rather than jump

241

on him, I took a step back and gave him two options: fight or surrender. To my surprise, he stood up and began flailing away, throwing wild, exhausting punches, not one of which came close to landing. Now he was scared, nervous, tired, and all I had to do was bob and weave. Finally, I hit him with a combination—left hook, right hand—forcing him backward into the cell door . . . which had been left ajar! He reeled into the door and tumbled out onto the tier with a *crash!* Suddenly everyone knew what was happening.

"Fight! Fight!" the other inmates shouted. And they began to gather around. I knew I had little time left to finish this matter, because soon the guards would descend upon us. So I grabbed my opponent by the feet and dragged him back into the cell, where I proceeded to hammer him repeatedly in the face, just blasted him over and over.

"You gonna cover that tattoo?"

"Help!" he shouted.

"Ain't nobody gonna help your sorry ass," I said. Then I hit him again, and I felt his cheekbone collapse beneath my fist. I punched him again. His nose broke, sending a geyser of blood into the air.

"Uuughhh," he moaned. "Please." I stopped hitting him. "Okay . . . I'll cover it."

I rolled off him and sat on the floor, trying to catch my breath. He was a bloody mess, as beaten and humiliated as a man could be. I stood up.

"All you had to do was cover that tattoo, but you had to go and be a tough guy. Now look at you . . . look at your face, man." He pulled himself up, wiped away some of the blood. "The only reason you got that tattoo is because you never thought you'd see a Hells Angel in your life, huh?"

He shrugged. "Never thought I'd see one in jail."

"Same fucking thing!"

He spit out a gob of something thick and red and extended his hand to me.

"I'm not shaking your hand," I said, pushing him away. "You've got until Sunday night to get rid of that thing." Then I walked out of the cell and into the yard, where Red Dog and Hammer were waiting for me.

"Man, you took care of business in two minutes," Hammer said with a smile. "From now on, I'm gonna call you the Two-Minute Warning."

The guards never came. I'm not sure why. Maybe they knew we were fighting and didn't care. So I got some fresh clothes from my brothers, did a quick change, and went about my routine. The next day, Saturday, Skeeter told me we had a little problem.

"They don't want anyone from their club being told what to do," he explained. "Especially by a Hells Angel."

"Why not?"

"They don't want him to lose his dignity."

"Dignity?" I said. "What dignity? His dignity is long gone. I beat it right the hell out of him." I was so upset by this news that I was prepared to march right back to this guy's cell and teach him another lesson. "You know what? Fuck Sunday night. You tell them if that tattoo isn't covered by seven o'clock tonight, we're gonna get it on."

So, seven o'clock came and I took a walk over to visit Skeeter, whose cellmate was a tattoo artist. And guess what? There was the asshole I'd beaten, sitting on the bunk, getting his tattoo covered. I walked up to him, grabbed his arm, twisted it around to get a good look. "I'll be back when it's done."

As promised, I returned an hour later. The words "Kill all Hells Angels" were now gone, obliterated by a giant blob of black ink.

"Okay?" he said, standing and offering his hand again.

"Yeah, fine. But I'm not shaking your hand."

"Why not?"

"Because you wanted to be a tough guy and all this could have been avoided."

Two days later I was transferred out. Not only were the guys from our rival club happy to see me go, but I think my own brothers were relieved, too: *Get this guy out of here, man—he starts too much shit!*

Despite spending nearly six years in prison, I never became institutionalized. That happens to a lot of people—jail becomes their world. They spend every waking moment thinking about their jobs, their cliques, their routines. I never let that happen to me. My body was behind bars, but my mind was always out on the street: on the back of a Harley . . . in bed with my wife . . . in the backyard of my home in New Rochelle, playing with Lisa. I learned to survive in jail and I did what I had to do in order to keep my sanity and pride, but I never accepted it as my life, never felt for a moment that it was anything more than a way station. I called home as much as I could. I wrote hundreds of letters to friends and relatives and former clients. Cher wrote to me; Liza wrote to me. Mickey sent not only letters but also books and magazines and other gifts. Their kindness touched me, kept me going in some of the darker moments. It helped me realize that life was worth living and that despite my surroundings—the cages and rifles and half-crazy convicts—I was not an animal.

Like anyone who survives prison with his sanity intact, I found pockets of dignity behind bars. In Petersburg, Virginia, home to one of the best vocational facilities in the federal system, I took a masonry class, mainly because I thought I might learn something that I could use while working on our house in New Rochelle. I sketched a picture for Kathy, a picture of a house that looked like ours, except this one had a facade of brick and stone and a circular driveway and round steps rising to the front door.

"This is what I'm going to do for you when I get home," I wrote on the back.

Eventually I made good on that promise. I completed the masonry class and used much of what I learned to remodel our home. Not only that, but I also received my high school equivalency diploma at Petersburg. We had a graduation ceremony and everything, complete with caps and gowns. I sent the diploma home to Kathy, along with a note that said: "Hey, I did it! I finally finished high school."

My last two years were relatively peaceful. I had a reputation for being not just strong and tough but fair. I was always one of the leaders of the biker

Anthony Truglia on the left and myself

factions, but I had friends from all walks of life. Unlike a lot of inmates, I was capable of having breakfast with the Aryan Brotherhood and lunch with the Black Muslims and sharing knowledge of the martial arts with the Latinos—without angering anyone. I spent a lot of time with the Italians, of course, not only because of my own heritage but also because the Italians were the best cooks. One New Year's Eve we made a big dinner in our cells. One guy fried up some steaks (stolen from the kitchen), another boiled macaroni, and I was in charge of the sauce. It takes some ingenuity to put together a meal like that in prison. I used a homemade stove, the primary component of which was a heating element stolen from a water heater by someone who worked in the plumbing department. (Nowhere is the phrase "where there's a will, there's a way" more appropriate than in prison.) I flipped over a tin garbage can and set the hot plate on top of it, and then I began cooking up this great sauce. I sliced up onions, garlic . . . poured in the crushed tomatoes . . . added the salt, pepper, spices. Oh, man, did it smell good.

Unfortunately, I didn't realize that the hot plate was melting the paint off the surface of the garbage can, and pretty soon my cell began to fill with an acrid smoke. I turned off the hot plate and tried to clean up, but it was too late. There was a silent fire alarm in every cell, and mine had already gone off. The next thing I knew, a handful of guards were at my door, laughing as I tried to hide the sauce and burning garbage can. They had caught me red-handed (so to speak).

The next day I was taken to the lieutenant's office to argue my case.

"What were you doing, Zito?" he asked.

"To tell you the truth, Lieutenant, we were having a nice Italian dinner and I was making the sauce."

"Yeah?" he said. "Well, I hope it was good, because you're going to the hole. And you know why?"

"Uh . . . because I was cooking in my cell?"

He leaned forward and pounded his fist on his desk. "No, you're going to the hole because you didn't invite us!"

Then he laughed out loud and I realized I'd caught a break. I wouldn't be going to the hole after all. Apparently, even corrections officers get a little softhearted around the holidays.

"Go on; get back to your cell," the lieutenant said.

I thanked him and turned to leave, but I stopped as I reached the doorway. "Sir?"

"Yeah?"

"Can I have my sauce back?"

He wagged his index finger and smiled. "Don't push it, Zito."

With thirty days left in my bid, I was in Otisville, New York, trying to keep a low profile and dreaming about going home. I was getting ready to leave when a food strike broke out. Naturally, I was one of the inmates blamed for instigating the strike. I guess they figured if I could lead the Hells Angels, I could put together a food strike. So they stuck me in the hole for a few days, then shipped my ass off to Oakdale, Louisiana, and added five months to my sentence.

I did the rest of my time quietly, made it down to the final few days, and started giving away all the stuff that clogged up my cell, stuff I never wanted to see again and which I wouldn't need on the outside. Then, on a Friday afternoon in the winter of 1990, I went to receiving and discharge to sign out my personal items—family photos, letters, things like that. Everything else was gone. I walked up to the guard and said, "I'm Charles Zito, 120-32-054." (You never forget the number.)

The guard laughed and said, honest to God, "Sorry, Charlie. You're not going anywhere today."

I started to boil, thinking he was trying to fuck with my mind for some strange, sick reason.

"What are you talking about? I'm maxed out. I'm done. You can't hold me anymore."

"Listen," he said. "Our job is to give you a hundred bucks, put you on a bus—"

I cut him off. "Right, so do it."

"Can't," he said. "Greyhound just went on strike. You're stuck here until Monday. Then we'll get you a plane ticket back home."

What the fuck?! This was like some twisted joke. I had to get my sneakers back, some of my clothes, and then I spent the next three days in my cell, trying to avoid any type of conflict. Short-timers always have to be wary of other inmates, especially lifers, trying to provoke them into fights. It's a form of entertainment for some prisoners, to mess with you just for the pure fun of it. One mistake and

I'd be in there for another six months, and there was no way I was going to let that happen.

Those were three of the longest days of my life, but I made it through. On Monday they brought me to the airport and I flew to New York, where my whole family was waiting for me—my wife, my daughter, my sisters, my mother. We all cried and hugged, and

My daughter, Lisa, and my wife, Kathy, welcome me home from prison.

then I went home to New Rochelle. I walked into the backyard, as I had so many times before, to greet my rottweiler, Champ. Failing at first to recognize me, he charged at me, teeth bared, snarling. So I got right down on the ground, on all fours, and let him smell me. Within a few seconds he started licking me, playing with me. Six years I'd been gone, since he was just a puppy, but he remembered.

I went into the garage, backed out my '57 Chevy, and started washing it in the driveway, with my daughter helping. Standing there together, soap splashing all over us, laughing, it almost felt like I'd never been gone, like it all had been a terrible dream. But it wasn't. Lisa was older now, a young woman. I'd missed her sixteenth birthday, her eighteenth birthday, her junior prom, and countless other important events. I'd lost almost six years of my life.

As I scrubbed the car, I felt a lump rising in my throat. Most people have no idea what freedom really means. But I did. And I would never take it for granted again.

21

YOU FIND OUT WHO YOUR FRIENDS ARE WHEN YOU'RE IN PRISON. THEY'RE
the ones who accept your phone calls, who don't pretend they've
never met you or worked with you or spent a long night with you at
some club. I was lucky. Most of my friends stood by me, as did the
majority of my clients. During my last week behind bars I made one
of my many calls to Mickey Rourke and, as always, he sounded happy
to hear from me. Sean Penn was visiting Mickey the day I called. I'd
never worked for Sean before, but I'd known him for some time and
I respected the hell out of him. He was a standup guy who took no
bullshit from anyone (good with his fists, too, which is always worth
a few points in my book). And he was a great actor and writer. But
it wasn't until that day that I realized just how honorable a man Sean
is.

"Listen, Chuck," he said. "I'm working on this movie, and we have
to do reshoots in New York. Why don't you come work for me?"

I was stunned. Sean owed me nothing, and yet he was willing to
offer me a job as soon as I was released from prison. His generosity,
compassion, and friendship allowed me to quickly resurrect my career as a bodyguard, and for that I will always be indebted to him.

The movie was *State of Grace*, a terrific (and underrated) story of
the Irish mob in New York City. I went to the city every day and
worked as a bodyguard for both Sean and his girlfriend (and future
wife), Robin Wright. During the daylight hours I felt comfortable and
productive, as if six years of hell had been wiped away and my life
had been returned to me. Nights were harder, though, because after
just a few days at home, during which I tried to reconnect with my
family, I was assigned to a halfway house. This was a condition of

249

my parole, and there was nothing I could do about it. For thirty days I had to sleep and eat with other parolees—drug addicts and thieves, mostly, who were trying to get back on their feet. It was a degrading, depressing journey that I took each night, from the movie set to this place that wasn't my home and that felt like a jail without the bars. But I did it and I did it without complaint, because the alternative was a return to prison and more time away from my family and my work. For once in my life, I swallowed my pride and did exactly what I was told.

Well, for the most part, anyway.

Another condition of my parole, which saddened and frustrated me, was a nonassociation clause: in short, wearing my patch, riding a motorcycle, even hanging out with anyone wearing a Hells Angels jacket—all of these constituted parole violations. So I had to stay away from all of my friends, guys I'd grown up with, even if they didn't have criminal records, even if they were completely clean. It killed me.

Of course, my friends understood; and I did sneak around a bit. There were times when I'd be in a restaurant and bump into a few of the guys from the club. Just by coincidence, you know? When my parole officer would ask me about it, I'd say, "Hey, what do you want me to do? Ignore them when we see each other in public?"

The day I fulfilled the requirements of my parole was one of the happiest days of my life. I put my Hells Angels patch on and went for a long ride. And I've never looked back.

Which is not to say I haven't known some controversy over the years. It comes with the territory. Like the time in early 1994, shortly after the second of my three serious motorcycle accidents, while driving my '87 Grand Marquis to my sister's house in New Rochelle, I noticed a bunch of guys on motorcycles near Hudson Park heading toward a restaurant called Dudley's, which had a reputation as a bikers' hangout. I wanted to see what was happening, so I made a U-turn and came back up the street. Several bikes were blocking my way, so I leaned on the horn a bit, just to get them to bear to the right so I could pass. As I drove past them, one of the bikers turned around and gave me a dirty look, but I just kept going.

At the stop light, at the intersection of Davenport and Pelham

Road, I looked in my rearview mirror and saw five bikers approaching from behind. Now, these guys were just weekend warriors, not affiliated with any club, and since I'd just come from the gym, I wasn't wearing anything that would identify me as a member of the Hells Angels—just workout gear. I suppose that gave them a measure of confidence, for it wasn't long before they were next to my car, five of them in one lane, me in the other, with the window down. The last of them to pull up was the one who had given me a dirty look when I drove by, and now he was staring at me again. As he inched forward, I could hear him talking to his buddies.

"There's that punk motherfucker," he said.

Well, I wasn't looking for a fight, but that's not the sort of insult that I can ignore, so I put my car in park, opened the door, and marched through the line of bikes. "Oh, shit!" I heard one of them say. "That's Chuck Zito." By the time the words had left his mouth I was face to face with his buddy, the biker who had disrespected me.

"Who's a punk motherfucker?" I said, and before he had a chance to answer, I hit him with a right hand. He went flying off his bike. I stood there waiting for him to get up so that I could beat him some more, but he had something else in mind . . . something more serious. He pulled a gun from his waistband. I jumped on top of him and began wrestling with him on the ground. I kept punching him with one hand, while I grabbed the gun with the other. I don't know how long it went on like that. I only know that suddenly the sirens were all around us. Then I heard the squealing of brakes and the sound of car doors slamming, and, almost in my ear, the distinctive click of a shotgun being primed.

"Hey, motherfuckers! Drop the gun, get to your feet! Both of you!"

We rolled apart and pulled ourselves up. There were several members of the New Rochelle Police Department on the scene now, but the only one who mattered was the one with the shotgun, which was aimed squarely at my opponent's chest; this scumbag, meanwhile, still had his gun pointed at me. I was the only one unarmed.

"Put the gun down—now!" the New Rochelle cop yelled.

"It's okay," the biker responded. "I'm a New York City cop." And with that he proceeded to slowly remove his wallet. Inside, to my dismay, was a badge.

Ah, fuck! Just what I needed. I just beat up an off-duty cop!

"All right, somebody tell me what's going on here," the New Rochelle cop said.

Given the circumstances, I decided that it was time to be diplomatic. "Just a little misunderstanding officer," I said. "No big deal."

I smiled, figuring if this guy was a New York cop, he'd want this to go away as quickly as possible, too. After all, he'd been the instigator. But I misjudged him. He was an even bigger asshole than I'd imagined. As I was trying to talk to the New Rochelle cop, I heard the New York cop call me a motherfucker again, and as I turned to face him, he threw a punch. Fortunately, he just missed my nose, which was still aching from having been broken in the motorcycle accident. Instead, his fist caught me in the mouth, which began to bleed.

"Now you've pissed me off," I said. "When these guys leave, it's me and you."

At that point, I expected the worst, that cops would take care of cops and I'd end up in jail. To my astonishment, that's not what happened at all. The New Rochelle cop ordered the New York cop to lean against one of the squad cars. Then he walked up to me and said, quietly but firmly, "Would you like to press charges?"

"You guys are fellow officers," I said.

The New Rochelle cop shook his head and frowned. "This guy ain't no cop to me. What he did was punk shit. You want to press charges; it's fine with me."

I glanced at the New York cop, then at the New Rochelle cop. "No, that's okay," I said. "I don't press charges. I get even."

The New Rochelle cop smiled. "Okay."

By this time, more officers had arrived, and they stayed on the scene until the New York cop and his buddies got on their bikes and rode away. I never did see him again, but that's okay. As far as I'm concerned, justice was served.

In December of 1994 we had a big party in Rockford, Illinois, to celebrate the conversion of a club known as the Hells Henchmen to the Hells Angels. We flew into Chicago's O'Hare International Airport, rented three vans, and drove eighty miles to Rockford, where we had a nice patchover ceremony and a typically exhausting, weekend-long Hells Angels party. The cops had us under surveillance the entire time, though I'm not really sure why or what they were looking for. (It's amazing to me that the FBI and other law enforcement agencies actually pay their officers to sit there and watch us have a good time.) As we left Rockford to return to O'Hare, our party split up. Two vans went one way; the third (which I was driving) went in a different direction. The cops tailed the other two vans all the way to Chicago and jacked up my brothers in the O'Hare terminal. I didn't realize this until after I had turned in my keys and paid my bill at the rental counter. We were walking toward the gate to catch our flight when a group of roughly ten cops came running at us, guns drawn.

"Down on the floor! *Now!*"

They accused us of trying to evade capture, of leading them on a dangerous high-speed chase. In truth, they were merely pissed because they'd lost track of one of our vans. Shit, I was driving that van and I'm telling you right now that I never even broke the speed limit. I didn't know the cops were following us, and I didn't care. Anyway, they searched every one of us, along with our vans, and found absolutely nothing. Nevertheless, they loaded us into a paddy wagon and brought us downtown, where they charged us with criminal disorderly conduct, even though we hadn't committed any crimes and hadn't behaved in a disorderly fashion. They lied about the high-speed chase, and then they claimed there was some sort of law in Illinois that made it illegal to wear gang-related clothing in airports.

Bullshit. Complete and utter bullshit.

What I did not need at that time was another arrest, even one that couldn't possibly stick. The next day my picture appeared in newspapers, in Chicago and New York and I was identified alternately as a "bodyguard," "stuntman," "friend of the stars." It was not the kind of publicity I wanted. It wasn't good for my career, and it wasn't good for my family. Kathy and Lisa had stood by me through my years in prison, and I was immensely grateful for their loyalty. But now here I was, going back to my old ways, hanging out with my old buddies, which I knew had the potential to get me in trouble, even if I didn't break any laws. It seemed at times as though I had two separate lives: one with my wife and daughter and one with the Hells Angels. If six years in prison had demonstrated to me just how much I loved my family, it also had strengthened the bond I felt with my brothers. They were there with me, day in and day out. I shared a cell with John the

Hells Angels on the set of *A Bronx Tale*. Left to right: Steve Kendall with the beard, Steve Bonge with the striped shirt, and behind him is Butch Garcia.
Credit: Peter Figetakis

Baptist. I shared a cell with Bert. I shared a cell with Lightfoot. Along the way, they became family, too.

We spent only ten hours in jail before posting bail. The judge dismissed the case, and it became apparent that the cops knew they had made a mistake and simply wanted the whole thing to go away. We weren't about to let that happen. Instead, we hired Ron Kuby, a prominent defense attorney, and sued the Chicago police. And you know what? We won. Granted, the out-of-court settlement wasn't much—only $250,000—but we felt vindicated nonetheless. I tried to pay back Kathy and Lisa by pumping my share—approximately nine grand—into improvements on the house. I'm sure they didn't see it as fair compensation for what I'd put them through (again!), but it was an important victory. For a change, justice was served.

Despite my continued allegiance to the Hells Angels (and the occasional brush with the law), my career in Hollywood blossomed. I worked as a stunt coordinator on a 1996 children's movie called *Santa with Muscles*, starring professional wrestler Hulk Hogan. That job not only led to future work in wrestling but also allowed me to pay back many of the people who had helped me in the past. You see, as stunt coordinator, I was in a position to assign work to more than thirty people, and, naturally, I hired all of my buddies. Some of them got SAG cards out of it and went on to do more stunt work.

In October, 1992, I filled a similar role in *A Bronx Tale,* starring Robert De Niro and Chazz Palminteri. There's a scene in that movie (the best scene, really) in which a group of mobsters, led by Palminteri, kick the shit out of a group of bikers in a barroom brawl. The bikers were Hells Angels from our Connecticut, Massachusetts, and New York City chapters, recruited by yours truly at De Niro's behest. I had read for a part in the movie, and though I didn't get the job, Bobby asked me if I could help him round up a few tough-looking guys for the big brawl. I was glad to do it, especially since it allowed several people to get their SAG cards. I did, however, make it clear to everyone on the set that my brothers were just acting.

"Anytime you guys want to try this in real life, you just let me know," I joked to Chazz as we set up for the barroom scene.

"No, that's OK, Chuck," he said with a laugh. "This is just for the movies."

The closing credits of *A Bronx Tale* include a note saying: "Thanks to Chuck Zito," which always makes me smile. But it's a hard movie for me to watch, because one of the bikers, a character called Red Beard, is played by my friend and brother Steve Kendall. Steve had a couple lines in the movie and did a terrific job (especially for a guy who had never acted before). He was proud of the work he did. Sadly, Steve never did get to see himself on-screen. He was on his way to Connecticut one night when a bus collided with his motorcycle which hit a retaining wall on the Bruckner Expressway in the Bronx. His death came just a few weeks before the movie was released.

In my world, you lose people now and then. And sometimes you save them; Even when they're not sure they want to be saved. Take Charlie Sheen, for example. Charlie is one of my all-time favorite clients. I know, I know . . . most people think of Charlie as just another notorious fuckup. But I'll tell you this—Charlie is a good guy.

The first time I met Charlie was in the mid 1990s. I'd gotten a call from the cinematographer on a movie called *The Chase,* which was being shot in Texas. Seems the movie company was having trouble with the local teamsters, many of whom were in the process of being fired and replaced by teamsters from California. Before the locals left, they started threatening everyone associated with the film. So I was brought in to work as a bodyguard for the director and cinematographer (I was also hired to do stunt work for Buddy Joe Hooker, the movie's stunt coordinator).

I flew in from New York and met some of my old stunt buddies at the airport. We rode together to the movie set and began working on the film. Not long after we started shooting, there was trouble. We happened to be playing highway patrol officers, so we each had our own police cruiser. A call came over the walkie-talkie that the local teamsters truck had to come through and we had to bear to the right so they could pass. Well, we all did as instructed, but I guess the vehicle behind me was a little slow to pull over, because the next thing I knew, there was a big commotion . . . people yelling, honking their horns. A truck filled with teamsters crept by, and right behind them was my friend and fellow stuntman Pete Antico, running after the teamsters. The truck stopped and at least six teamsters jumped off and got right in Pete's face. I jumped out of my car and ran over next to Pete. When Pete saw me, he knew right away I had his back, no questions asked. Later I would find out that one of the teamsters had yelled at Pete and disrespected him. But I didn't need an explanation. Pete was my friend. There was no way I was going to let him fight this battle alone.

"I'm not just some extra," Pete told the teamsters. "I'm a stuntman doing his job."

"I don't give a fuck who you are," one of the teamsters said. "I will—"

Before he could finish the sentence, Pete hit him with a right hand to the jaw, followed by an elbow to the temple—all in one motion. The teamster went down hard. Instantly another teamster went to move on Pete, but I stepped in and hit him with a ridge hand to the throat. He, too, went right down, flopping and gasping for air like a fish pulled from a lake.

The rest of them froze. "Whoa, these guys ain't stuntmen," one of them said. And then they backed off.

Meanwhile, sitting in his car, watching the whole episode unfold, was the star of *The Chase*, Charlie Sheen. A few weeks later, after the movie had wrapped and I'd returned to New York, I received a call from Charlie, wondering if I'd be interested in working for him.

"How much do you get paid?" he asked.

"Five hundred dollars a day."

"A thousand dollars?!"

"No, five hundred," I repeated.

"A thousand dollars?!" Charlie said again. "Man, there must be something wrong with this phone."

I took a deep breath. "Charlie . . . I get five hundred a day. What are you doing?"

There was laughter on the other end of the line. "Chuck," he said. "I'd like you to come work for me, and I'll pay you a thousand dollars a day."

"Guess you got yourself a bodyguard," I said.

I flew to California to meet with Charlie, and then we took a private jet to Phoenix, to begin working on a new movie. We hit it off right away. I don't know that I've ever had a client with a bigger heart. It's true that Charlie has had difficulties with drugs and alcohol, but he is without question the most generous man I've ever worked with.

One night while we were in Arizona we went to a local car show (like me, Charlie was a big car enthusiast). As we were walking around, Charlie spotted a '63 Buick LeSabre convertible, in mint condition, and he just fell in love with it. So he walked up to the owner, an elderly gentleman, and said, "This is a great car. Do you want to sell it?"

The old man thought for a moment and said, "I suppose for the right price I'd consider it."

"How much do you want?"

"I'd need at least twelve grand."

Charlie smiled and said, "You got a ride home tonight?"

I pulled him aside. "Charlie, what are you doing, man? We can get this car for seven or eight grand—max."

Charlie waved me off casually. "It's okay. Let him have the money."

Within five minutes Charlie had written a check for $12,000 and was driving back to the hotel in a '63 Buick LeSabre. The next day I saw a black woman, one of the production assistants on the movie, driving out of the hotel parking lot in Charlie's new car. When I asked Charlie what had happened, he just shrugged his shoulders.

"Her car broke down, and she doesn't have the money for a new one," he said. "So I gave her mine."

"You mean you let her borrow it?"

"No, it's hers now."

I gave him a pat on the back. "Charlie, from now on I'm calling you E," I said.

"E?"

"Uh-huh. E . . . as in Elvis, because you're the only man I know who just gives stuff away to people he barely knows."

Despite his admitted weakness for whiskey and women, Charlie was a guy who usually stayed out of trouble when I was around him. He liked to train with me, and that kept him clean. Unfortunately, our relationship has been something of a roller-coaster ride. We went our separate ways around the time Charlie got married to his first wife, a model named Donna Peele. They'd met in Central Park one night when Charlie was filming a commercial for a Japanese company. At the end of the shoot Charlie took her back to his home in Malibu. Three days later I got a phone call.

"Chuck, it's Charlie." He sounded happy, excited. With Charlie, that was not always a good thing. He had mood swings, and sometimes he did crazy things when he was in a manic state. This was precisely such a case. "I just want you to be the first to know—I'm getting married!"

Although I wanted to be happy for him, I couldn't lie. "Jesus, Charlie," I said. "Are you out of your mind? You've known this woman a week."

"I know, I know," he said. "But you've gotta trust me . . . she's the one. I can feel it."

"Don't do it, Charlie. Please. It won't last six months."

Two weeks later we started work on another movie, and already it was apparent that there was trouble in paradise. I picked up Charlie at five o'clock in the morning, and Donna was there waiting, fully dressed, ready to join us. They had a little discussion about whether it was appropriate for Donna to be on the set, and quickly the discussion escalated into an argument. I founded myself standing there, watching this ugly little scene, saying to myself, *Oh, boy, Charlie . . . this ain't gonna work.*

And, of course, it didn't. Donna was a gorgeous, jealous woman unaccustomed to dating someone like Charlie. He was a big movie star, a good-looking guy with tons of money. It was only natural that women would be attracted to him. And they were. Everywhere Charlie went, young beautiful women were sure to follow. That drove Donna crazy. Her jealousy and the stress it caused in their relationship wreaked havoc on Charlie's work. He was distracted. He flubbed his lines. Finally, even though it probably wasn't my place, I decided to have a little talk with Donna.

"You have to relax," I told her. "This man comes home to you every night. He loves you. Those other women that hang around the set? They don't mean shit to Charlie."

Predictably, Donna didn't exactly appreciate my getting involved in her personal business. When Charlie first told me of his impending wedding plans, he also asked me to be his best man. Shortly thereafter he told me there had been a change, that he had been best man at another friend's wedding and now felt obliged to reciprocate. "But I'd still like you to be in the wedding party," he said.

No problem, I told him. I was honored to be involved in any way (even though I knew the union wouldn't last). As it happened, though, I was not part of the wedding party. In fact, I wasn't even invited to the wedding. Charlie never called, never explained. We simply went our separate ways. I didn't really hold it against him. I knew his nuts were in a vise, that his wife didn't like me and that his first obligation was to her. I just wish he'd called to explain it to me—man to man.

A year passed. I got a call from Brett Michaels, who had been the lead singer for a big 1980s band called Poison. Brett had turned his attention to writing and had recently finished a screenplay for a movie called *No Code of Conduct*. The film was about to begin shooting, and he wanted to know whether I'd be interested in playing a small role. It was only a week's worth of work, he explained, but both Charlie Sheen and his father, Martin Sheen, had already signed on.

"Sure," I said. "I'd be happy to do it."

As often happens in Hollywood, my part shrank. A week of work became a day. I called Brett and told him it wasn't worth my time. Then I thought about it some more and decided maybe there was a reason I'd been offered this part . . . and maybe it had nothing to do with my ambitions as an actor. Maybe it was time to patch things up with Charlie.

So I flew to Texas, where the movie was being filmed, and drove out to the set. Charlie had his own trailer, in front of which sat Charlie's new bodyguard, a mountainous man, probably six-foot-3, 300 pounds. As I approached, he stood up and crossed his arms, as if he was looking for trouble. Fortunately, Charlie had seen me coming. He opened the door to his trailer and yelled, "Hey, Chuck! Come on up."

We shook hands and embraced like family.

"I came out here for one reason, Charlie," I said. "To make up with you. Life is too short. We shouldn't have any hard feelings."

Charlie nodded, said he felt the same way. I couldn't help but notice that Donna was nowhere to be found. They'd already split, Charlie explained. The marriage had been a huge mistake. I said I was sorry and that I hoped he was doing okay. We talked for a little while. The conversation was smooth, comfortable, just as it had always been. So comfortable, in fact, that Charlie invited me to work for him again. I'd have to peacefully coexist with his current bodyguard for a few weeks, but then it would be just the two of us again.

A couple weeks later I went to Charlie's house in Malibu. My first night there I was sleeping downstairs, in the guest quarters, when I heard the bodyguard screaming.

"Chuck! Come quick! It's Charlie!"

I ran upstairs and found Charlie unconscious. There had been a party earlier in the night, with several girls, but I fell asleep before it got too wild. I didn't know what Charlie had ingested, but knowing his history and judging by his appearance—white as a sheet, barely breathing—it seemed obvious he'd suffered some sort of overdose. When paramedics arrived they confirmed that diagnosis. Before leaving the house I picked up the phone and called Charlie's father.

"Mr. Sheen," I said. "Charlie's had some kind of a drug overdose. We're on our way to the hospital."

"My wife and I will meet you there," he answered.

I took a lot of heat at the hospital, first from Martin Sheen, who walked up to me at Charlie's bedside and said, with fire in his eyes, "I don't want you around my son anymore."

Now, I didn't really know Martin at the time. We'd met, said hello a few times, but that's about it. I knew he was in pain, that it had to be incredibly difficult to see his son in that condition. Nevertheless, I felt compelled to set the record straight.

"Mr. Sheen," I said. "You don't know anything about me, other than the fact that I'm a Hells Angel. Regardless of what you think that means, I don't drink, I don't smoke, and I have never taken a drug in my life. Charlie is a good friend of mine, and I just want to help him."

Martin stepped back, gave me a long, hard look. A recovering alcoholic himself, I think he knew when he was being lied to and when he was being told the truth.

"I'm sorry," he said, extending a hand. "I didn't know that. I thought you were supplying my son with drugs."

"No way," I said. "I'd never do anything to hurt Charlie."

While Martin and I were starting to bond, Charlie woke up; naturally, his first reaction was outrage.

"Who called you?" Charlie said to his father.

I stepped in and took the blame, or the credit . . . whatever you want to call it. "I didn't know what was happening, Charlie," I said. "I thought you might die, and I wanted your parents to know what was going on."

Charlie spent four days in the hospital, during which his parents and I repeatedly tried to convince him that he needed help. I didn't leave the hospital the entire time. I put my chair across the door and sat there, because I knew Charlie wanted to put on his shoes and run. He wasn't quite ready to admit he had a problem. Slowly, though, we began to wear him down. Charlie went to his first support group meeting while he was in the hospital. I accompanied him. It was kind of funny, actually, all these people standing up and talking about their problems and how they were addicted to this drug or that drug or how alcohol had ruined their lives. And there I was the guy with the Hells Angels patch, and I was the only person in the room who had always been sober!

On the fourth day we went for a walk outside so that Charlie could smoke a cigarette. As we got close to the garage, I could see Charlie's eyes starting to dance. I'd seen it before. It was a mischievous look.

"Come on," he said as we approached his Lincoln. "Give me my keys. We're getting out of here."

He looked so sad, standing there in his pajamas, trying to make a getaway.

"Charlie," I said. "We're not going anywhere."

"This is my car," he said, his voice starting to rise. "Now give me the fucking keys!"

"No."

"God damn it, Chuck! You work for me! And I want to leave—now!"

"You know what, Charlie?" I said. "I don't work for you anymore. I work for your mom and dad . . . and we're going back into the hospital."

With that, Charlie went ballistic. He started screaming, jumping around. "This is bullshit, man! I'm gonna kill you!"

I smiled. "Careful now, Charlie. That sounds like a threat. And if you threaten me . . ." I started to walk toward him. . . . "I'll have to defend myself."

He jumped back and held up his hands. "Okay, I get the point."

So we went back to his room, and pretty soon Mr. and Mrs. Sheen arrived. The plan was to discharge Charlie and take him to a rehabilitation center in Malibu called Promises. On the way we stopped off at Charlie's house so that he could pick up enough clothes for a thirty-day visit. I had my doubts about whether he could make it, but when we arrived, and I volunteered to spend the first night with him, he surprised me with his resolve.

"Thanks anyway," he said. "But I need to do this on my own."

I told him that I was proud of him and that I loved him and that I'd stop by to visit in a few days. Then I left with Mr. and Mrs. Sheen.

Five hours later, damned if I didn't get a phone call from Promises. Charlie had jumped the wall and escaped! No wonder he hadn't wanted me to spend the night with him—he had no intention of staying.

The cops caught up with him on the Pacific Coast Highway and took him to a local lockup. He was still in the back of the police cruiser when I got to Malibu. As they took him out of the car, I could see just how angry he was. He blamed this on me, as if I had betrayed him. And I didn't blame him. He was scared. He was hurt. In his mind, anyway, he was all alone.

As they took him out of the car and led him to jail, I said goodbye. "I hope you do the right thing, buddy."

Charlie looked back. He didn't say a word.

I've not spoken to Charlie since. He spent a couple days in jail, then went straight to rehab. His recovery and subsequent career resurrection have become the stuff of Hollywood legend. He's a big star again, with a leading role on one of television's best sitcoms, *Spin City*. As far as anyone can tell, he's been clean and sober for years.

And I couldn't be happier for him. As I said, he's one of the good guys, and he deserves his success.

With Mr. and Mrs. Martin Sheen at their home in Malibu

I once sent him a letter in which I tried to explain my actions. I told him his health and well-being were more important to me than money. I told him I missed him and that I understood his anger, but that given the same set of circumstances . . . I would do the same thing all over again. "I'm not sorry I took you to the hospital," I wrote. "And I'm not sorry I called your mom and dad. I'm just glad you're happy and healthy and doing well."

He didn't write back. But that's okay. Someday maybe we'll reconnect. Or maybe not.

I still keep in touch with Charlie's parents. As a matter of fact, I ran into Martin at an awards show not too long ago. He was a nominee as well as a presenter. I was there with my colleagues from HBO. Martin saw me from across the room and immediately came over. He hugged me and said aloud, to everyone within earshot, "This is the man who saved my Charlie's life." We talked for a few minutes, and then we said good-bye. Before leaving, Martin pressed something into the palm of my hand: a rosary.

My daughter, Lisa, age two

22

I HAVE A KNACK FOR FINDING TROUBLE AT THE MOST INOPPORTUNE TIMES.
Like when I was working as a stuntman on the movie *Heat,* in 1995.
We were filming in Los Angeles, and one night after work I went to
the Rainbow Bar & Grill with a few other stuntmen and Hells Angels.
We took a table in the back, tried to keep a low profile. After a while
I got up to go to the men's room and found my path blocked. There
was nothing unusual about that at the Rainbow, which was usually
packed to the rafters. So I simply said, "Excuse me," and tried to
squeeze through.

Most people, I find, are reasonable in these situations. They step
aside and go on with their little party. In every bar, however, there
are people who have had a little too much to drink and who begin to
lose the ability to tell right from wrong. These are the people who get
on my nerves and who, for some reason, I seem to find with alarming
regularity.

"Excuse me," I said to the pack of six guys swigging beer in the
aisle.

No reaction.

"Excuse me," I repeated, this time with greater volume.

Still no reaction.

"Excuse me!"

Finally, one of them turned around and stared at me, angrily, as if
I were some kind of jerk-off giving him a hard time.

Well, that's all it took. I walked right through their pack, nudging
several of them out of the way in the process.

"Hey, don't push me, pal," said the guy who had given me the hairy
eyeball.

I stopped. "I asked you three times to move out of the way."

"Fuck you," he said.

That, of course, was my invitation to punch him in the face, which was precisely what I did. Before he had even hit the floor, one of his friends jumped in. I decked him, too. Before he hit the floor, however, someone else hit me in the face with a beer bottle, right across my eyebrow. The moment it struck, I knew I was in trouble. Blood began streaming down my face. As I reached out and grabbed another of their party and threw him down, someone kicked me in the face. Now there was blood coming from my mouth, too.

And then it was over. The bouncers swarmed and pulled us apart. My friends came, too.

"What happened?" one of them said.

"I was fighting six guys while you were eating dinner, that's what happened."

Once outside, I caught up with one of their party and gave him a few more shots, just so he'd remember me. Then I went to the hospital. The emergency room docs said I was lucky, that I could have been blinded. They removed shards of glass from my eye, then shaved my eyebrow and closed the wound with a dozen stitches.

It was five o'clock in the morning before I was discharged. We were supposed to start shooting at seven, so I put on a hat and dark glasses and went straight to the set. One of the first people I ran into was Robert De Niro, the film's star.

"Jesus, Chuck, what happened to your lip?" he said.

"Bobby," I said. "Forget about my lip." I lowered my glasses.

"Holy shit!" Bobby yelled. "Are you okay?"

"For a guy who fought six guys by himself just a few hours ago, yeah, I'm doing all right. But I'd like to keep it quiet."

"Of course," he said.

Fortunately, I was just one of a hundred bit players in the movie's most famous scene: a protracted shoot-out between the cops and De Niro's gang of thieves. I was one of the good guys, but not so good that I warranted a close-up. I finished the shoot, got paid, and cashed the check.

Come to think of it, I've had quite a few brawls at the Rainbow. There was one time when I never even made it through the front door. It started when I pulled into the parking lot off Sunset Boulevard.

There was already a lot of traffic in front of the Rainbow because of something that had happened next door at the Roxy—fire trucks and police cars clogged the roadway. A crowd of onlookers had naturally gathered, including my friends Mario, Tony, and Michael (who, incidently, owns The Rainbow).

I was driving Pete Antico's black BMW with blacked-out windows. As I pulled into the lot, someone punched the window of Pete's car. Well, by now you know I have a short fuse, so you can probably guess what happened next. I put the car in park and hopped out. Actually, I didn't really "hop." See, I left out one little detail: Thanks to another of my motorcycle accidents, I was wearing a cast on my leg at this time. So I *hobbled* out of the car . . . and saw this skinhead who punched my window walking across Sunset Boulevard.

"Hey, asshole!" I yelled as I shuffled toward him.

He stopped, turned, and waited. And there we were, in the middle of Sunset Boulevard, surrounded by cop cars, fire trucks, and a whole bunch of people. "Why did you punch my window?" I asked. "You want to get knocked out?"

He responded by trying to head-butt me. But I moved just in time, so instead of hitting my nose, which definitely would have hurt, he hit my mouth, which of course began to bleed. Then I hit him with a right hand on the chin, and he fell face first onto the ground, right next to one of the police cars. I reached down to grab him—he had no hair, so I yanked him up by the ears and proceeded to bang his face against the bumper of the car. Finally, a cop saw what was happening and pulled me off the guy. The cop was about to arrest me when Mario, Tony, and Michael came running over and said they had witnessed the whole incident.

"This poor guy's got a broken leg, and that skinhead there hit him first," they explained.

A few minutes later another cop arrived on the scene, a sergeant who (luckily for me) happened to be an ex–New Yorker. He listened to my friends' version of the fight, then looked at the skinhead, who was trying to stand up, hamburger face and all, and shrugged. "That's what I call street justice," the sergeant said. Then he told me to take off. Not wanting to wait until he changed his mind, I hobbled into the Rainbow as quickly as I could, leaving the skinhead behind me, sniveling to the cops.

When it comes to interpersonal relationships, my motto is at once simple and rigid: *Treat me good, I'll treat you better; treat me bad . . . I'll treat you worse.*

I mean that with all my heart. I'm as good and true a friend as you're likely to find. But you don't want me as an enemy. The world is a small place, and I have a long and vivid memory.

Consider the phone call I received from Charlie Sheen in 1996. He was in a bar, and he'd run into someone who said he knew me.

"This guy says he once dated your daughter," Charlie said.

"Oh, yeah? Put him on."

The guy got on the phone and introduced himself as "Johnny." He sounded drunk and full of himself, and while I had no idea who he was, had no recollection of Lisa having dated anyone named Johnny, I didn't like his attitude.

"Why are you telling Charlie any of my business?" I said. "Don't fuckin' talk about my family."

"Hey, take it easy," Johnny said. "We have another mutual acquaintance." Then he proceeded to drop the name of a wise guy from the Bronx, as if that meant he'd have some sort of immunity from me. That, of course, was a mistake.

"This conversation ends now," I said. "When I see you in person, we'll take it up again."

It was 1997 before we spoke again. I was sitting in front of Mulberry Street Pizza in Beverly Hills, hanging out with a bunch of my friends—Johnny C., Pete Antico, Jay Accavone, Tom Patty, Giuseppe Franco, and the owner of the place, Richie Palmer—when I noticed a group of five guys walking toward us. As they drew near, one of them stepped forward, a kid who looked to be in his mid-to late twenties, and said, "Hey, Chuck, how are you?"

I had no idea who he was, but I said hello anyway, and then he proceeded to sit down and bend my ear like we were old buddies. He told me about some movie he was working on and how his career was going great. I kept staring at him, trying to place the face.

Who is this guy, and how does he know me?

After about five minutes of small talk, the guy said, "Good to see you, Chuck," and excused himself. As he started to walk away, he paused and turned. "Oh," he added. "I'm really sorry about what happened with Charlie that night."

"Charlie who?"

"Charlie Sheen. You know . . . in the bar . . . when we called you."

Son of a bitch. . . .

I looked hard at his face, and suddenly it came into focus. He was older now, but I remembered. The last time I'd seen him he was just a teenager, scrambling to get out of my house after making an unauthorized visit to Lisa. It was 1984. Lisa was only thirteen years old at the time, and Kathy and I had forbidden her to have male guests when we weren't home. This kid—Johnny—had violated that rule on two occasions, the second time narrowly escaping my wrath by jumping out a second-story window and climbing down a tree in my backyard. He'd had the good sense to never come around again after that. I didn't know what had happened to him, and frankly I didn't care. But now . . . here he was.

"You're that guy?" I said, standing up. "You're the one who talked to Charlie about my daughter?"

"Uhhhh . . . yeah."

I closed the space between us. "Who did you mention to me on the phone that night?"

"What do you mean?"

"You said we had a mutual acquaintance. Remember? What was his name?"

"Oh," Johnny said. "You mean . . ."

As soon as he repeated the name, I slapped him in the face. He stumbled backward, hurt and scared, and started to run away.

"Don't make me chase you!" I shouted.

He stopped in his tracks and walked back in my direction.

"Listen," I said. "Don't ever drop anyone's name around me. And don't ever talk to anyone about me or my daughter. You got that?"

"Yes, sir," he said.

And then I let him go. It had taken thirteen years, but I'd finally tracked that kid down and taught him a much-needed lesson: In the immortal words of the Bronx Bomber, Joe Louis, the second-greatest boxer in history (after Muhammad Ali, of course), "You can run, but you can't hide."

Fast-forward to February 5, 1998, and a night that will live in infamy (well, in some circles, anyway). The night I taught Jean-Claude Van Damme the difference between reel life and real life. But first . . . a little background.

I first met Jean-Claude in 1992. He'd been a legitimate martial artist at one time, a black belt who had competed successfully in Belgium. But now his attention was focused squarely on Hollywood. We were introduced at a beauty pageant sponsored by Hawaiian Tropic. I'd been hired to do security (the pageant coincided with a big motorcycle event known as Bike Week); Jean-Claude was one of three celebrity judges (the others were Chad McQueen and O. J. Simpson). When the week ended, Jean-Claude asked me if I'd be interested in working as his personal bodyguard and I accepted. But it became apparent to me fairly quickly that our relationship wouldn't last. Not that he wasn't respectful to me—he was. We trained together, sparred a few times, and generally got along all right. But I just didn't hit it off with him the way I usually did with my clients. More often than not, I became friends with the people who hired me. I genuinely liked them, and they liked me.

When you're spending that much time together, you have to develop a certain rapport, and I never felt like I had that with Jean-Claude. Why? I don't know. It's hard to explain. For one thing, I didn't like his demeanor, his attitude. I'd worked with some of the biggest stars in the world, and most of them made a concerted effort to put other people at ease. They were comfortable with their celebrity, and they didn't wield it arrogantly. They were nice to the small people who crossed their paths on a daily basis: the limo drivers, the hotel maids, waiters, and waitresses. And, especially, to their fans. In other words, they seemed to realize how fortunate they were.

Jean-Claude, on the other hand, acted like the world owed him something. He wasn't gracious. In fact, sometimes he could be downright mean. I was accustomed to working with stars who were considerate of other people. Being with Jean-Claude made me uncomfortable, so, after a few weeks, we parted ways. There was no big scene, no fight, nothing. It was a mutual decision.

Over the course of the next few years our paths crossed a few times, and there always seemed to be tension between us. It's hard to explain, but I always got the feeling that Jean-Claude felt insecure around me. He was defensive, unfriendly. There wasn't any open animosity, nothing on the surface. But I could tell he didn't like me. Maybe he didn't like the fact that when we worked together sometimes I'd get more attention than he did. Maybe it had something to do with him being an actor who fashioned himself as a real tough guy. I was the tough guy, the street guy, and he knew it. To be perfectly candid, I think Jean-Claude felt threatened by me.

Anyway, by February of 1998 it had been several years since we'd had a meaningful conversation. As far as I was concerned, we were neither friends nor enemies, just two men who once had worked together. I guess Jean-Claude felt differently. We ran into each other one night at Scores, an upscale New York strip club where I like to hang out. I was sitting there, eating my steak, minding my own business, when Jean-Claude walked in with Mickey Rourke and a few of his buddies. I figured, *Hey, life's too short; why hold grudges?* So I went over to Jean-Claude, pulled up a chair, and said hello. Right away he copped an attitude.

"Hey . . . Chuck Zi-to," he said, barely making eye contact. Now, I know my last name, so it was pretty obvious that he was trying to be an asshole. But I just decided to stay away from him. I didn't want or need any trouble.

A little while later, though, I was approached by a guy named Frankie, one of the club's bouncers, who had seen me talking with Jean-Claude.

"Hey, Chuck," he said. "Why are you wasting any time with that prick?" "What do you mean?"

"I just heard him talking about you in the bathroom."

I looked over at Jean-Claude, who was in the process of getting a lap dance from some long-legged honey.

"What did he say?"

"I asked him for an autograph and told him we had a mutual friend—Chuck Zito. And he started laughing, saying you had no heart, shit like that."

"Oh, yeah?"

"Yeah. You ask me, that guy's a scumbag."

I knew the bouncer and I trusted him. There was no way he was lying. So I pulled my chair next to Jean-Claude, looked at the girl wriggling in his lap, and said, "Sweetheart, do me a favor. Take your shoes for a walk." She got up and left, leaving me and Jean-Claude sitting just inches apart, staring at each other. We were surrounded by other people, but the music was loud, the place was jumping, and I'm not sure anyone realized we were on the edge of a brawl.

"Jean-Claude, were you just talking about me in the bathroom?"

He didn't respond at first. Then he slowly removed his glasses, tucked them into his breast pocket, and leaned even closer, and I thought, *Why the hell is he taking his glasses off? Unless he wants to fight.*

"Yeah. So what?"

"You tell Frankie I had no heart?"

"Uh-huh."

I didn't want to disrespect the people who owned the club, and I didn't want to disrespect Mickey, who came with Jean-Claude. But I couldn't just let this go. In all honesty, I have to say that I was amazed Jean-Claude was being such a jerk. So I gave him one more chance to explain his actions.

"Why would you say that?" I asked.

He lowered his head. "Because you're full of shit."

Shocked, I reached out and grabbed him by the arm. The music was blaring, and I thought perhaps I'd misheard him. "Excuse me, Jean-Claude. Did you say I'm full of shit?"

"No . . . I said you're *fucking* full of shit!"

And with that I hit him—twice. A straight right and a left hook. *Bam-bam!* Jean-Claude's chair flipped over backward, and he landed in the lap of my friend Kevin Lubic. As Jean-Claude tried to scramble to his feet, I started screaming at him.

"You fuckin' scumbag! I got no heart? You got no heart! This ain't the movies, asshole; this is the street. And I own the fucking street!"

I started hitting him with everything I had. Jean-Claude barely even tried to fight back. He just tried to shield himself. When he covered his head, I hit him in the body. When he covered his body, I hit him in the face. It went on like that for about thirty seconds, until the bouncers jumped in, Mickey jumped in, and all of my buddies jumped in and pulled me off Jean-Claude. He was tossed out of the club, and I left on my own—quickly—before the police arrived. I went straight to the hospital, because even though he hadn't landed a punch, I'd managed to hurt myself. I could feel my hand throbbing. Sure enough, X rays showed a broken bone.

This was no small matter, since I was scheduled to start work on *Oz* the following Monday (the fight happened on a Thursday night). Through a friend, a photographer named Brian Hamill, I'd met Tom Fontana, the head writer and producer of *Oz*, a few months earlier, at the premier of an HBO movie called *Only in America*. We'd talked a little, and when Tom found out I'd been in prison and that I'd done a little acting and a lot of stunt work, he asked me if I'd be interested in reading for *Oz*. I couldn't say yes fast enough. Two weeks later I was offered the part of Chucky Pancamo, an Italian mobster. (Interesting aside: The character's name was originally Sam Pancamo, but they changed it to Chucky when I got the role. I guess they were worried I wouldn't answer to Sam.)

Now, though, I was afraid I'd blown my big chance. I couldn't let the doctors cast me, because then everyone would know I'd gotten into a fight and I might lose the job. So I decided to tough it out, stay quiet, and hope the incident blew over. Fat chance! The next morning there was a huge photo of Jean-Claude on the cover of the *New York Post*, along with a shrieking headline:

JEAN-CLAUDE VAN SLAMMED!
Muscled Macho Action-Star Decked at Scores

Even worse, the accompanying story referred to me as "Chuck Zito, star of *Oz*."

Star?! I haven't worked a day yet? Oh, Christ, I'm gonna get fired before I film a scene.

But Tom Fontana is about the coolest guy around. Laughing, he came right up to me when I walked onto the set Monday morning and said, "Hey, Chuck. Couldn't you have hit the guy after the show aired? Would have been better publicity."

Interestingly enough, my career has been soaring ever since. I'm in my fourth season on *Oz*, which has been widely recognized as one of the best shows on television. Aside from the time I woke up in my cell after taking a little nap on the set and began to have flashbacks about being in prison (for a few terrifying moments I thought I'd never left), the *Oz* experience has been terrific. No one else associated with the show has done time, so they frequently ask me for input. *Oz* is a great prison soap opera and many of the stories have a basis in truth, but it *is* television and the drama is intentionally heightened. Sometimes I have to remind the producers and writers that convicts don't routinely kick the shit out of guards and, while prisons are indeed brutal and dehumanizing places, the murdering and molesting of inmates isn't quite as common as *Oz* might indicate. Generally speaking, though, it's an accurate depiction of life behind bars.

Tom has been happy with my work, which is one reason that I've lasted four years. *Oz* has a reputation for killing off important characters, but Chucky Pancamo is alive and well. When he first hired me, Tom said, "Chuck, before we're through, you're gonna be begging me to get off this show."

"I don't think so, Tom. This is a big deal to me."

"Yeah, but I'm going to push you and your character. I'm going to take you places you've never been."

"That's fine," I said. "But there's something you should know. I don't do rapes, and I don't get raped."

Tom laughed. "Come on, Chuck; it's just acting."

"Yeah? Well, if I have to stick my tongue down some other guy's throat to be a great actor, then I guess I'll never win an Academy Award."

So far, so good. Chucky Pancamo is a nasty guy, but he's kept his dick in his pants for four seasons.

Around the same time that I started doing *Oz*, I became a semi-regular on the *Howard Stern Show*. When Howard heard about my fight with Jean-Claude, he wanted me to be a guest. I turned him down for a while, because I didn't want the publicity, but when I found out Jean-Claude was giving interviews about the incident, I figured I'd better tell my side of the story. Anyway, I respect Howard because he speaks his mind and tells it like it is. I'm the same way. I did his show a dozen times in two years, and listeners seemed to respond well to my appearances.

Most of them, anyway.

We ran into a little trouble when some callers began making jokes about the Hells Angels and a few people from the club tried, unsuccessfully, to call in and respond. Howard's show is all about controversy and laughter, and I understand that. But some people don't realize that making fun of the Hells Angels is serious shit. You don't do it unless you're prepared to fight. A few people in the club were really pissed at Howard, but I straightened it out. I went on the show that Friday, not knowing until I got there that it was Howard's birthday.

"Some people are pretty upset with you," I told him. "But it's okay, now. My present to you, Howard, is that you're not going to get beat up today."

We went back and forth a bit, talked about the procedure for taking calls and putting listeners on the air. Everything was fine until Robin Quivers, Howard's sidekick, got involved.

"We don't know who's calling until we put them on the air," Robin said. Now, I know that's not true. They screen their calls and make a determination as to whether the caller will be funny or interesting.

"Robin, stay out of this," I said. "I'm talking to Howard."

Well, Robin didn't like that one bit. She started yelling at me, saying, "You don't tell us what to do. This is our radio show!"

"Not today it isn't!" I said.

Anyway, it all blew over and I still consider Howard a friend and I respect him immensely; his show, and the exposure it offered, is a big reason for the success I've enjoyed in recent years. It was after one of my appearances on the Stern show that a producer from Las Vegas named Howard Cohen called me and said he had an interesting idea for a reality-based television show about a "judge" who makes house calls. Sort of a cross between *The People's Court* and *Death Wish*, the show would feature a tough guy—played by me—settling disputes without having to deal with the annoying constraints of the judicial system. The show's participants would have to agree to abide by whatever decision was rendered by the judge. When Howard first ran the idea by me, I thought he was nuts. But within a month it became a reality. We filmed a pilot for USA Network in which I rode my Harley and wore sunglasses and a long leather duster. Television series often wind up in development hell, of course, but someday soon *Chuck Zito's Street Justice* could be coming into your living room. Believe me, it'll be like nothing you've ever seen. If you thought Judge Judy was a hard-ass, wait until you get a load of me.

It's funny the way things turn out. I thought the fight with Jean-Claude would be a career killer, but it proved to be a career *maker*.

There was a place in the world for a legitimate tough guy, I discovered, as when the honchos at World Championship Wrestling offered me a recurring role. I played a manager type, rather than an in-ring character (al-

That's me with my shihan, Chris Colombo.
Credit: Ralph Corwin

though there was talk of having me become a wrestler as well). The highlight of my WCW career came in Knoxville, Tennessee, in the spring of 1998. Hulk Hogan, the WCW's biggest star, had called me up one night and asked me if I could round up a bunch of my brothers to escort him and his upstart faction, known as the New World Order (which supposedly was at war with the lords of the WCW), into the ring. I said, "Sure, no problem." Then I went out and recruited eighteen Hells Angels from New York, Kentucky, Illinois, and North Carolina.

We roared into the arena in two lines, nine guys on each side, Hulk and the New World Order in the center. We were supposed to dismount from our bikes and stand in the center of the ring while Hulk and the NWO conferred. Eric Bischoff, the head of the WCW, had told us that the fans might start throwing soda cans and bottles at us. "Be on your toes," he had said.

"Listen," I warned him. "If me or anyone of my brothers gets hit, we'll start stabbing and slabbing."

"Jesus," Eric said. "I don't want another Altamont."

"Well, if we get hit, it *will* be."

Eric contemplated this possibility for maybe a second or two before coming to a decision. "Don't get off the bikes. Just circle the ring and go back behind the stage."

So we circled the ring once, made a lot of noise, and then rode back out. As the crowd went wild, Hulk took the microphone.

"First of all, I want to thank Chuck Zito, the Van-Damminator, and Mel from the Windy City, and their brothers for showing up tonight," he said. "The WCW says they've got a bunch of football players on their side. But that doesn't matter. They could have the army and the navy, for all I care. Because we've got the Hells Angels! Ain't nobody stopping us now!"

That was kind of cool, I have to admit. But not nearly as cool as hanging out with Muhammad Ali backstage at a Billy Joel concert. Many years earlier I had taken my wife and daughter to visit Ali at his Deer Lake Training Camp, where he was preparing for a title fight in Zaire against George Foreman. The champ took us into his home then and treated us like family, which only confirmed what I'd already believed about him: that he was not only a great fighter but also a great man. Here's a guy who refused to serve in the armed services during the Vietnam War, even though he never would have seen combat. He was perfectly safe. But serving would have meant turning his back on his own beliefs, and he wouldn't do that. Instead, he forfeited three of the best years of his life. This was a man who was stripped

of his dignity, his title, his livelihood. Thirty years ago he was one of the most hated men in America. But he persevered. He clung to his beliefs. And look at him today. He's a hero, and deservedly so.

We shook hands and chatted a little after the concert. Despite the Parkinson's disease that has ravaged his body, Ali's mind and wit remain as sharp as ever. A photographer asked us to pose together. "I want to get a shot of the Greatest and the Toughest," he said. So we each went into a little boxer's stance and put our fists up. We stood toe-to-toe, staring into each other's eyes, as a roomful

Trying to re-create my father's stance
Credit: Big Joe Kaplan

of people looked on. Just before the photographer snapped his picture, Ali leaned into me and said, out loud:

"Did you call me a nigger?"

Holy shit! Here's Muhammad Ali, the fastest thing on two feet, trying to intimidate me, playing with me.

I hesitated, then snarled back at him, "You heard me right!"

The camera clicked and lights flashed as a smile came to Ali's face. He cupped a hand warmly around the back of my head.

"I like that," he said. "I like that."

EPILOGUE

IF YOU STUDY THE MARTIAL ARTS FOR ANY LENGTH OF TIME, YOU CAN'T HELP but be affected to some degree by Eastern philosophy, including the belief that there is a balance to the universe. I find it interesting that opportunities sometimes arise out of unfortunate circumstances and that moments of utter despair can give way to happiness and clarity. Everything has a way of evening out.

A little more than a month after my fight with Jean-Claude, just as my career was really starting to take flight, I got a phone call from my sister informing me that our father had died. I knew he was in a nursing home and his health had been deteriorating for some time, but his death still came as something of a shock. You see, there was a great deal of unfinished business between me and my dad. I hadn't seen him in thirteen years, since the time he came to visit me when I was incarcerated at MCC. Our family was going through a rough time then, and not simply because I was in jail. My father had re-married and moved to Sun City, Arizona, ostensibly for health reasons, although my sisters and I believed he was talked into relocating by his new wife, a woman named Pat who always seemed jealous of Dad's family; she hated him spending any time with us, and I think she wanted to put distance between his two lives.

In 1986, during one of my sister Rosanne's trips to Arizona, she and Pat had a serious falling-out. I'm not exactly sure of the details, but it had something to do with Pat yelling at Rosanne's three kids for being too rambunctious, and of course Rosanne took offense to that. She left early and returned to New York, swearing that she'd never set foot in Pat's house again. After Rosanne returned, I talked with my father on the phone from the federal prison in Petersburg,

Virginia. He was planning to come and visit, which made me happy, but I told him we had to have a little conversation about what had happened with Rosanne. He immediately stiffened.

"That's none of your business," he said. "That's between me and Rosanne and Pat."

"It *is* my business," I said. "Rosanne is my sister, and you're my father."

"That's right, I'm your father. And I'm telling you to stay out of it."

The conversation deteriorated after that, eventually becoming a full-scale argument. I told my father that I was looking forward to seeing him, but that Pat wasn't welcome.

"Oh, really?" he said. "That's my wife you're talking about."

"I know, but until I find out what happened between her and Rosanne, I don't want to see her."

"Fine," he said. "Then I'm not coming, either."

I was hurt, of course, but mainly I was just pissed off. I'd gotten over the damage my father had done when I was a kid, in part because I'd grown up and now understood that no one was perfect, that everyone fucked up now and then. (Hell, I was in prison—how could I not understand that?) Nevertheless, I refused to cut my father any slack on this issue. This was a man who had always preached about the importance of family, of respecting and protecting those who share your blood. The truth was, he talked a better game than he played. And while I still loved him and admired him on many levels, I found myself at that moment consumed by anger.

"Okay, then don't come."

There was a long pause, as if my father was searching for precisely the right words, the ones that would do the most damage. And he found them.

"You better learn some respect, you muscle-bound freak."

It was true that I'd gotten bigger behind bars. Like a lot of inmates, I'd taken up serious weight lifting as a way to increase my strength and keep my sanity. I'd put on more than twenty pounds of muscle, which made people far less likely to mess with me; more important, the exercise gave me a productive outlet for my energy and emotion. My father knew that. But he wanted to hurt me. And now I wanted to hurt him.

"I'm a freak? If that's the way you feel, then have a good life."

I hung up the phone and went back to my cell. At the time, I had no idea that I'd never speak to my father again. I did my time and earned my release. He never came to visit, never tried to call. And I didn't call him.

Years went by. My Aunt Connie used to tell me I should let it go, that I should take a trip to Arizona and visit my father while there was still time. She was right, too. I should have.

My wife, daughter, and mom during a prison visit in Petersburg, Virginia

Life is too damn short to hold grudges. But I'd pick up the phone, think about what I'd say, and then remember our previous conversation and I'd get pissed all over again and slam the receiver back in its cradle.

Even as my father grew older and more feeble and we'd get reports about his failing health and signs of senility, I refused to reach out. Eventually something happened. There was an altercation between Pat and my father, and the police were called to intervene. He was placed in a nursing home.

And then, on March 20 1998, the call came. Dad had passed away. But here's the real kicker: by the time we found out, he'd been dead almost two weeks! Pat had arranged a funeral and put him in the ground before even giving his own children the courtesy of a phone call. There was nothing left for us to do but say a prayer. I still think that was a horrible, mean-spirited thing for Pat to have done, but I don't really hold her responsible for my being estranged from my father. That was my doing . . . and his. We should have patched things up. I guess I just thought he'd always be around. I thought he'd live forever.

Even though we had no funeral, we held a memorial at Immaculate Conception in Tuckahoe, New York. I had mass cards made up featuring my dad in his boxing pose and I gave them to all my relatives and friends. The card included a verse from the Bible that I thought was appropriate.

In loving memory of Charles Zito, Sr.
aka
Al LaBarba
January 30, 1920–March 12, 1998
"Whereas once I was blind . . . now I can see"
—John 9:25

I thought my mother would live forever, too. She's the rock of our family, in many ways tougher than my father. She raised three kids, mostly on her own, always working, fighting, struggling to survive. I was the most difficult child, of course, but she's long since forgiven me for any pain I might have caused her. And I love her more than I can express.

One of the most difficult days of my life occurred in 1995, when I got a phone call from my sister Rosanne telling me that something was wrong with Mom and that I should come right away. I ran out the door of my house at 240 Davenport Avenue, jumped into my car, and drove about a hundred miles an hour through Westchester County. By the time I got to Mom's house in Bronxville, the ambulance had already arrived and paramedics were working on her. Her eyes were open as she lay back on the stretcher, but she was thoroughly unresponsive.

"Mom," I said. "What's wrong?"

She didn't say a word, just stared blankly, as if I were a complete stranger.

I followed the ambulance to the hospital emergency room in New Rochelle, where doctors quickly determined that Mom had suffered a stroke. It was too soon, they said, to know the extent of the damage. But she was only sixty-four years of age, and the doctors said that was a factor in her favor. She was young enough, and strong enough, to recover.

I called Kathy from the hospital. She was in Florida on business and told me she'd catch the next flight out. By that evening she'd come home and rushed to my side. I don't mind admitting that I was a wreck. I couldn't imagine life without Mom; I couldn't imagine losing her or, even worse, watching her suffer.

That night I stayed in the hospital, right by my mother's bed. I did that a lot over the next few weeks. I'd just lie there by her side, watching her as she slept, thinking about all we'd been

My wife and daughter

through and how she'd been the most consistent presence in my life. She'd been so strong for me; now it was my turn to be strong for her.

Over the course of several months, Mom steadily improved. Her speech and memory had been the areas most severely affected, so she had to undergo extensive therapy. For the longest time she couldn't talk at all, and she seemed not to recognize anyone, even her own kids. One night, though, when I arrived at the hospital, my sisters were already in the room, along with one of Mom's nurses.

"Gloria," the nurse said. "Do you know who these people are?"

Mom looked around the room, slowly turning her head and making eye contact with each one of us.

"It's my Chucky," she said. "And Rosanne . . . and Cindy."

Crying like babies, we all gathered around Mom and hugged her as hard as we could, just as she had hugged us so many times in the past.

It took a few years, but Mom eventually recovered almost 100 percent of her speech and memory. There were setbacks along the way. Mom had seizures that not only scared the hell out of all of us but also pissed her off, because each time she had an episode she was restricted from driving for a full year. Mom didn't like losing her freedom and independence, and I don't blame her. But she's well now, thank God, and we hope to have her with us for a long, long time.

Part of a son's duty, of course, is to avoid making some of the mistakes his father made. God knows I wasn't a perfect father or husband. But I wasn't the worst, either. One of the best days of my life was December 12, 1998, the day Lisa got married. I missed her sixteenth birthday, I missed her eighteenth birthday, I missed her senior prom and her high school graduation, and I can never atone for that. But I was there that day at the Roosevelt Hotel when she married a young man named Jonathan Cohen. It was a wonderful day. A perfect day.

Well, almost.

You see, I got a little upset before the wedding. Lisa was taking a bit longer than usual to get dressed—okay, she was taking quite a bit longer than usual—and some of the guests and members of the wedding party began to get restless. Fifteen minutes went by.

No Lisa. . . .

Thirty minutes.

Still no Lisa. . . .

Forty-five minutes.

The groom's parents became agitated. His grandmother became agitated. And, finally, the groom himself became agitated.

"Jonathan," I said. "Do you love her?"

"Of course," he answered.

"All right then, remember that. This is the most important day of her life, and she's trying to make herself beautiful. And she's doing it for you. So what if it takes her a little longer?"

To help pass the time, the wedding photographer suggested taking a few pictures of the groom with his current and future family. I should

have been gracious about the whole thing and just straightened my tie and put on a smile. Instead, I told the photographer to go ahead without me. "I'll wait until my wife and daughter come downstairs," I said. "Then I'll have some photos taken with *my* family."

In retrospect, I realize that was not the right thing to do. But boy, it seemed like the right response at the time. And it felt good to say it. Unfortunately, even though I was trying to defend their honor, my wife and daughter got mad at me, which left me with a bad attitude for much of the night. I sulked during the ceremony and the first part of the reception. It wasn't until it came time for the traditional father-daughter dance and the band played "Daddy's Little Girl" that everything came into focus. I held Lisa in my arms, whirled her around the room, and stared at her in wonder . . . this tiny child who had grown into the most beautiful young woman in the world. Where had the years gone?

I'd spent so much time fighting and riding and defending my own set of beliefs—so much time doing the things that came naturally to me. But there was a peacefulness now, a tranquility. At that moment I couldn't think of anywhere else I wanted to be. There was no wanderlust, no anger, none of the self-righteous indignation that so often got me in trouble. I was happy, content.

The feeling passed, of course. It always does.

Not long ago, after hearing about my latest late-night TKO, someone asked me if I'd ever stop fighting the good fight (whatever that means), if I'd always insist on living life by my own peculiar and inflexible set of rules, regardless of the consequences.

My initial response was, "I hope not. I'm getting too old for this shit."

Upon further reflection, though, I realized something: I'll never get too old for it. For better or worse, this is who I am.

You got a problem with that?